THE CRAFTWORKER'S
YEAR BOOK 1999

formerly
The Craftsman's Directory

compiled and published by
THE WRITE ANGLE PRESS
44 Kingsway, Stoke-on-Trent
Staffordshire ST4 1JH

Editorial: 01782 749919
Advertising and Trade Sales: 0181 298 0234
Information and Credit Card Sales: 0181 770 7087 and 0181 298 0929

D1806016

ISBN 0 9520737 9 X

©**The Write Angle Press 1999**

This book shall not, by way of trade or otherwise be lent, resold, hired out or otherwise circulated without the publisher's prior consent in writing, in any form of binding/cover etc. other than that in which it is here published and without similar conditions being imposed on the subsequent purchaser.

No part of this publication may be reproduced, stored in a retrieval system or transmitted in any form or by any means electronic, mechanical or photographic without the express, prior, written permission of the publisher: **The Write Angle Press**

Eastern Events 1999 schedule at National Trust Properties

April 2nd, 3rd, 4th and 5th
The Craft Show, Blickling Hall, Norfolk

May 1st, 2nd and 3rd
The Craft Show for Calke, Calke Abbey, Derbyshire

May 29th, 30th and 31st
**Felbrigg Coast & Country Show, Felbrigg Hall,
Nr Cromer, Norfolk**

June 19th and 20th
The Craft Show, Erddig, near Wrexham

August 5th and 6th
**Oxburgh Children's Extravaganza, Oxburgh Hall,
King's Lynn, Norfolk**

September 24th, 25th and 26th
The Craft Show, Chilford Vineyard, Linton, Cambridge *

November 5th, 6th and 7th
The Craft Show, Marks Hall, Coggeshall, Essex *

December 10th, 11th and 12th
Crafts for Christmas, Blickling Hall, Norfolk

* = not National Trust Properties

**Our policy is to always offer the public an extremely
high standard of design and display**

For further information or to book any of the above please contact

Eastern Events Ltd

*Diggens Farm House, Aylsham, Norfolk NR11 6UB
Tel: 01263 734711 or Fax: 01263 735134*

e-mail:eastern.events@paston.co.uk   http://www.paston.co.uk/easternevents

THE CRAFTWORKER'S
YEAR BOOK 1999

cover illustration
Brian Grimwood

data conversion consultant
Arthur Strong

distribution
Nice Bureau

type and layout
The Write Angle Press

film processing
Bureau 2000

printing
Crewe Colour Printers

BRITISH CRAFT

JUST ARTS and CRAFTS

Traditional Crafts Limited
Presents 1999 Events

Great Hall, Kempton Park Racecourse, Sunbury on Thames	20th & 21st March
Rosebery Suites, Epsom Racecourse, Surrey	17th & 18th April
Hyde End, Great Missenden, Bucks **Marquee Event**	23rd, 24th & 25th April
Bowley Showground, Horspath, Oxford **Marquee Event**	5th & 6th June
Hyde End, Great Missenden, Bucks **Marquee Event**	1st, 2nd & 3rd October
Rosebery Suites, Epsom Racecourse, Surrey	16th & 17th October
Great Hall, Kempton Park Racecourse, Sunbury on Thames	20th & 21st November
Chatham Historic Dockyard, Kent	27th & 28th November
Rosebery Suites, Epsom Racecourse, Surrey	4th & 5th December

*All events signposted, ample free parking and refreshments
All events open 10am-5pm*

Traditional Crafts Limited was formed by Craftworkers for Craftworkers, with the aim of keeping the Craft Industry alive. To present to the public genuine hand made crafts of a good quality and to ensure there are no bought in or mass produced goods. To qualify for these Events you must make the product you sell and be prepared to demonstrate such to one of our representatives who are mainly craftworkers

BUILDING FOR CRAFTWORKERS AND THEIR INDUSTRY

Enquiries to
TRADITIONAL CRAFTS LIMITED
The Thames Sovereign, Box 31 MBM, Manor Lane, Rochester, Kent ME1 3HS
Tel/Fax: 01634 849778

4

ABOUT THIS BOOK

The Craftworker's Year Book (formerly The Craftsman's Directory) will next year celebrate 20 continuous years in print, having long ago become recognised as the essential annual handbook for professional craftspeople. We constantly reappraise the content of the book, always endeavouring to add more and more useful information as it becomes available and this final edition of the 'old' millennium is no exception.

For the main list of events, listed chronologically beginning on page 6, we have spread our net wider to feature a whole host of shows, spectaculars and specialist activities which have now introduced craft sales sections. This has meant that while the number of traditional craft fairs has actually reduced slightly, this 1999 list actually contains over 100 more events than last year's book.

As always, after the date, event and venue, you will find the name of the organiser, whose full details are carried in the comprehensive contact section beginning on page 145. Here, too, we have made improvements. We have now added both email and website addresses for all those organisations who have them and we now also give the average price that they charge the public for admission to their events. Attendance figures are something mentioned to us from time to time by readers: the reason that we do not list them next to the events is that in most cases they are at best speculative and at worst totally misleading.

Our section on representative bodies in the crafts, beginning on page 185, has been completely revamped. Firstly, we have split these organisations into five subsections, according to how they are constituted – associations and federations; guilds and clubs; societies; quangos and regional bodies; and, finally, a few of their European counterparts. Email addresses and websites have again been added, in addition to which we have asked these groups about member-ship criteria, i.e. whether or not they are selective, if you have to pay an annual fee and what, if any, regional boundaries affect eligibility.

In our directory of publications (see page 205), we have included more information than ever before on magazines of interest to craftworkers. The publishers have given us details on how and where you can buy these magazines, and on what prices they are currently charging. Many of them have very kindly agreed to issue free sample copies for appraisal, with this being noted at the end of their entry.

Just a word of warning on the Web and Email addresses – people do change their Internet providers fairly readily it seems and while we have taken every care in gathering this information it can for this reason become rapidly out of date.

Finally, we have throughout the last year exerted pressure on our many contacts to submit all their data at an earlier stage so that we could draw together all useful information into a single volume, without the need for the usual updating supplement, and subsequently brought to you at a much reduced price.

We feel that these changes have resulted in a more comprehensive, more user friendly year book, designed to be an invaluable aid to your business in the coming year. We do hope you agree.

All the information in The Craftworker's Year Book is published at no cost, so if you know of any organisation not currently listed but who may be eligible, then please let us have their details or ask them to contact us direct.

May we take this opportunity to wish you a successful trading year and, as always, to thank our advertisers for their continued support.

CRAFT SHOWS, FAIRS, FESTIVALS AND EXHIBITIONS

Details of around 1900 events are listed below and while no effort is spared in the accurate preparation of this listing, mistakes can occur and details may be subject to change. We accept information submitted to us in good faith and as such we cannot accept any liability for loss, financial or otherwise, that may occur as a result of any error or omission in this work. **We strongly recommend that readers contemplating a visit to any events listed contact the organiser before starting out to be sure that both date and venue remain unchanged.**

Jan 1   **CRAFT FAIR/The Village Hall, Groby, Leics**
County Crafts

Jan 2   **CRAFT MARKET/Fisher Hall, Guildhall Place, Cambridge, Cambs**
Balthazar

Jan 2-3   **CRAFT FAYRE/Blakemere Craft Centre, Chester Road, Sandiway, Northwich, Cheshire**
Blakemere Craft Centre   *See display advertisement*

Jan 3   **CRAFT FAIR/Northwood Stadium, Keelings Road, Northwood,Hanley, Stoke-on-Trent, Staffs**
Archer Promotions

Jan 3   **NEW YEAR CRAFT SALE/Warwickshire County Cricket Ground, Edgbaston, Birmingham, West Midlands**
Hobby Horse Design & Craft Fairs

Jan 7-9   **CRAFT & ANTIQUE FAIR/The Guild Hall, York, North Yorks**
Lancastrian Fairs

Jan 8-10   **THE KNIT, STITCH & CREATIVE CRAFTS SHOW/Kings Hall, Belfast**
Nationwide Exhibitions (UK) Ltd

Jan 9   **CRAFT & GIFT FAIR/The Harlington Centre, High Street, Fleet, Hants**
Aquarius Fairs

Jan 9   **CRAFT MARKET/Fisher Hall, Guildhall Place, Cambridge, Cambs**
Balthazar

Jan 9   **DUNSTABLE CRAFT MARKET/Methodist Church Hall, Ashton Square, Dunstable, Beds**
Dunstable Craft Market

Jan 9   **ARTS & CRAFTS FAIR/Town Hall, Brackley, Northants**
Falcon Fairs

Jan 9-10   **CRAFT FAYRE/Blakemere Craft Centre, Chester Road, Sandiway, Northwich, Cheshire**
Blakemere Craft Centre   *See display advertisement*

Jan 9-10   **CRAFT FAIR/Brigade Hall, Bakewell, Derbys**
Cottage Creations Craft Fairs

Buckingham Publicity

Buckingham House, 11 High Street, Old Portsmouth, Hampshire, PO1 2LP.

Most of our quality events are held in the main rooms of stately homes and extend into marquees or pavilions.
We provide a real opportunity to promote and sell high quality goods and services to a
discerning visitor in these very lucrative markets. Quality exhibitors are invited to take part in our superior Home
Design & Interiors Exhibitions which also feature a crafts section. We offer a reduced deposit system for those
booking a series of events and the high profile of our shows is assured by extensive advertising campaigns.

Please telephone to discuss the suitability of our shows for you.

• Exhibition Portfolio - 1999 •

Chilford Halls Home Design and Interiors, *Linton, Cambridgeshire* ....**Jan 22 - 24**

Woburn Abbey Home Design and Interiors, *Bedfordshire*............................**Jan 29 - 31**

Hartham Park Home Design and Interiors, *Corsham, Wiltshire*........................**Feb 5 - 7**

Loseley Park Home Design and Interiors, *Guildford, Surrey*..........................**Feb 26 - 28**

Holdenby House Home Design and Interiors, *Northamptonshire*....................**March 5 -7**

Goodwood House Home Design and Interiors, *Chichester, West Sussex*...... **April 16 -18**

Elton Hall Home Design and Interiors, *Peterborough.*.....................................**May 7 - 9**

Leigh Court Home Design and Interiors, *Abbots Leigh, Bristol*.....................**May 14 - 16**

Ingatestone Hall Home Design and Interiors, *Chelmsford, Essex*...................**June 4 - 6**

Hampshire Show, *Royal Victoria Country Park, Netley, Southampton* ....**August 13 - 15**

Avington Park Home Design and Interiors, *Winchester, Hampshire*..............**Sept 24 - 26**

Knebworth House Home Design and Interiors, *Hertfordshire*.........................**Oct 1 - 3**

Coughton Court Home Design and Interiors, *Alcester, Warwickshire* ....**Nov 5 - 7**

Stansted House Home Design and Interiors, *Rowlands Castle, Hampshire*......**Nov 19 - 21**

Fawley Court Home Design and Interiors, *Henley-on-Thames, Oxon.*............**Nov 26 - 28**

Goodwood Christmas Craft and Gift Fayre, *Chichester, West Sussex*................**Dec 4 - 5**

Goodwood House

Loseley Park

PLEASE WRITE OR TELEPHONE FOR FULL DETAILS AND BOOKING FORMS
SALES OFFICE (01705) 677200   FAX (01705) 677300

Jan 10   **CRAFT, DESIGN & GIFT FAIR/Bromsgrove Market Hall, Worcs**
Cottage Industries Association   *See display advertisement*

Jan 10   **CRAFT & GIFT FAIR/Barton Village Hall, nr Preston, Lancs**
Golden Age Fairs

Jan 10   **CRAFT & ANTIQUE FAIR/Community Centre, Hebden Bridge, West Yorks**
Lancastrian Fairs

Jan 10   **DOLLS HOUSE FAIR/Quality Clock Hotel, Welwyn, Herts**
R J Exhibitions

Jan 10-13   **CUMBREX '99 TRADE FAIR/Bowness-on-Windermere, Cumbria**
Northern Exhibitions

Jan 13-24   **ANNUAL WINTER EXHIBITION OF SOCIETY OF DESIGNER CRAFTSMEN/The Mall Galleries, London**
Society of Designer Craftsmen

Jan 14-17   **THE 14TH KNITTING, NEEDLECRAFT, DESIGN & HOBBYCRAFTS EXHIBITION/Sandown Exhibition Centre, Esher, Surrey**
Nationwide Exhibitions (UK) Ltd

Jan 16   **CRAFT MARKET/Fisher Hall, Guildhall Place, Cambridge, Cambs**
Balthazar

Jan 16   **CRAFT FAIR/Burgh Hall, Peebles**
Border Fairs

Jan 16-17   **CRAFT FAYRE/Blakemere Craft Centre, Chester Road, Sandiway, Northwich, Cheshire**
Blakemere Craft Centre   *See display advertisement*

Jan 16-17   **CRAFT & GIFT FAIR/Wyndley Garden Centre, Warwick Road, Knowle, Warks**
Cottage Industries Association   *See display advertisement*

Jan 17   **CRAFT FAIR/Congleton Town Hall, High Street, Congleton, Cheshire**
Archer Promotions

Jan 17   **TEDDY BEAR FAIR/Cresta Court Hotel, Altrincham, Cheshire**
Brentwood Fairs

Jan 17   **CRAFT FAIR/Olde House Trading Post, Chesterfield, Derbys**
Cottage Creations Craft Fairs

Jan 17   **CRAFT FAIR/The Bosworth College, Desford, Leics**
County Crafts

Jan 17   **ARTS & CRAFTS FAIR/Woburn Village Hall, Woburn, Beds**
Falcon Fairs

Jan 17   **CRAFT & ANTIQUE FAIR/Community Centre, Hebden Bridge, West Yorks**
Lancastrian Fairs

Jan 17-20   **THE SCARBOROUGH GIFTS TRADE FAIR/The Southlands Hotel and The Red Lea Hotel, Scarborough, North Yorks**
Northern Exhibitions

jewellery

Ceramics

CRAFTS

If you are looking to sell to trade and corporate buyers in Scotland and elsewhere, Made in Scotland's events are the major opportunities. The Highland Trade Fair has been established for nearly 30 years, and has become a vibrant trade event with a legendary social scene! Scotland's International Trade Fair is divided into sectors, including a special area devoted to crafts from Scotland and elsewhere, with its own targeted marketing effort

The Highland Trade Fair
24th-27th October 1999, Aviemore

Scotland's International Trade Fair
23rd -26th January 2000, Glasgow

MADE IN
SCOTLAND

Please send me details as an exhibitor ☐ as a buyer ☐

Name... Company ....

....

Postcode .... Tel no ....

Return to: Made in Scotland Ltd, The Craft Centre, Beauly,
Inverness-shire IV4 7EH Tel: 01463 782578 Fax: 01463 782409

| Jan 17-26 | **WELSH CRAFTS AT SHOWCASE DUBLIN/Dublin, Eire** |
| | Wales Craft Council |

| Jan 21-24 | **SCOTLAND'S INTERNATIONAL TRADE FAIR/Scottish Exhibition & Conference Centre, Glasgow** |
| | Made in Scotland Ltd *See display advertisement* |

| Jan 22-24 | **CHILFORD HALLS HOME DESIGN & INTERIORS EXHIBITION/Chilford Halls, Linton, Cambs** |
| | Buckingham Publicity *See display advertisement* |

| Jan 23 | **CRAFT MARKET/Fisher Hall, Guildhall Place, Cambridge, Cambs** |
| | Balthazar |

| Jan 23 | **CRAFT FAIR/Volunteer Hall, Galashiels, Selkirkshire** |
| | Border Fairs |

| Jan 23 | **JANUARY CRAFT SALE/Town Hall, Dover, Kent** |
| | East Kent Fairs *See display advertisement* |

| Jan 23-24 | **CRAFT FAYRE/Craft Centre, Chester Road, Sandiway, Northwich, Cheshire** |
| | Blakemere Craft Centre *See display advertisement* |

| Jan 24 | **CRAFT FAIR/Community Centre, Kinver, nr Stourbridge, West Midlands** |
| | Central Promotions *See display advertisement* |

| Jan 24 | **CRAFT FAIR/The Quality Inn, Loughborough, Leics** |
| | County Crafts |

| Jan 24 | **CRAFT & ANTIQUE FAIR/Community Centre, Hebden Bridge, West Yorks** |
| | Lancastrian Fairs |

| Jan 24-27 | **WALES SPRING FAIR/Llandudno, Gwynedd** |
| | Wales Craft Council |

| Jan 27 | **CRAFT FAYRE/Craft Centre, Chester Road, Sandiway, Northwich, Cheshire** |
| | Blakemere Craft Centre *See display advertisement* |

| Jan 27-28 | **CRAFT FAIR/Brigade Hall, Bakewell, Derbys** |
| | Cottage Creations Craft Fairs |

| Jan 29-31 | **WOBURN ABBEY HOME DESIGN & INTERIORS EXHIBITION/Woburn Abbey, Woburn, Beds** |
| | Buckingham Publicity *See display advertisement* |

| Jan 30 | **CRAFT MARKET/Fisher Hall, Guildhall Place, Cambridge, Cambs** |
| | Balthazar |

| Jan 30 | **CRAFT FAIR/Tewkesbury Town Hall, Tewkesbury, Glos** |
| | Craft in Action |

| Jan 30 | **CRAFT FAIR/Guildhall, Plymouth, Devon** |
| | Kevin Murphy Craft Fairs |

| Jan 30 | **ANTIQUE & CRAFT FAIR/Memorial Hall, Darras Road, Ponteland, Northumberland** |
| | Quintet Promotions |

Dalesway

FESTIVALS OF CRAFT
FASHION
AND DESIGN

Calendar of Events for 1999

Harewood House, Leeds   29th-31st May

Dalkeith Palace, Nr Edinburgh   3rd-4th July

Floors Castle, Kelso   24th-25th July

St. Andrews, Fife   30th July - 2nd August

Aberdeen, Exhibition & Conference Centre
5th-7th November

Floors Castle, Kelso   13th-14th November

Eastwood House, Glasgow   19th-21st November

Harewood House, Leeds   26th-28th November

For booking information call Gary Bates at.
Dalesway Festivals Ltd
The All England Jumping Course
London Road, Hickstead, West Sussex RH17 5NX
Tel: 01273 833884 Fax: 01273 835556
E-Mail:- dalesway@btinternet.com

Jan 30-31	**CRAFT FAYRE/Blakemere Craft Centre, Chester Road, Sandiway, Northwich, Cheshire** Blakemere Craft Centre *See display advertisement*
Jan 30-31	**ANNUAL EXHIBITION OF THE BRITISH TOYMAKERS GUILD/Chelsea Old Town Hall, Kings Road, Chelsea, London SW3** British Toymakers Guild
Jan 30-31	**AYLESBURY CRAFT WEEKEND/Civic Centre, Aylesbury, Bucks** Living Heritage Craft Shows Ltd *See display advertisement*
Jan 30-31	**THE CRAFT GUILD SALE/Greenwood Room, Martin Mere Wildfowl & Wetlands Trust Centre, Burscough, nr Ormskirk, Lancs** The Craft Guild of West Lancashire
Jan 31	**CRAFT FAIR/Biddulph Leisure Centre, Thames Drive, off Congleton Road, Biddulph, Staffs** Archer Promotions
Jan 31	**DOLL FAIR/Nostell Priory, nr Wakefield, West Yorks** East Midlands Doll Fairs
Jan 31	**CRAFT FAIR/Passage House Hotel, Newton Abbot, Devon** Kevin Murphy Craft Fairs
Jan 31	**CRAFT & ANTIQUE FAIR/Community Centre, Hebden Bridge, West Yorks** Lancastrian Fairs
Jan 31	**CRAFT & ANTIQUE FAIR/Gargrave Village Hall, nr Skipton, North Yorks** Lancastrian Fairs
Feb 4	**CRAFT FAIR/Daresbury Park Hotel, Daresbury, Warrington, Cheshire** Creative Crafts Association *See display advertisement*
Feb 5-7	**HARTHAM PARK HOME DESIGN & INTERIORS EXHIBITION/Corsham, Wilts** Buckingham Publicity *See display advertisement*
Feb 6	**CRAFT MARKET/Fisher Hall, Guildhall Place, Cambridge, Cambs** Balthazar
Feb 6	**CRAFT FAIR/Burgh Hall, Peebles** Border Fairs
Feb 6	**ARTS & CRAFTS FAIR/Town Hall, Towcester, Northants** Falcon Fairs
Feb 6	**ART & CRAFT FAIR/The Arts Centre, Biddick Lane, Fatfield, Washington, Tyne & Wear** The Arts Centre
Feb 6-7	**CRAFT FAYRE/Blakemere Craft Centre, Chester Road, Sandiway, Northwich, Cheshire** Blakemere Craft Centre *See display advertisement*
Feb 6-7	**CRAFT FAYRE/Trentham Gardens, Stone Road (A34), Trentham, Stoke-on-Trent, Staffs** Cheshire Fayre *See display advertisement*

CREATIVE 99

3 - 5 April 1999

Finished crafts plus fine art, craft and hobby supplies

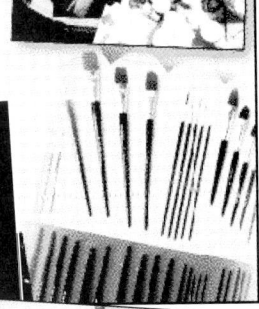

Alexandra Palace, London

For booking information call Gary Bates at:
Marathon Event Management Limited
The All England Jumping Course, London Road, Hickstead,
West Sussex RH17 5NX.
Tel: 01273 833884 Fax: 01273 835556
Email: marathon@btinternet.com

THE BRIGHTON CHRISTMAS CRAFT FAIR

For booking information call Gary Bates at:
Marathon Event Management Ltd
The All England Jumping Course, London
Road, Hickstead, West Sussex RH17 5NX
Tel: 01273 833884 Fax: 01273 835556 Email: marathon@btinternet.com

MARATHON
EVENT
MANAGEMENT
LIMITED

The Brighton Centre, Kings Road, Brighton, Sussex

5 - 7 November 1999

The Festive Table and The Alexandra Palace Christmas Craft Fair

Alexandra Palace
3 - 5 December
1999

For booking
information call Joel
Piveteau/Dee Leek at:

**Marathon Event
Management Limited**
The All England
Jumping Course,
London Road,
Hickstead,
West Sussex
RH17 5NX.

Tel: 01273 833884
Fax: 01273 835556
Email: marathon@
btinternet.com

Feb 6-7   **CLACTON CRAFT WEEKEND/Highfields Holiday Park, London Road,**
          Clacton-on-Sea, Essex
          Living Heritage Craft Shows Ltd   *See display advertisement*

Feb 6-7   **CROYDON CRAFT WEEKEND/John Ruskin College, Selsdon Park Road,**
          Selsdon, South Croydon, Surrey
          Living Heritage Craft Shows Ltd   *See display advertisement*

Feb 6-7   **CRAFT FAIR/Castle Combe, Wilts**
          Rainbow Fair

Feb 6-7   **FORT PURBROOK CRAFT FAYRE/Portsdown Hill, Cosham, nr Portsmouth,**
          Hants
          Woodland Crafts   *See display advertisement*

Feb 7   **CRAFT FAIR/Northwood Stadium, Keelings Road, Northwood,Hanley, Stoke-**
          on-Trent, Staffs
          Archer Promotions

Feb 7   **BOURNEMOUTH & POOLE DOLLS HOUSE & MINIATURE FAIR/Pavilion**
          Theatre, Westover Road, Bournemouth, Dorset
          Bournemouth & Poole Dolls House & Miniature Fair

Feb 7   **CRAFT FAIR/Windmill Village Hotel, Allesley (A45), Coventry, Warks**
          Central Promotions   *See display advertisement*

Feb 7   **CRAFT FAYRE/The Belgrave Hotel, Torquay, Devon**
          Cherrycraft Fayres & Festivals

Feb 7   **CRAFT FAIR/Rivermead Complex, Richfield Avenue, Caversham, nr Reading,**
          Berks
          Cottage Craft Fairs   *See display advertisement*

Feb 7   **CRAFT & GIFT FAIR/Barton Village Hall, nr Preston, Lancs**
          Golden Age Fairs

Feb 7   **CRAFT FAIR/Dunkenhalgh Hotel, Clayton-le-Moors, nr Accrington, Lancs**
          Heritage Fairs

Feb 7   **CRAFT FAIR/Chase Hotel, Ross-on-Wye, Herefordshire**
          Kevin Murphy Craft Fairs

Feb 7   **CRAFT & ANTIQUE FAIR/Ground Floor Centre, Hebden Bridge, West Yorks**
          Lancastrian Fairs

Feb 7   **ARTS & CRAFTS SHOW/Lauderdale House, Highgate Hill, London N6**
          Lauderdale Arts & Crafts

Feb 7   **ANTIQUE & CRAFT FAIR/Seaburn Centre, Seaburn, Sunderland, Tyne & Wear**
          Quintet Promotions

Feb 7   **DOLLS HOUSE FAIR/Plinston Hall, Letchworth, Herts**
          R J Exhibitions

Feb 7-11 **FOCAL POINT (DESIGN & PROFFSSIONAL CRAFTS) AT THE SPRING FAIR**
          BIRMINGHAM/National Exhibition Centre, Birmingham
          Focal Point

MGA FAIRS

George and Marion Aldis
PO Box 282, Overstone
Northampton NN6 0SD   Phone: 01604 642185
EMail: GMAldis@AOL.com

1999
BEAUTIFUL BRITISH CRAFTS

Quality Events
in lovely surroundings by organisers who care for
their exhibitors and public alike

Lamport Hall, Northamptonshire

May 2nd & 3rd, Crafts Festival and Garden Show
September 11th &12th, Autumn Crafts Festival

Stanford Hall (nr Rugby), Leicestershire

October 2nd & 3rd, Crafts in Stanford Hall (Lady Fair)

Ragley Hall, Warwickshire

March 13th & 14th, Spring Craft Festival
October 9th &10th, Autumn Craft Festival
November 27th & 28th, Yuletide Craft Festival

Elton Hall, Peterborough, Cambridgeshire
April 17th &18th and September 18th &19th

Prices for 1999 between £75 and £98 per weekend per single stand
depending on the venue. NO VAT. No charge for electricity. Tables
£3.75. Absolutely no bought-in craft goods. Write or phone or EMail

Feb 7-11	**RURAL CRAFTS ASSOCIATION AT THE SPRING FAIR BIRMINGHAM/**

Feb 7-11   **RURAL CRAFTS ASSOCIATION AT THE SPRING FAIR BIRMINGHAM/ National Exhibition Centre, Birmingham, West Midlands**
Rural Crafts Association   *See display advertisement*

Feb 7-11   **WELSH CRAFTS AT THE SPRING FAIR BIRMINGHAM/National Exhibition Centre, Birmingham, West Midlands**
Wales Craft Council

Feb 7-11   **SPRING FAIR BIRMINGHAM/National Exhibition Centre, Birmingham, West Midlands (main organiser)**
Trade Promotion Services Ltd

Feb 11-13   **CRAFT & ANTIQUE FAIR/The Guild Hall, York, North Yorks**
Lancastrian Fairs

Feb 13   **CRAFT & GIFT FAIR/The Harlington Centre, High Street, Fleet, Hants**
Aquarius Fairs

Feb 13   **CRAFT MARKET/Fisher Hall, Guildhall Place, Cambridge, Cambs**
Balthazar

Feb 13   **DUNSTABLE CRAFT MARKET/Methodist Church Hall, Ashton Square, Dunstable, Beds**
Dunstable Craft Market

Feb 13   **ARTS & CRAFTS FAYRE/Winter Gardens, Weston-super-Mare, North Somerset**
Fountain Fayres & Exhibitions

Feb 13   **CRAFT FAIR/Guildhall, Salisbury, Wilts**
Kevin Murphy Craft Fairs

Feb 13   **CRAFT FAIR/ Leisure Centre, Recreation Ground Road, Tenterden, Kent**
M B County Fairs

Feb 13   **CRAFT & GIFT FAIR/Barnet Library, Stapylton Road, Barnet, Herts**
Marie Margaret Promotions

Feb 13   **DOLLS HOUSE & MINIATURES FAIR/Somerset Hall, Portishead, North Somerset**
Rita Daniels/Posset Fundraisers

Feb 13   **VALENTINE'S CRAFT FAIR/Nantwich Civic Hall, Market Street, Nantwich, Cheshire**
Stancie Kutler Crafts

Feb 13-14   **CRAFT FAYRE/Blakemere Craft Centre, Chester Road, Sandiway, Northwich, Cheshire**
Blakemere Craft Centre   *See display advertisement*

Feb 13-14   **CRAFT FAIR/Brigade Hall, Bakewell, Derbys**
Cottage Creations Craft Fairs

Feb 13-14   **CRAFTS AT SHERBORNE/Sherborne School, Sherborne, Dorset**
Craft Carnival

Feb 13-14   **CRAFT FAIR/Market Hall, Hawes, North Yorks**
Keld Craft Fairs

Heart of England CRAFTWORKERS

Marquees and Pavilions for 1999

Harrogate Spring Flower Show	22-25 April
Mitsubishi Badminton Horse Trials	6-9 May
The Devon County Show	20-22 May
The Royal Bath and West Show	2-5 June
The South of England Show	10-12 June
BBC Gardeners World Live	16-20 June
The Lincolnshire Show	23-24 June
The Royal Show	5-8 July
The Great Yorkshire Show	13-15 July
Holkham Country Fair	17-18 July
Newport and District Agricultural Show	17 July
The Royal Welsh Show	19-22 July
Country Landowners Association Game Fair	30 July-1 August
The Bakewell Show	4-5 August
Lulworth Horse Trials and Country Fair	7-8 August
The United Counties Show	12-13 August
The Pembrokeshire Show	17-19 August
Chatsworth Country Fair	4-5 September
Harrogate Autumn Flower Show	17-19 September

Further major shows were being finalised at the time this advert was going to print. Please ring for details of these

Please send an SAE for a copy of our 1999 brochure including photographs of your work if you have not exhibited with us before

01905 21702 or Fax on 01905 29285

105 St Georges Lane, Worcester WR1 1QS

P R O M O T I N G   C R A F T S   T H R O U G H O U T   B R I T A I N

Feb 13-14	**NORWICH CRAFT SHOW/Norwich Sports Village Hotel, Norwich Ring Road, Norwich, Norfolk** Living Heritage Craft Shows Ltd _See display advertisement_
Feb 13-14	**CRAFT FAIR/Newark Showground, Newark, Notts** Rainbow Fair
Feb 13-14	**LIVE CRAFTS SHOW/Ascot Exhibition Centre, Ascot, Berks** The Exhibition Team Ltd _See display advertisement_
Feb 13-14	**CRAFT FAIR/The Pavilion, Buxton, Derbys** Town & Country Craft Fairs
Feb 14	**DOLLS HOUSE & MINIATURE FAIR/Cresta Court Hotel, Altrincham, Cheshire** Brentwood Fairs
Feb 14	**CRAFT FAIR/Kingfisher Hotel, Wall Heath (A44), nr Kingswinford, West Midlands** Central Promotions _See display advertisement_
Feb 14	**CRAFT, DESIGN & GIFT FAIR/Bromsgrove Market Hall, Worcs** Cottage Industries Association _See display advertisement_
Feb 14	**DOLL FAIR/The Belfry, Wishaw, Sutton Coldfield, West Midlands** East Midlands Doll Fairs
Feb 14	**DOLLS, DOLLSHOUSES & MINIATURES SHOW/Hilton National Hotel, Grove Way, Milton Keynes (handmade British miniatures only)** Four Seasons Fairs
Feb 14	**CRAFT FAIR/Westland S&SC, Yeovil, Somerset** Kevin Murphy Craft Fairs
Feb 14	**CRAFT & ANTIQUE FAIR/Ground Floor Centre, Hebden Bridge, West Yorks** Lancastrian Fairs
Feb 14	**CRAFT FAIR/Agricultural Hall, Maidstone, Kent** M B County Fairs
Feb 14	**CRAFT & GIFT FAIR/Marton Hotel & Country Club, Middlesbrough, Cleveland** Quality Craft & Gift Fairs _See display advertisement_
Feb 14	**DOLLS HOUSES, DOLLS & MINIATURES FAIR/Royal Chace Hotel, The Ridgeway, Enfield, Middx** Quality Craft Fairs
Feb 14-17	**NORTH-EASTERN SPRING GIFTS TRADE FAIR/North-Eastern Exhibition Centre, Newcastle upon Tyne, Tyne & Wear** Northern Exhibitions
Feb 16	**CRAFT FAIR/White Hart Inn, Hawes, North Yorks** Keld Craft Fairs
Feb 18-21	**THE 8TH NORTH WEST KNITTING, NEEDLECRAFT & HOBBYCRAFTS EXHIBITION/G-Mex Centre, Manchester** Nationwide Exhibitions (UK) Ltd

MARY HOLLAND CRAFT FAIRS

to be held at

The Leisure Centre, University of Keele
Newcastle-under-Lyme, Staffordshire
21st, 22nd, 23rd May 1999 and
1st, 2nd and 3rd October 1999

The National Trust, Petworth Park, West Sussex
29th, 30th and 31st May 1999
Bank Holiday Weekend

Mentmore Towers, Mentmore
Leighton Buzzard, Bedfordshire
28th, 29th, 30th August 1999
Bank Holiday Weekend

The Medieval Abbey Buildings, Abingdon, Oxon
14th to 18th and
20th to 24th October 1999

Craftspeople and artists from all over the country will be
exhibiting and selling their work at these prestigious craft
shows. All the venues are distinctive and offer opportunities
to relax and enjoy the exhibition sites.

Refreshments are available all day and visitors can also
picnic and stroll in the grounds of Petworth Park
and Mentmore Towers

**All enquiries: MCHF Ltd, PO Box 43, Abingdon, Oxon
OX14 2EX. Tel/Fax 01235 521873**

| Feb 19-21 | **CRAFT IN ACTION SHOW/Lincolnshire Showground, Grange-de-Lings, nr Lincoln, Lincs** |
| | The Exhibition Team Ltd — *See display advertisement* |

Feb 19-21   **CRAFT IN ACTION SHOW/Lincolnshire Showground, Grange-de-Lings, nr Lincoln, Lincs**
The Exhibition Team Ltd   *See display advertisement*

Feb 20   **CRAFT MARKET/Fisher Hall, Guildhall Place, Cambridge, Cambs**
Balthazar

Feb 20   **TYNESIDE DOLLS HOUSE & MINIATURES FAIR/Gateshead Civic Centre, Regent Street, Gateshead, Tyne & Wear**
Dolly Domain Fairs

Feb 20   **CRAFT & ANTIQUE FAIR/The Guild Hall, York, North Yorks**
Lancastrian Fairs

Feb 20   **WELLS SPRING CRAFT SHOW/Wells Town Hall, Wells, Somerset**
West Country Craft Fairs   *See display advertisement*

Feb 20-21   **CRAFT FAYRE/Blakemere Craft Centre, Chester Road, Sandiway, Northwich, Cheshire**
Blakemere Craft Centre   *See display advertisement*

Feb 20-21   **CRAFT FAYRE/Fenton Manor, Fenton, Stoke-on-Trent, Staffs**
Cheshire Fayre   *See display advertisement*

Feb 20-21   **CRAFT, DESIGN & GIFT FAIR/Wyndley Garden Centre, Warwick Road, Knowle, Warks**
Cottage Industries Association   *See display advertisement*

Feb 20-21   **CRAFT FAIR/Haydock Park Racecourse Exhibition Centre, St Helens, Merseyside**
Creative Crafts Association   *See display advertisement*

Feb 20-21   **CRAFT FAIR/St William's College, York, North Yorks**
Keld Craft Fairs

Feb 20-21   **BRENTWOOD CRAFT WEEKEND/Shenfield Sports Centre, Brentwood Green, Essex**
Living Heritage Craft Shows Ltd   *See display advertisement*

Feb 20-21   **MAIDENHEAD CRAFT WEEKEND/Magnet Leisure Centre, A4 Town Centre, Maidenhead, Berks**
Living Heritage Craft Shows Ltd   *See display advertisement*

Feb 20-21   **CRAFT FAIR/Kings Hall, Herne Bay, Kent**
M B County Fairs

Feb 21   **CRAFT SHOW/The Belfry, Wishaw, Sutton Coldfield, West Midlands**
CFL Craft Shows

Feb 21   **CRAFT FAIR/Albrighton Hall Hotel, Ellesmere Road, Shrewsbury, Salop**
Central Promotions   *See display advertisement*

Feb 21   **CRAFT FAIR/Spelthorne Leisure Centre, Knowle Green, Staines, Middx**
Cottage Craft Fairs   *See display advertisement*

Feb 21   **CRAFT FAIR/Peel Centre, Dronfield, Sheffield (Mayor's Charity 1999)**
Cottage Creations Craft Fairs

DULWICH CONTEMPORARY CRAFT FAIRS

is one of the few craft event organisers with a selection procedure carried out by an independent team of experienced craftworkers, artists and lecturers.

In conducting the selection, the committee look not only for **skill** *and* **design ability** *in the craftsworkers invited to attend but a* **talent** *to* **display, light** *and* **present** *their work.*

The events this year are held on **May 1st***,* **November 27th** *and* **December 11th.**

This attention to **quality, design, detail** *and* **display** *has made The Dulwich Craft Fairs consistently popular with a discerning public willing and able to pay for design flair and skill in craft work.*

To retain a variety of craft types the organisers are seeking early applications from crafts people producing quality work.

Write, please, with a CV, photographs of work and previous displays to: **Nicholas Keogh, 25 Tewkesbury Avenue, Forest Hill, London SE23 3DG. Tel: 0181 291 0024**

DULWICH STYLE DULWICH QUALITY

Feb 21   **ARTS & CRAFTS FAIR/Woburn Village Hall, Woburn, Beds**
Falcon Fairs

Feb 21   **DOLLS, DOLLSHOUSES & MINIATURES SHOW/Swallow Hotel, Old Shire Lane, Waltham Abbey (handmade British miniatures only)**
Four Seasons Fairs

Feb 21   **CRAFT FAIR/Leisure Centre, Chepstow, Gwent**
Kevin Murphy Craft Fairs

Feb 21   **CRAFT FAIR/Hinchingbrooke House, Huntingdon, Cambs**
Kingfisher Promotions

Feb 21   **CRAFT & ANTIQUE FAIR/Ground Floor Centre, Hebden Bridge, West Yorks**
Lancastrian Fairs

Feb 21   **CRAFT & GIFT FAIR/St George Swallow Hotel, Harrogate, North Yorks**
Quality Craft & Gift Fairs   *See display advertisement*

Feb 25-27   **CRAFT & ANTIQUE FAIR/The Guild Hall, York, North Yorks**
Lancastrian Fairs

Feb 26-28   **LOSELEY PARK HOME DESIGN & INTERIORS EXHIBITION/Loseley Park, Guildford, Surrey**
Buckingham Publicity   *See display advertisement*

Feb 26-29   **THE QUILT FAIR/South of England Showground, Ardingly, nr Haywards Heath, West Sussex**
Quilt Events Ltd

Feb 27   **CRAFT MARKET/Fisher Hall, Guildhall Place, Cambridge, Cambs**
Balthazar

Feb 27   **CRAFT FAIR/Corn Exchange, Melrose, Roxburghshire**
Border Fairs

Feb 27   **ANTIQUES, CRAFTS & COLLECTABLES FAIR/The Parish Hall, Culcheth, nr Warrington, Cheshire**
Gem Fairs

Feb 27   **ANTIQUE & CRAFT FAIR/Hedworth Hall, Westoe, South Shields, Tyne & Wear**
Quintet Promotions

Feb 27-28   **CRAFT FAYRE/Park Farm Garden Centre, Landford, Salisbury, Wilts**
Avocet Crafts

Feb 27-28   **CRAFT FAYRE/Blakemere Craft Centre, Chester Road, Sandiway, Northwich, Cheshire**
Blakemere Craft Centre   *See display advertisement*

Feb 27-28   **CRAFT FAIR/The Ingestre Suite, County Showground, Weston Road, Stafford, Staffs**
Central Promotions   *See display advertisement*

Feb 27-28   **CRAFT FAIR/Brigade Hall, Bakewell, Derbys**
Cottage Creations Craft Fairs

Cottage Industries Association
1999 Craft, Design & Gift Fairs
25 Hughes Av., Wolverhampton, West Midlands WV3 7AU

1999 VENUES

MARCH 13-14	**MOTHERS DAY WEEK-END CRAFT FAIR** Percy Throwers Gardening Centre, Shrewsbury	4,000	(c)
APRIL 2-3-4-5	**JARDINERIE GARDEN PLACE EASTER HOLIDAY** Craft Fair. Hampton in Arden, Kenilworth Rd (A452)	6,000	(c)
MAY 1-2-3	**MAY BANK HOLIDAY CRAFT FAIR** Percy Throwers Gardening Centre, Shrewsbury	6,000	(e)
MAY 30-31	**BIRMINGHAM LORD MAYOR'S SHOW** Spring Bank Holiday, Cannon Hill Park	50,000	(c)
MAY 30-31	**LICHFIELD SUMMER FLOWER SHOW** Beacon Park (Town centre)	10,000	(e)
JUNE 5-6	**WALSALL SUMMER SHOW** Bosty Lane Airport, Aldridge	16,000	(c)
JUNE 26-27	**WADDINGTON INTERNATIONAL AIRSHOW** More information on request	120,000	(c)
AUG 5-6-7-8	**BRISTOL INTERNATIONAL BALLOON FIESTA** Ashton Court, Bristol – the largest show in Europe (British Crafts only)	500,000	(c)
AUG 28-29-30	**NATIONAL FISHING CHAMPIONSHIPS** Crown Meadow, River Avon, Evesham	40,000	(c)
SEPT 3-4-5	**BIRMINGHAM CITY NATIONAL DOG SHOW** Perry Park (A34)	40,000	(c)

(c) confirmed attendance (e) estimated attendance. **Caravan parking available at all events.**

ALSO GARDEN CENTRE TWO-DAY MARQUEE EVENTS THROUGHOUT THE YEAR

BYRKLEY PARK
(Burton-on-Trent)

DOBBIES GARDEN WORLD
(A5 Penkridge, Cannock)

HURRANS GARDEN CENTRE
(Leigh Sinton, nr Malvern)

HURRANS GARDEN CENTRE
(Newport, South Wales)

HURRANS GARDEN CENTRE
(West Hagley, nr Stourbridge)

JARDINERIE GARDEN PLACE
(Hampton-in-Arden)

**PERCY THROWERS GARDENING
CENTRE** (Shrewsbury)

WILLIAM WHEATS GARDEN CENTRE
(Little Aston, A452)

WYNDLEY GARDEN CENTRE (Knowle)

WYEVALE GARDEN CENTRE
(Strawberry Fields, Farm Shop Complex
Donnington, Telford)

Garden Centre Attendances between 3,000-6,000
50 EVENTS SPECIALLY SELECTED FOR THEIR POPULARITY
Tel/Fax: Jean or John Jeater 01902 332901 or 07957 31462

Feb 27-28	**CRAFT, DESIGN & GIFT FAIR/Byrkley Park Garden Centre, Rangemore, Burton-on-Trent, Staffs**	
	Cottage Industries Association	*See display advertisement*
Feb 27-28	**CRAFT FAIR/St William's College, York, North Yorks**	
	Keld Craft Fairs	
Feb 27-28	**GRIMSBY CRAFT WEEKEND/The Grimsby Auditorium, Cromwell Road, Grimsby, North East Lincs**	
	Living Heritage Craft Shows Ltd	*See display advertisement*
Feb 27-28	**CRAFT FAIR/Sevenoaks Community Centre, Otford Road, Sevenoaks, Kent**	
	M B County Fairs	
Feb 27-28	**LIVE CRAFTS SHOW/Brooklands, Weybridge, Surrey**	
	The Exhibition Team Ltd	*See display advertisement*
Feb 28	**CRAFT FAIR/Biddulph Leisure Centre, Thames Drive, off Congleton Road, Biddulph, Staffs**	
	Archer Promotions	
Feb 28	**CRAFT FAIR/Village Hotel, Whiston, nr Prescot, Merseyside**	
	Creative Crafts Association	*See display advertisement*
Feb 28	**DOLL FAIR/Kelham Hall, Newark, Notts**	
	East Midlands Doll Fairs	
Feb 28	**CRAFT FAIR/The Country Park Inn, Hessle Foreshore, nr Hull, East Yorks**	
	Holland Fairs	
Feb 28	**CRAFT FAIR/Mayflower Centre, Plymouth, Devon**	
	Kevin Murphy Craft Fairs	
Feb 28	**CRAFT & ANTIQUE FAIR/Gargrave Village Hall, nr Skipton, North Yorks**	
	Lancastrian Fairs	
Feb 28	**CRAFT & ANTIQUE FAIR/Ground Floor Centre, Hebden Bridge, West Yorks**	
	Lancastrian Fairs	
Feb 28	**CRAFT FAIR/Stone Manor Hotel, Stone, nr Kidderminster, Worcs**	
	Laurel Crafts	
Feb 28	**CRAFT FAIR/Durham County Cricket Club, Chester-le-Street, Co Durham**	
	Quintet Promotions	
Feb 28-March 2	**THE GREAT YORKSHIRE SPRING GIFTS TRADE FAIR/Great Yorkshire Showground, Wetherby Road, Harrogate, North Yorks**	
	Northern Exhibitions	
Feb 28-March 2	**RURAL CRAFTS ASSOCIATION AT BETA/National Exhibition Centre, Birmingham, West Midlands**	
	Rural Crafts Association	*See display advertisement*
March 5-7	**HOLDENBY HOUSE HOME DESIGN & INTERIORS EXHIBITION/Holdenby, nr Northampton, Northants**	
	Buckingham Publicity	*See display advertisement*

BLAKEMERE CRAFT CENTRE

CRAFT FAIR EVENTS '99

STALL PRICES FROM £35 PER WEEKEND INCLUDING RATES, HEAT AND LIGHT

BLAKEMERE is a large family attraction set around a restored Edwardian Stable Block in the heart of the Cheshire countryside. It is open for 12 months of the year and attracts around 100,000 visitors per annum.

With permanent Craft Shops, an Aquatic & Falconry Centre and large Indoor Children's Playbarn it offers a wonderful family day out.

CRAFT FAIRS are situated in the large loft areas of the Stable Block and are held every weekend and the last wednesday of the month. With free admission and parking to all events, Blakemere can be an ideal solution to your 1999 programme.

Prime Retail Location

Indoor Weekend Craft Fairs

Indoor Children's Playbarn

Excellent Coffee Shop & Restaurant

Aquatic & Falconry Centre

Craft Shops

Craft Workshops

FREE ADMISSION & PARKING

	A49 ▲ WARRINGTON
CHESTER	MANCHESTER
◄ A556	A556 ►
	BLAKEMERE CRAFT CENTRE
	A49 ▼ WHITCHURCH

OPENING TIMES

Tues - Fri:
10am - 5pm
Sat & Sun:
10am - 5.30pm
Bank Holidays:
10am - 5.30pm
Mondays closed

CHESTER RD, SANDIWAY, NORTHWICH CW8 2EB. TEL: 01606 883261

March 6	**CRAFT MARKET/Fisher Hall, Guildhall Place, Cambridge, Cambs** Balthazar
March 6	**CRAFT FAIR/Burgh Hall, Peebles** Border Fairs
March 6	**CRAFT FAIR/Community Centre, Pond Road, Shoreham-by-Sea, West Sussex** Craft Developments
March 6	**ARTS & CRAFTS FAIR/Town Hall, Towcester, Northants** Falcon Fairs
March 6	**CRAFT & GIFT FAIR/Barnet Library, Stapylton Road, Barnet, Herts** Marie Margaret Promotions
March 6	**DOLLS HOUSES, DOLLS & MINIATURES FAIR/The Rhodes Centre, Bishop's Stortford, Herts** Quality Craft Fairs
March 6	**CRAFT & GIFT FAYRE/Ferneham Hall, Fareham, Hants** Something Special Craft & Gift Fayres
March 6	**ART & CRAFT FAIR/The Arts Centre, Biddick Lane, Fatfield, Washington, Tyne & Wear** The Arts Centre
March 6-7	**SPRING CRAFT & GIFT FAIR/Purbeck Hall, Bournemouth International Centre, Dorset** BIC Exhibitions
March 6-7	**CRAFT FAYRE/Blakemere Craft Centre, Chester Road, Sandiway, Northwich, Cheshire** Blakemere Craft Centre *See display advertisement*
March 6-7	**CRAFT FAYRE/Trentham Gardens, Stone Road (A34), Trentham, Stoke-on-Trent, Staffs** Cheshire Fayre *See display advertisement*
March 6-7	**CRAFT FAIR/Brigade Hall, Bakewell, Derbys** Cottage Creations Craft Fairs
March 6-7	**CRAFT, DESIGN & GIFT FAIR/Dobbies Gardening World, A5, Penkridge, nr Cannock, Staffs** Cottage Industries Association *See display advertisement*
March 6-7	**ARTS, CRAFTS & COUNTRY SHOPPING FAIR/Hagley Hall, nr Stourbridge, West Midlands** Countrywide Events
March 6-7	**CRAFT FAIR/Cliffs Pavilion, Station Road, Westcliff-on-Sea, Southend, Essex** Hallmark Fairs
March 6-7	**CRAFT FAIR/St William's College, York, North Yorks** Keld Craft Fairs
March 6-7	**DERBY CRAFT WEEKEND/Assembly Rooms, Market Place, Derby, Derbys** Living Heritage Craft Shows Ltd *See display advertisement*

Woodland Crafts
Quality Craft Shows For Genuine Craftworkers

BUSY SHOWS - FRIENDLY ATMOSPHERE
VENUES WITH A DIFFERENCE
HIGH QUALITY CRAFTS - DEMONSTRATIONS
CRAFT SUPPLIES AND KITS - FOOD STALLS
ENTERTAINMENT AND EXTRA ATTRACTIONS
EXTENSIVE PUBLICITY - SIGNPOSTING

1999 CRAFT SHOWS AND OUTDOOR EVENTS IN HAMPSHIRE AND SUSSEX

FEB 6-7	FORT PURBROOK, NR. PORTSMOUTH
MAR 9-14	COUNTY MALL SHOPPING CENTRE, CRAWLEY
MAR 16-21	FAREHAM SHOPPING CENTRE, HANTS.
MAR 20-21	FORT BROCKHURST, NR. FAREHAM, HANTS.
APR 3-5	FORT PURBROOK EASTER CRAFT SHOW
APR 10-11	LANCING COLLEGE CRAFT SHOW, SUSSEX
APR 20-25	FAREHAM SHOPPING CENTRE, HANTS.
MAY 1-3	HEAVY HORSE WEEKEND, SOUTHSEA
MAY 29-31	FORT PURBROOK CRAFT SHOW
JUNE 5-6	FORT BROCKHURST, NR. FAREHAM, HANTS.
JUNE 8-13	COUNTY MALL SHOPPING CENTRE, CRAWLEY
JUNE 15-20	FAREHAM SHOPPING CENTRE, HANTS.
JULY 10-11	QUEEN ELIZABETH COUNTRY PARK SHOW
AUG 6-8	PORTSMOUTH AND SOUTHSEA SHOW
AUG 7-8	VICTORIAN FESTIVAL, WORTHING, SUSSEX
AUG 10-15	COUNTY MALL SHOPPING CENTRE, CRAWLEY
AUG 28-30	INTERNATIONAL KITE FESTIVAL, SOUTHSEA
AUG 28-30	FORT PURBROOK CRAFT SHOW
SEPT 4-5	SHOREHAM AIRSHOW , SHOREHAM, SUSSEX
OCT 9-10	FORT PURBROOK CRAFT SHOW
OCT 12-17	COUNTY MALL SHOPPING CENTRE, CRAWLEY
NOV 6-7	FORT PURBROOK CRAFT SHOW
NOV 20-21	FORT BROCKHURST CHRISTMAS CRAFT SHOW
DEC 3-5	FORT PURBROOK CHRISTMAS CRAFT SHOW

EXTRA CRAFT DEMONSTRATORS NEEDED!!
**If you are a demonstrator with an interesting craft
of any type, we would like to hear from you.**

EXHIBITORS, PLEASE RING OR WRITE FOR DETAILS AND FULL
CALENDER OF EVENTS TO: Woodland Crafts, Dept CB, "Butskiln",
Street End, Sidlesham Common, Chichester, W. Sussex PO20 7QD
TEL/FAX: 01243 641306

March 6-7	**CRAFT FAIR/Windsor Racecourse, Windsor, Berks** Rainbow Fair

March 6-7   **CRAFT FAIR/Windsor Racecourse, Windsor, Berks**
Rainbow Fair

March 6-7   **CRAFT FAIR/Garson Farm, West End Village, nr Esher, Surrey**
VBR Crafts

March 7   **CRAFT & GIFT FAIR/Rotherwick Hall, nr Basingstoke, Hants**
Aquarius Fairs

March 7   **CRAFT FAIR/Northwood Stadium, Keelings Road, Northwood, Hanley, Stoke-on-Trent, Staffs**
Archer Promotions

March 7   **DOLLS HOUSE & MINIATURE FAIR/The Marine Hall, The Esplanade, Fleetwood, Lancs**
Brentwood Fairs

March 7   **CRAFT SHOW/Morley Hayes, Morley, Derbys**
CFL Craft Shows

March 7   **CRAFT FAIR/The Leisure Centre, Ounsdale Road, Wombourne, West Midlands**
Central Promotions   *See display advertisement*

March 7   **CRAFT FAYRE/The Belgrave Hotel, Torquay, Devon**
Cherrycraft Fayres & Festivals

March 7   **CRAFT FAIR/Oasis Leisure Centre, North Star Avenue, Swindon, Wilts**
Cottage Craft Fairs   *See display advertisement*

March 7   **CRAFT FAIR/Park Royal International Hotel, Stretton, Warrington, Cheshire**
Creative Crafts Association   *See display advertisement*

March 7   **DOLL FAIR/Woburn Abbey, M1 Junction 13, Beds**
East Midlands Doll Fairs

March 7   **CRAFT & GIFT FAIR/Barton Village Hall, nr Preston, Lancs**
Golden Age Fairs

March 7   **CRAFT FAIR/Gargrave Village Hall, Gargrave, nr Skipton, North Yorks**
Heritage Fairs

March 7   **ARTS & CRAFTS FAIR/Grassington Town Hall, Grassington, nr Skipton, North Yorks**
Jean Bryon

March 7   **CRAFT FAIR/Ely Maltings, Ely, Cambs**
Kingfisher Promotions

March 7   **CRAFT & ANTIQUE FAIR/Ground Floor Centre, Hebden Bridge, West Yorks**
Lancastrian Fairs

March 7   **ARTS & CRAFTS SHOW/Lauderdale House, Highgate Hill, London N6**
Lauderdale Arts & Crafts

March 7   **CRAFT FAIR/The Heath Hotel, Bewdley, Worcs**
Laurel Crafts

Living Heritage Craft Shows

1999 Programme of Events

NEW SHOWS IN 1999

With nearly 20 years experience of organising quality Craft Shows, Living Heritage are now inviting applications from quality Craftsmen and Women for their 1999 series of events.

All of the established shows are there, including Knebworth, Woburn Abbey, Broadlands, Blenheim Palace, Blake Hall and many more, plus the exciting new events listed here.

Call us now for our 1999 programme, our finest yet & enjoy a successful year of shows with Living Heritage.

Programme Hotline:

01283 820548

**PO Box 36
Uttoxeter
Staffs. ST14 8PY**

**Tel: 01283 820548
Fax: 01283 821200**

January 30th & January 31st
October 16th & 17th
Aylesbury Civic Centre

February 13th & 14th
**Norwich Sports
Village Hotel**

February 27th & 28th
October 23rd & 24th
Grimsby Auditorium

March 13th & 14th
October 9th & 10th
Hop Farm Museum
Kent

April 17th & 18th
July 17th & 18th
Stoneyhurst College
nr Preston

May 1st, 2nd & 3rd
August 28th, 29th & 30th
Somerley Estate
Ringwood

June 12th & 13th
Hughenden Manor
High Wycombe

July 10th & 11th
Ashridge Estate
Berkhampstead

July 24th & 25th
**Royal International
Air Tattoo**

October 9th & 10th
**Telford International
Exhibition Centre**

29

March 7	**CRAFT & GIFT FAIR/Ramside Hall Hotel, Carrville, Co Durham**
	Quality Craft & Gift Fairs *See display advertisement*

March 7   **CRAFT FAIR/Leisure World, Cowdray Avenue, Colchester, Essex**
R&S Fairs

March 7   **CRAFT FAIR/Pittville Pump Rooms, Cheltenham, Glos**
Town & Country Craft Fairs

March 7   **DOLLS HOUSE, DOLLS, TOYS & MINIATURES FAIR/Exmouth Pavilion, Exmouth, Devon**
West of England Fairs

March 7   **CRAFT FAIR/Pavilion Theatre, Worthing, West Sussex**
Worthing Leisure

March 11-13   **CRAFT & ANTIQUE FAIR/The Guild Hall, York, North Yorks**
Lancastrian Fairs

March 12-14   **THE QUILT FAIR/The Belfry Halls, Brugge, BELGIUM**
Quilt Events Ltd

March 13   **CRAFT & GIFT FAIR/The Harlington Centre, High Street, Fleet, Hants**
Aquarius Fairs

March 13   **CRAFT MARKET/Fisher Hall, Guildhall Place, Cambridge, Cambs**
Balthazar

March 13   **DUNSTABLE CRAFT MARKET/Methodist Church Hall, Ashton Square, Dunstable, Beds**
Dunstable Craft Market

March 13   **ARTS & CRAFTS FAIR/Town Hall, Brackley, Northants**
Falcon Fairs

March 13   **CRAFT FAYRE/St Mary's Centre, Grassmere Close, Felpham, West Sussex**
Good Ideas Craft Fayres

March 13   **CRAFT FAIR/Wyvern Hall, Swallows Leisure Centre, Central Avenue, Sittingbourne, Kent**
M B County Fairs

March 13   **CRAFT FAIR/Market Hall, Abergavenny, Monmouthshire**
Monmouthshire County Council

March 13   **POSSET CRAFT FAYRE/Somerset Hall, Portishead, North Somerset**
Portishead Supporters

March 13-14   **CRAFT FAIR/Hawkshead Market Hall, nr Ambleside, Cumbria**
Aphrodite

March 13-14   **CRAFT FAYRE/Balmer Lawn Hotel, Brockenhurst, Hants**
Avocet Crafts

March 13-14   **CRAFT FAYRE/Blakemere Craft Centre, Chester Road, Sandiway, Northwich, Cheshire**
Blakemere Craft Centre   *See display advertisement*

1999  **1999**

DIANE MORRIS

Quality CRAFT & GIFT FAIRS

HELD IN FIRST CLASS HOTELS/BANQUETING SUITES • MIN 50+ EXHIBITORS

HARROGATE

ST. GEORGE SWALLOW HOTEL
Half Term February 21st
Bank Holiday May 2nd/3rd
Bank Holiday May 30th/31st
Half Term October 24th
Nov 28th (Coincides with Knitting & Stitching Show)

NEW VENUE

Free Entry Fairs in the Newly Refurbished
SUN PAVILION - VALLEY GARDENS
Cornwall Road, Harrogate
Fathers Day June 20th, July 18th and August 15th

LEEDS

PUDSEY CIVIC HALL: May 23rd, December 19th
HILTON NATIONAL, GARFORTH: Half Term October 17th, December 12th
VILLAGE HOTEL, OTLEY ROAD: November 14th

MIDDLESBROUGH

MARTON HOTEL & COUNTRY CLUB
Valentines Day (With Wedding Fair): February 14th
Halloween (With Wedding Fair) October 31st

NEW VENUE ### THE ORMESBY SPRING GARDEN SHOW
Ormesby Hall (Craft Marquee with wooden floor)
May 15th/16th

NEW VENUE ### TEESSIDE FESTIVAL OF TRANSPORT
Ormesby Hall (Craft Marquee with wooden floor)
Bank Holiday August 29th/30th

DURHAM

RAMSIDE HALL HOTEL, CARRVILLE: March 7th, November 21st

All Fairs 10am - 5pm
• REALISTIC STAND RATES • SUBSTANTIAL SUPPORT ADVERTISING •
• UNRIVALLED PROMOTIONS • RAC SIGNPOSTING FOR ALL FAIRS •
"WE TARGET THE BUYING PUBLIC"
for full year's programme and booking form, telephone:
MRS DIANE MORRIS, QUALITY CRAFT & GIFT FAIRS, LEEDS
TEL: 0113 - 2671896 FAX: 0113 - 2300225

March 13-14	**CRAFT SHOW/Kelham Hall, Newark, Notts** CFL Craft Shows	
March 13-14	**CRAFT FAIR/Brigade Hall, Bakewell, Derbys** Cottage Creations Craft Fairs	
March 13-14	**CRAFT, DESIGN & GIFT FAIR/Percy Thrower's Gardening Centre, Shrewsbury, Salop** Cottage Industries Association	*See display advertisement*
March 13-14	**CRAFT FAIR/White Hart Inn, Hawes, North Yorks** Keld Craft Fairs	
March 13-14	**COOMBE ABBEY CRAFT SHOW/Coombe Abbey, Coventry, Warks** Living Heritage Craft Shows Ltd	*See display advertisement*
March 13-14	**HOP FARM CRAFT SHOW/Hop Farm Country Park, Beltring, Paddock Wood, nr Tonbridge, Kent** Living Heritage Craft Shows Ltd	*See display advertisement*
March 13-14	**SPRING CRAFT FESTIVAL/Ragley Hall, Alcester, Warks** MGA Fairs	*See display advertisement*
March 13-14	**MINIATURA - THE DOLLS' HOUSE SHOW/NEC, Birmingham, West Midlands (March 13, limited visitor number, pre-booked)** Miniatura Dolls House Shows	
March 13-14	**CRAFT FAIR/Newstead Abbey, Mansfield, Notts** Oak Craft Fairs	*See display advertisement*
March 13-14	**CRAFT & GIFT FAIR/Towerlands Centre, Panfield Road, Braintree, Essex** Towerlands Centre	
March 13-17	**RURAL CRAFTS ASSOCIATION AT BRIGHTER HOMES 99/Dublin, Eire** Rural Crafts Association	*See display advertisement*
March 14	**CRAFT FAIR/Congleton Town Hall, High Street, Congleton, Cheshire** Archer Promotions	
March 14	**TEDDY BEAR & DOLL FAIR/University of Liverpool, Carnatic Conference Park, North Mossley Hill Road, Liverpool** Brentwood Fairs	
March 14	**CRAFT FAIR/The Manor Hotel, Hartlebury Road, Stourport, Worcs** Central Promotions	*See display advertisement*
March 14	**CRAFT FAIR/Kings Hall, Herne Bay, Kent** East Kent Fairs	*See display advertisement*
March 14	**CRAFT FAIR/Knights Barn, King's Lynn, Norfolk** Kingfisher Promotions	
March 14	**CRAFT & ANTIQUE FAIR/Ground Floor Centre, Hebden Bridge, West Yorks** Lancastrian Fairs	
March 14	**CRAFT FAIR/The Inn on the Lake, Shorne, nr Gravesend, Kent** M B County Fairs	

East Kent Fairs 1999

Excellent Fairs around the Kent Coast

Over twenty events held throughout the year in prestige and well attended venues around Kent and its coastline.

Sat **January 23rd DOVER** Town Hall 'The January Craft Sale'
Sun **March 14th HERNE BAY** Kings Hall
Sat/Sun **March 20th & 21st FOLKESTONE** Leas Cliff Hall
Sat/Sun **March 27th & 28th TENTERDEN** Leisure Centre
Sat **April 3rd DOVER** Easter Craft Fair Town Hall
Saturday **May 1st SANDWICH** Guildhall
May 29th, 30th, 31st Spring Bank Holiday, **THE GREAT EAST KENT GARDEN SHOW** 16th year **DEAL**
Sat/Sun **September 11th/12th FOLKESTONE** Leas Cliff Hall

Christmas Craft Fairs
Sat/Sun **October 23rd/24th MARGATE** Winter Gardens
Sat **October 30th DEAL** Astor Theatre
Sat/Sun **November 6th & 7th HERNE BAY** Kings Hall
Sat/Sun **November 13th & 14th FOLKESTONE** Leas Cliff Hall
Sat/Sun **November 20th & 21st TENTERDEN** Leisure Centre
Sat/Sun **November 27th & 28th GRAVESEND** Woodville Halls
Sat/Sun **Dec 4th & 5th DOVER** Town Hall
Sat **December 11th SANDWICH** Guildhall

for full details of this exciting, reasonably priced programme phone **John Payne** on **01304 201644** or write to

East Kent Fairs, 134/135 London Road, Dover CT17 0TG

March 14	**CRAFT FAIR/Lyndhurst Community Centre, Lyndhurst, Hants**
	Oakleaf Craft Fairs *See display advertisement*

March 14   **CRAFT FAIR/Lyndhurst Community Centre, Lyndhurst, Hants**
Oakleaf Craft Fairs   *See display advertisement*

March 14   **CRAFT FAIR/Royal Chace Hotel, The Ridgeway, Enfield, Middx**
Quality Craft Fairs

March 14   **CRAFT FAIR/Lumley Castle, Chester-le-Street, Co Durham**
Quintet Promotions

March 14-15   **WELSH GIFT FAIR/Cardiff International Arena**
Oyster Exhibitions

March 19-21   **THE QUILT FAIR/The MacRobert Pavilion, Royal Highland Showground, Ingliston, Edinburgh**
Quilt Events Ltd

March 20   **CRAFT MARKET/Fisher Hall, Guildhall Place, Cambridge, Cambs**
Balthazar

March 20   **CRAFT FAIR/Town Hall, Jedburgh, Roxburghshire**
Border Fairs

March 20   **DESIGN IN ACTION/The Art Workers' Guild, London**
Society of Designer Craftsmen

March 20   **FORT BROCKHURST CRAFT FAYRE/nr Fareham, Hants**
Woodland Crafts   *See display advertisement*

March 20-21   **CRAFT FAIR/Hawkshead Market Hall, nr Ambleside, Cumbria**
Aphrodite

March 20-21   **CRAFT FAYRE/Blakemere Craft Centre, Chester Road, Sandiway, Northwich, Cheshire**
Blakemere Craft Centre   *See display advertisement*

March 20-21   **CRAFT, DESIGN & GIFT FAIR/Hurrans Garden Centre, West Hagley, nr Stourbridge, Worcs**
Cottage Industries Association   *See display advertisement*

March 20-21   **ARTS, CRAFTS & COUNTRY SHOPPING FAIR/Tatton Park, Knutsford, Cheshire**
Countrywide Events

March 20-21   **CRAFT FAIR/Leas Cliff Hall, Folkestone, Kent**
East Kent Fairs   *See display advertisement*

March 20-21   **CRAFT FAIR/St William's College, York, North Yorks**
Keld Craft Fairs

March 20-21   **CRAFTS AT THE MANOR HOUSE/The Manor House, Aldermaston, Berks**
Living Heritage Craft Shows Ltd   *See display advertisement*

March 20-21   **CRAFT FAIR/Sandwich Leisure Centre, Sandwich, Kent**
M B County Fairs

Please remember to mention The Craftworker's Year Book to event organisers when you contact them

THE NATIONAL CRAFTS FAIR

National House
28 Grosvenor Road
Richmond, Surrey
TW10 6PB
Tel: 0181 940 4608
Fax: 0181 891 0115
Mobil: 0370 626424

1999 CHANNEL ISLAND NATIONAL CRAFT FAIRS

Established in the Islands for Twelve Years, in the UK since 1981

27th September to 3rd October
Fort Regent Leisure Centre, St. Helier, Jersey

6th to 9th October
Beau Séjour Leisure Centre, St Peter Port, Guernsey

possible also 10th October if Sunday trading is in force

We are always looking for new and interesting craftworkers
Why not ring us on 0181 940 4608 or 0370 626424

No craftworker invited without
personal inspection at a craft fair of your choice

No bought in goods or imports

If your product is different, original, well made and well
presented we would like to hear from you.

Easy payment plan, a happy atmosphere and some of the best
fairs in the country go to make membership of the
National Crafts Fair well worthwhile.

Your contact is: **Anthony James**

March 20-21   **THE ST IVES SPRING CRAFTS FAIR/St Ivo Recreation Centre, St Ives, Cambs**
Romor Exhibitions Ltd   *See display advertisement*

March 20-21   **RURAL CRAFTS ASSOCIATION AT THE NATIONAL SHIRE HORSE SHOW/ Peterborough, Cambs**
Rural Crafts Association   *See display advertisement*

March 20-21   **SPRING CRAFT FAIR/Stapehill Abbey, Crafts & Gardens, 276 Wimborne Road West, Stapehill, nr Wimborne, Dorset**
Stapehill Abbey, Crafts & Gardens

March 20-21   **LIVE CRAFTS SHOW/Bletchley Park, Bletchley, Bucks**
The Exhibition Team Ltd   *See display advertisement*

March 20-21   **JUST ARTS & CRAFTS/Great Hall, Kempton Park Racecourse, Sunbury-on-Thames, Middx**
Traditional Crafts Ltd   *See display advertisement*

March 21   **CRAFT FAIR/Manor House Hotel, Audley Road, Alsager, Staffs**
Archer Promotions

March 21   **CRAFT FAIR/Lordsbridge Arena, Barton, Cambs**
Cambridge Craft Fairs

March 21   **CRAFT FAIR/Leisure Centre, Clewer Mead, Stovell Road, Windsor, Berks**
Cottage Craft Fairs   *See display advertisement*

March 21   **CRAFT FAIR/Keresforth Hall, Barnsley, South Yorks**
Cottage Creations Craft Fairs

March 21   **CRAFT, DESIGN & GIFT FAIR/Bromsgrove Market Hall, Worcs**
Cottage Industries Association   *See display advertisement*

March 21   **CRAFT FAIR/Lancaster University Conference Centre, Lancs**
Creative Crafts Association   *See display advertisement*

March 21   **ARTS & CRAFTS FAIR/Woburn Village Hall, Woburn, Beds**
Falcon Fairs

March 21   **CRAFT FAIR/Beverley Leisure Centre, Flemingate (opposite Army Museum), Beverley, East Yorks**
Holland Fairs

March 21   **CRAFT FAIR/Exmouth Pavilion, Exmouth, Devon**
J M Evans

March 21   **CRAFT & ANTIQUE FAIR/Gargrave Village Hall, nr Skipton, North Yorks**
Lancastrian Fairs

March 21   **CRAFT & ANTIQUE FAIR/Ground Floor Centre, Hebden Bridge, West Yorks**
Lancastrian Fairs

March 21   **CRAFT FAIR/Royal Derwent Hotel, Allensford, Co Durham**
Quintet Promotions

March 21   **CRAFT FAIR/St Herberts Parish Hall**
West Pennine Promotions

Cottage Craft Fairs

FIRST CLASS VENUES ◆ AFFORDABLE FEES
Quality Presentation ◆ Extensive Promotional Support
Professional Signposting ◆ Mobile Advertising

RIVERMEAD COMPLEX Reading Berks
Feb 7 Apr 5 May 31 Sept 19 Nov 20/21 Dec 12
LODDON VALLEY CENTRE Reading Berks
Apr 11 Oct 17 Dec 5
WINDSOR CENTRE Windsor Berks
Mar 21 Oct 24
OASIS CENTRE Swindon Wilts
Mar 7 Oct 10
SPELTHORNE CENTRE Staines Middx
Feb 21 Sept 26 Nov 28
WYCOMBE CENTRE High Wycombe Bucks
May 3 Aug 30
HALTON SPECTACULAR Aylesbury Bucks
June 26

SAE please (A5 9x6 min)
Cottage Craft Fairs
122 Sevenoaks Road Orpington BR6 9JZ
Tel: 01689 852121

March 23	**CRAFT FAIR/White Hart Inn, Hawes, North Yorks** Keld Craft Fairs
March 26-28	**THE QUILT FAIR/Chilford Hall Vineyard, Linton, Cambs** Quilt Events Ltd
March 27	**CRAFT MARKET/Fisher Hall, Guildhall Place, Cambridge, Cambs** Balthazar
March 27	**CRAFT FAIR/Corn Exchange, Haddington, East Lothian** Border Fairs
March 27	**LEEDS DOLL & TEDDY FAIR/Pudsey Civic Hall, New Pudsey, nr Leeds, West Yorks** Dolly Domain Fairs
March 27	**ARTS & CRAFTS FAIR/Buckingham Community Centre, Bucks** Falcon Fairs
March 27	**CRAFT FAIR/Victoria Hall, Bourton-on-the-Water, Glos** M&B Crafts
March 27-28	**CRAFT FAYRE/Birmingham Craft Centre, Chester Road, Sandiway, Northwich, Cheshire** Blakemere Craft Centre *See display advertisement*
March 27-28	**CRAFT FAYRE/Fenton Manor, Fenton, Stoke-on-Trent, Staffs** Cheshire Fayre *See display advertisement*
March 27-28	**CRAFT, DESIGN & GIFT FAIR/Wyevale Garden Centre & Farm Shop, Telford, Salop** Cottage Industries Association *See display advertisement*
March 27-28	**CRAFT, FOOD & GIFTS FAIR/Beaumanor Hall, Loughborough, Leics** Countrywide Events
March 27-28	**CRAFT FAIR/Haydock Park Racecourse Exhibition Centre, St Helens, Merseyside** Creative Crafts Association *See display advertisement*
March 27-28	**CRAFT FAIR/Leisure Centre Sports Hall, Tenterden, Kent** East Kent Fairs *See display advertisement*
March 27-28	**CRAFT & GARDENING EVENT/Warwickshire County Cricket Ground, Edgbaston, Birmingham, West Midlands** Hobby Horse Design & Craft Fairs
March 27-28	**CRAFTS AT THE YORKSHIRE DESIGNER LIVING SHOW/Knavesmere Suite, York Race Course, North Yorks** Jean Welch Shows *See display advertisement*
March 27-28	**MID SUSSEX CRAFT SHOW/South of England Centre, Ardingly, nr Haywards Heath, West Sussex** Living Heritage Craft Shows Ltd *See display advertisement*
March 27-28	**CRAFT FAIR/Chatham Girls Grammar School, Rainham Road, Chatham, Kent** M B County Fairs

CRAFTS  CRAFTS

PROFESSIONAL ORGANISERS OF QUALITY EVENTS
1999

20th year
MARCH 20th - 21st
THE ST. IVES, SPRING CRAFTS FAIR
St. Ives Cambs
Up to 80 Stands

20th year
APRIL 4th - 5th
THE BEDFORD EASTER CRAFTS FAIR *Bank Holiday*
Corn Exchange, Bedford
Up to 60 stands

9th year
MAY 1st - 3rd *Bank Holiday*
THE MILTON KEYNES
GARDEN SHOW
Walton Hall, Milton Keynes, Bucks
Up to 150 stands
(Includes large crafts marquee)

10th year
MAY 29th - 31st *Bank Holiday*

THE WREST PARK GARDEN SHOW
Silsoe, Beds
Up to 150 stands
(Includes large crafts marquee)

5th year
JUNE 5th - 6th

THE WOBURN ABBEY
GARDEN SHOW
Woburn, Beds
up to 150 stands
(includes large crafts marquee)

10th year
AUGUST 28th - 30th *Bank Holiday*
THE WREST PARK
CRAFTS FESTIVAL
Silsoe, Beds
Up to 200 stands
(includes traditional craft demonstrations)

3rd year
OCTOBER 17th
THE ST. IVES TEDDY BEAR FAIR
St. Ives, Cambs
Up to 70 stands

20th year **NOVEMBER 20th - 21st**
THE ST. IVES CHRISTMAS CRAFTS FAIR
St. Ives, Cambs
Up to 80 stands

STANDS AVAILABLE FROM £25 PER DAY

All enquires to Dept. CY, Romor Exhibitions Limited,
PO Box 448, Bedford, Beds MK40 2ZP

Tel: 01234 345725   Fax: 01234 328604

March 27-28	**CRAFT FAIR/Fritton Lake, Norfolk** Rainbow Fair
March 27- April 5	**THE TORBAY SPRING CRAFTS FESTIVAL/Lower Union Street, Torquay, Devon (provisional and marquee)** Cherrycraft Fayres & Festivals
March 27- April 18	**THE SUSSEX GUILD EXHIBITION/The Towner Art Gallery, High Street, Eastbourne Old Town, Eastbourne, East Sussex** The Sussex Guild
March 28	**CRAFT FAIR/Biddulph Leisure Centre, Thames Drive, off Congleton Road, Biddulph, Staffs** Archer Promotions
March 28	**CRAFT FAIR/The Moat House Hotel, M54 Junction 5, Telford, Salop** Central Promotions *See display advertisement*
March 28	**CRAFT FAIR/Aston Hall, Aston, Sheffield, South Yorks** Cottage Creations Craft Fairs
March 28	**CRAFT FAIR/Lacock Village Hall, Lacock, nr Chippenham, Wilts** Countrycraft
March 28	**CRAFT FAIR/Dog & Fox Hotel, High Street Wimbledon, Wimbledon Village, London** Eden Crafts
March 28	**CRAFT FAIR/Courage Hall, Brentwood Boys School, Middleton Hall Lane, Brentwood, Essex** Hallmark Fairs
March 28	**CRAFT FAIR/Great Hall, Worksop College, Manton, Worksop, Notts** Heathfield Craft Fairs
March 28	**CRAFT FAIR/The Jarvis International Hotel, Willerby, nr Hull, East Yorks** Holland Fairs
March 28	**CRAFT & ANTIQUE FAIR/Ground Floor Centre, Hebden Bridge, West Yorks** Lancastrian Fairs
March 28	**CRAFT FAIR/The Bellhouse Hotel, Oxford Road (A40), Beaconsfield, Bucks** Midas Fairs
March 28	**CRAFT FAIR/Southwater Village Centre, Southwater, nr Horsham, West Sussex** Southwater Promotions
March 31	**CRAFT FAYRE/Blakemere Craft Centre, Chester Road, Sandiway, Northwich, Cheshire** Blakemere Craft Centre *See display advertisement*
March 31- April 1	**CRAFT FAIR/Market Hall, Hawes, North Yorks** Keld Craft Fairs
April 2	**CRAFT FAIR/Otford Village Memorial Hall, nr Sevenoaks, Kent** Goldfinch Crafts

1999
PREMIER EVENTS

Beaumanor Hall Loughborough, Leics	November 6 & 7
Coughton Court Alcester, Warks	August 21 & 22
Elton Hall Peterborough, Cambs	July 17 & 18
Haddon Hall Bakewell, Derbyshire	June 26 & 27
Hanbury Hall Droitwich, Worcs	September 18 & 19
Ingestre Hall Stafford	April 4 & 5 + August 7 & 8
Newstead Abbey Mansfield, Notts	March 13 & 14 + November 27 & 28
Tatton Park Knutsford, Cheshire	May 2 & 3 + November 20 & 21

For a full colour brochure of our 1999 quality fairs
please send a 9" x 6" SAE for
a priority booking form to:
**Oak Craft Fairs, 7 Sandstone Ave., Walton,
Chesterfield, Derbys S42 7NS
Telephone: 0956 493260 or 01246 569698**

New customers please send photographs of your craft display

| April 2 | **CRAFT FAIR/Westland S&SC, Yeovil, Somerset** |
| | Kevin Murphy Craft Fairs |

| April 2 | **CRAFT & ANTIQUE FAIR/Victoria Hall, Settle, North Yorks** |
| | Lancastrian Fairs |

| April 2-3 | **ARTS & CRAFTS FAYRE/Winter Gardens, Weston-super-Mare, North Somerset** |
| | Fountain Fayres & Exhibitions |

| April 2-5 | **EASTER CRAFT FAIR/Town Hall, Grange-over-Sands, Cumbria** |
| | Aphrodite |

| April 2-5 | **CRAFT FAYRE/Blakemere Craft Centre, Chester Road, Sandiway, Northwich, Cheshire** |
| | Blakemere Craft Centre   *See display advertisement* |

| April 2-5 | **CRAFT, DESIGN & GIFT FAIR/Jardinerie Garden Place, Kenilworth Road (A452), Hampton-in-Arden, West Midlands** |
| | Cottage Industries Association   *See display advertisement* |

| April 2-5 | **CRAFT FAIR/Norfolk Showground, Dereham Road, New Costessey, nr Norwich, Norfolk** |
| | Country Cottage Crafts |

| April 2-5 | **THE CRAFT SHOW/Blickling Hall, Blickling, nr Norwich, Norfolk** |
| | Eastern Events Ltd   *See display advertisement* |

| April 2-5 | **MEDWAY CRAFT SHOW/Cobham Hall, Cobham, nr Gravesend, Kent** |
| | Living Heritage Craft Shows Ltd   *See display advertisement* |

| April 2-5 | **CHILLI COUNTRY CRAFTS/Chilli Showground, A2 nr Dover, Kent** |
| | M B County Fairs |

| April 2-5 | **CRAFT FAIR/Thoresby Park, nr Newark, Notts** |
| | Rainbow Fair |

| April 2-5 | **LIVE CRAFTS SHOW/Marlborough College, Marlborough, Wilts** |
| | The Exhibition Team Ltd   *See display advertisement* |

| April 2-5 | **CRAFT FAIR/The Pavilion, Buxton, Derbys** |
| | Town & Country Craft Fairs |

| April 2-5 | **CITY OF WELLS 7TH ANNUAL CRAFT FESTIVAL/Wells Town Hall, Wells, Somerset** |
| | West Country Craft Fairs   *See display advertisement* |

| April 3 | **CRAFT MARKET/Fisher Hall, Guildhall Place, Cambridge, Cambs** |
| | Balthazar |

| April 3 | **CRAFT FAIR/Burgh Hall, Peebles** |
| | Border Fairs |

| April 3 | **CRAFT FAIR/Village Hall, Pagham, nr Bognor Regis, West Sussex** |
| | Craft Developments |

| April 3 | **EASTER CRAFT FAIR/Town Hall, Dover, Kent** |
| | East Kent Fairs   *See display advertisement* |

Garden
and Kite
Festival

"events with Magic"

Regular craft shows at beautiful Harrogate's famous Crown Hotel and other events and venues

Events where
People meet
People
in a busy happy
atmosphere
designed for
them to enjoy
and discover
GREAT SHOPPING

Christmas
Festival
of designer gifts,
fine foods.
Quality events with a lively
Christmas atmosphere

Almost 10 years' experience of making events work for you.
Jean Welch Shows, Knaresborough, North Yorks
phone/fax 01423 867144 for 1999 brochure.

| April 3 | **CRAFT FAIR/Bridport Arts Centre, Bridport, Dorset** |
| | J M Evans |

| April 3 | **CRAFT FAIR/Guildhall, Salisbury, Wilts** |
| | Kevin Murphy Craft Fairs |

| April 3 | **EASTER FAYRE/Southend-on-Sea, Essex** |
| | Special Events - Southend Borough Council |

| April 3 | **ART & CRAFT FAIR/The Arts Centre, Biddick Lane, Fatfield, Washington, Tyne & Wear** |
| | The Arts Centre |

| April 3-4 | **CRAFT FAIR/Lyndhurst Community Centre, Lyndhurst, Hants** |
| | Oakleaf Craft Fairs *See display advertisement* |

| April 3-4 | **EASTER CRAFT FAIR/Springfields, Camelgate, Spalding, Lincs** |
| | Springfields Exhibition Centre |

| April 3-5 | **CRAFT FAIR/The Village Hall, Bolton Abbey, nr Skipton, North Yorks** |
| | CFL Craft Shows |

| April 3-5 | **CRAFT FAYRE/Gawsworth Hall, Macclesfield, Cheshire** |
| | Cheshire Fayre *See display advertisement* |

| April 3-5 | **CRAFT FAIR/Brigade Hall, Bakewell, Derbys** |
| | Cottage Creations Craft Fairs |

| April 3-5 | **EASTER CRAFTS SHOW/Tenants Hall, Tatton Park, Knutsford, Cheshire** |
| | Countrywide Events |

| April 3-5 | **EASTER CRAFTS AT LARMER TREE/Larmer Tree, nr Shaftesbury, Wilts** |
| | Craft Carnival |

| April 3-5 | **CRAFT, HOME, INTERIORS & DESIGN SHOW/Sandown Park, Esher, Surrey** |
| | Four Seasons (Events) Ltd |

| April 3-5 | **CRAFT FAIR/St William's College, York, North Yorks** |
| | Keld Craft Fairs |

| April 3-5 | **NOSTELL PRIORY CRAFT SHOW/Nostell Priory, A638 Doncaster Road, nr Wakefield, West Yorks** |
| | Living Heritage Craft Shows Ltd *See display advertisement* |

| April 3-5 | **CREATIVE 99/Alexandra Palace, North London** |
| | Marathon Event Management Ltd *See display advertisement* |

| April 3-5 | **FORT PURBROOK CRAFT FAYRE/Portsdown Hill, Cosham, nr Portsmouth, Hants** |
| | Woodland Crafts *See display advertisement* |

| April 3-5 | **YORKRAFT FAIR/Pickering Over Sixties Club, Pickering, North Yorks** |
| | Yorkraft Fairs |

| April 4 | **CRAFT FAIR/Northwood Stadium, Keelings Road, Northwood, Hanley, Stoke-on-Trent, Staffs** |
| | Archer Promotions |

CRAFT FAIRS ™

PRESTIGIOUS NEW VENUES FOR 1999

NATIONAL AGRICULTURAL CENTRE
STONELEIGH – WARWICKSHIRE

16th and 17th October

THE ARTS CENTRE
WARWICK UNIVERSITY – COVENTRY
14th November

In addition to our regular and well established events at

Stafford, Telford, Shrewsbury, Llangollen, Stourport, Tamworth and Kinver

CENTRAL PROMOTIONS

JOIN THE FUN CONTACT US NOW

5 FORSYTHIA CLOSE, TELFORD, SHROPS. TF2 9TA

Telephone
01952 200992

| April 4 | **CRAFT FAIR/Corn Exchange, Melrose, Roxburghshire** |
| | Border Fairs |

| April 4 | **CRAFT FAYRE/The Belgrave Hotel, Torquay, Devon** |
| | Cherrycraft Fayres & Festivals |

| April 4 | **CRAFT & GIFT FAIR/Barton Village Hall, nr Preston, Lancs** |
| | Golden Age Fairs |

| April 4 | **CRAFT FAIR/Exmouth Pavilion, Exmouth, Devon** |
| | J M Evans |

| April 4 | **CRAFT FAIR/Goodwood Racecourse, nr Chichester, West Sussex** |
| | Mascot Craft & Gift Fairs |

| April 4 | **ANTIQUE & CRAFT FAIR/Seaburn Centre, Seaburn, Sunderland, Tyne & Wear** |
| | Quintet Promotions |

| April 4-5 | **CRAFT SHOW/The Belfry, Wishaw, Sutton Coldfield, West Midlands** |
| | CFL Craft Shows |

| April 4-5 | **CRAFT FAIR/Royal International Pavilion, Ruthin Road, Llangollen, Clwyd** |
| | Central Promotions *See display advertisement* |

| April 4-5 | **CRAFT FAIR/Lacock Village Hall, Lacock, nr Chippenham, Wilts** |
| | Countrycraft |

| April 4-5 | **CRAFT FAIR/Beaumanor Hall, Woodhouse Eaves, nr Loughborough, Leics** |
| | Heathfield Craft Fairs |

| April 4-5 | **CRAFT FAIR/Dunkenhalgh Hotel, Clayton-le-Moors, nr Accrington, Lancs** |
| | Heritage Fairs |

| April 4-5 | **COUNTRY CRAFTS WEEKEND/Audley End House, Saffron Walden, Essex** |
| | Hobby Horse Design & Craft Fairs |

| April 4-5 | **ARTS & CRAFTS FAIR/ Town Hall, Grassington, nr Skipton, North Yorks** |
| | Jean Bryon |

| April 4-5 | **CRAFT FAIR/Wood Green Animal Shelters, Godmanchester, Cambs** |
| | Kingfisher Promotions |

| April 4-5 | **CRAFT & ANTIQUE FAIR/Gargrave Village Hall, nr Skipton, North Yorks** |
| | Lancastrian Fairs |

| April 4-5 | **CRAFT & ANTIQUE FAIR/Ground Floor Centre, Hebden Bridge, West Yorks** |
| | Lancastrian Fairs |

| April 4-5 | **ARTS & CRAFTS SHOW/Lauderdale House, Highgate Hill, London N6** |
| | Lauderdale Arts & Crafts |

| April 4-5 | **CRAFT FAIR/Stone Manor Hotel, Stone, nr Kidderminster, Worcs** |
| | Laurel Crafts |

| April 4-5 | **HOP FARM COUNTRY SHOW/Hop Farm Country Park, Beltring, Paddock Wood, nr Tonbridge, Kent** |
| | Living Heritage Craft Shows Ltd *See display advertisement* |

WEST COUNTRY CRAFT FAIRS' 1999 PROGRAMME OF EVENTS

WELLS TOWN HALL, WELLS, SOMERSET
"ENGLAND'S SMALLEST CITY"
*20th February, 2nd, 3rd, 4th & 5th
April (Easter Weekend),
13th November (Annual Christmas Craft Fair)*

ROYAL SHAKESPEARE THEATRE, STRATFORD-UPON-AVON, WARWICKSHIRE
*23rd May, 30th May, 27th June, 11th July, 18th July,
8th August, 22nd August, 29th August (Bank Holiday), 12th
September, 28th November (Annual Christmas Craft Fair)*

MARINE THEATRE, LYME REGIS, DORSET
*29th May (Bank Holiday), 24th July (Mid-Summer Craft Fair),
28th August (Bank Holiday),
4th December (Christmas Craft Fair)*

ROYAL SPA CENTRE, LEAMINGTON SPA, WARWICKSHIRE
*3rd May (May Day Craft Fair),
14th November (Annual Christmas Craft Fair)*

THE CORN EXCHANGE, DORCHESTER, DORSET
20th November (Annual Christmas Craft Fair)

LYNDHURST PARK HOTEL, LYNDHURST, NEW FOREST, HAMPSHIRE
5th December (Annual Christmas Craft Fair)

ENQUIRIES TEL: 01749 677049

April 4-5	**CRAFT FAIR/Ingestre Hall, Weston Road, Stafford, Staffs**
	Oak Craft Fairs *See display advertisement*

April 4-5	**THE BEDFORD EASTER CRAFT FAIR/Corn Exchange, Bedford, Beds**
	Romor Exhibitions Ltd *See display advertisement*

April 4-5	**RURAL CRAFTS ASSOCIATION AT THE SELBY GAME FAIR/Selby, North Yorks**
	Rural Crafts Association *See display advertisement*

April 4-5	**CRAFT FAIR/Civic Hall, Ramsbottom, nr Bury, Lancs**
	West Pennine Promotions

April 5	**CRAFT FAIR/Rivermead Complex, Richfield Avenue, Caversham, Reading, Berks**
	Cottage Craft Fairs *See display advertisement*

April 5	**ARTS & CRAFTS FAIR/Woburn Village Hall, Woburn, Beds**
	Falcon Fairs

April 5	**CRAFT & GIFTS MARQUEE AT THE EASTER EXTRAVAGANZA/Avenham Park, Preston, Lancs**
	Golden Age Fairs

April 5	**CRAFT FAIR/Much Hadham Village Hall, nr Ware, Herts**
	Isabel Hospice Craft Fairs

April 5	**CRAFT FAIR/Pavilion, Weymouth, Dorset**
	Kevin Murphy Craft Fairs

April 5	**CRAFT FAIR/Market Hall, Abergavenny, Monmouthshire**
	Monmouthshire County Council

April 5	**CRAFT FAIR/The Post House, Brentwood, Essex**
	Quality Craft Fairs

April 5	**CRAFT FAIR/Park Hotel, Seafront, Tynemouth, Tyne & Wear**
	Quintet Promotions

April 5	**DOLLS HOUSE FAIR/Moat House Hotel, Borehamwood, Herts**
	R J Exhibitions

April 5	**EASTER CRAFT FAIR/The Argory, Derrycaw Road, Moy, Dungannon, Co Armagh**
	The National Trust, The Argory

April 6-8	**CRAFT FAIR/White Hart Inn, Hawes, North Yorks**
	Keld Craft Fairs

April 8-11	**NATIONAL NEEDLECRAFT SHOW/Olympia 2, Hammersmith Road, Kensington, London W14**
	Future Publishing

April 9-11	**COTSWOLDS CRAFTS SPRING SHOW/The Great Tythe Barn, Tetbury, Glos**
	Cotswold Craftsmen

April 10	**CRAFT & GIFT FAIR/The Harlington Centre, High Street, Fleet, Hants**
	Aquarius Fairs

The **MELTON MOWBRAY** *Show*

THE REGIONS BIGGEST *Free* SHOW
Best attendance 60,000

Bank Holiday Monday
31st May 1999

CRAFT MARQUEES
also Outdoor Craft Stands

BEST ENTERTAINMENT
From top military and civilian acts in non-stop main arena programme *also* second arena *and* live music stage

Preparations are already being made for the MILLENNIUM SHOW - 30th May

Book now for this unique event

Organiser: D. Whitehouse, MBE,
P.O. Box 5421, Melton Mowbray, Leics LE13 0WT
Tel/Fax: 01664 500335 (day)
01664 560606 (eves/weekends)

| April 10 | **CRAFT MARKET/Fisher Hall, Guildhall Place, Cambridge, Cambs** |
| | Balthazar |

| April 10 | **CRAFT FAIR/Municipal Hall, Biggar, Lanarkshire** |
| | Border Fairs |

| April 10 | **DUNSTABLE CRAFT MARKET/Methodist Church Hall, Ashton Square, Dunstable, Beds** |
| | Dunstable Craft Market |

| April 10 | **ARTS & CRAFTS FAIR/Town Hall, Towcester, Northants** |
| | Falcon Fairs |

| April 10 | **CRAFT & GIFT FAIR/Barnet Library, Stapylton Road, Barnet, Herts** |
| | Marie Margaret Promotions |

| April 10 | **CRAFT FAIR/Market Hall, Abergavenny, Monmouthshire** |
| | Monmouthshire County Council |

| April 10 | **CRAFT & GIFT FAYRE/Ferneham Hall, Fareham, Hants** |
| | Something Special Craft & Gift Fayres |

| April 10-11 | **CRAFT FAIR/Hawkshead Market Hall, nr Ambleside, Cumbria** |
| | Aphrodite |

| April 10-11 | **CRAFT FAYRE/Blakemere Craft Centre, Chester Road, Sandiway, Northwich, Cheshire** |
| | Blakemere Craft Centre   *See display advertisement* |

| April 10-11 | **CRAFT, DESIGN & GIFT FAIR/Wyndley Garden Centre, Lichfield Road, Sutton Coldfield, West Midlands** |
| | Cottage Industries Association   *See display advertisement* |

| April 10-11 | **CRAFT FAIR/Gateshead Central Library, Prince Consort Road, Gateshead, Tyne & Wear** |
| | Gateshead Fairs |

| April 10-11 | **CRAFTS AT THE BASC GAMEKEEPERS' FAIR/Shugborough Hall, Shugborough Estate, nr Stafford, Staffs** |
| | Laurel Crafts |

| April 10-11 | **CRAFT FAIR/Capesthorne Hall, Macclesfield, Cheshire** |
| | Rainbow Fair |

| April 10-11 | **CRAFT FAYRE/Lancing College, Lancing, West Sussex** |
| | Woodland Crafts   *See display advertisement* |

| April 11 | **DOLLS HOUSE & MINIATURE FAIR/Knights Hill Village Conference Centre, King's Lynn, Norfolk** |
| | Brentwood Fairs |

| April 11 | **CRAFT FAIR/Loddon Valley Leisure Centre, Chalfont Way, Lower Earley, nr Reading, Berks** |
| | Cottage Craft Fairs   *See display advertisement* |

| April 11 | **CRAFT FAIR/Olde House Trading Post, Chesterfield, Derbys** |
| | Cottage Creations Craft Fairs |

THE ROYAL INTERNATIONAL AIR TATTOO

CRAFT FAIR  CRAFT FAIR

weekend of 24th & 25th July 1999 RAF Fairford, Gloucester

Visit the Summer's most spectacular outdoor event.
With over 150,000 visitors you cannot afford to miss this
outstanding business opportunity.

For further information please contact either:

Mr Tom Watts
Exhibition Manager
Royal International Air Tattoo 99
Building 15, RAF Fairford
Gloucester GL7 4DL
Tel: 01285 713300 Ext 3391
Fax: 01285 713268

Mr Lyndon Short
Commercial Director
Living Heritage Craft Shows Ltd
PO Box 36 Uttoxeter
Staffs ST14 8PY
Tel: 01283 820548
Fax: 01283 821200

BOOK EARLY TO GUARANTEE PRIME SITES

CREATIVE CRAFTS ASSOCIATION

Quality Craft Fairs in the North West and North Wales

Haydock Park Racecourse Exhibition Centre
20/21 February, 27/28 March, 11/12 September,
23/24 October & 4/5 December

Lancaster University Conference Centre
21 March & 28 November

St. Helens Show 30 July to 1 August

Floral Hall Southport 11 April & 10 October

Theatre Clwyd, Mold 5 April, 17 October

Also events in Blackpool, Lytham, Altrincham, Warrington, Chester
and throughout the North West each weekend in 1999

EXCELLENT LOCATIONS – REALISTIC STAND FEES
FOR FULL 1999 LIST SEND SAE

**Creative Crafts Association, Primrose Cottage, Howards Lane, Eccleston
St. Helens, Lancs WA10 5QD. Tel: 01744 750606**

April 11	**CRAFT FAIR/Lacock Village Hall, Lacock, nr Chippenham, Wilts** Countrycraft
April 11	**CRAFT FAIR/Floral Hall, The Promenade, Southport, Merseyside** Creative Crafts Association *See display advertisement*
April 11	**DOLL FAIR/Hinchingbrooke House, Huntingdon, Cambs** East Midlands Doll Fairs
April 11	**CRAFT & ANTIQUE FAIR/Ground Floor Centre, Hebden Bridge, West Yorks** Lancastrian Fairs
April 16-18	**GOODWOOD HOUSE HOME DESIGN & INTERIORS EXHIBITION/** **Goodwood, nr Chichester, West Sussex** Buckingham Publicity *See display advertisement*
April 16-18	**CRAFT FAIR/Suffolk Showground, Bucklesham Road, Ipswich, Suffolk** Country Cottage Crafts
April 16-18	**THE MIDLANDS WOODWORKING & WOODTURNING EXHIBITION/** **Warwickshire Exhibition Centre, Fosse Way, Leamington Spa, Warks** Meridienne Exhibitions Ltd
April 16-18	**CRAFT FAIR/Sandringham Park, Norfolk** Rainbow Fair
April 17	**CRAFT MARKET/Fisher Hall, Guildhall Place, Cambridge, Cambs** Balthazar
April 17	**DOLL & TEDDY FAIR/Rivington Hall Barn, Horwich, nr Bolton, Lancs** Brentwood Fairs
April 17	**DOLLSHOUSE, MINIATURES, TEDDY & DOLL FAIR/Arts Centre, Vane** **Terrace, Darlington, Co Durham** Caile Fairs
April 17	**CRAFT FAIR/Steyning Centre, Fletchers Croft, Steyning, West Sussex** Craft Developments
April 17	**MUSIC & CRAFT FAYRE OF NATIONAL FOLK MUSIC FESTIVAL/Sutton** **Bonnington Campus, Sutton Bonnington, nr Loughborough, Leics** R J Heydon
April 17-18	**CRAFT FAIR/Hawkshead Market Hall, nr Ambleside, Cumbria** Aphrodite
April 17-18	**CRAFT FAYRE/Craft Centre, Chester Road, Sandiway, Northwich, Cheshire** Blakemere Craft Centre *See display advertisement*
April 17-18	**CRAFT FAYRE/Quarry Bank Mill, Styal, Cheshire** Cheshire Fayre *See display advertisement*
April 17-18	**CRAFT FAIR/Brigade Hall, Bakewell, Derbys** Cottage Creations Craft Fairs
April 17-18	**CRAFT, DESIGN & GIFT FAIR/Hurrans Garden Centre, Newport, Gwent** Cottage Industries Association *See display advertisement*

Oakleaf Crafts

THE ONLY NEW FOREST BASED CRAFT FAIR ORGANISER

Welcomes you to join them for the 1999
Craft Fair season in this popular tourist area.

**Authentic craft fairs run by crafts people
for genuine craft workers.**

STRICTLY NO BOUGHT IN GOODS

Organisers of quality assured fairs for over fourteen years

**For details please send LARGE S.A.E. to
Oakleaf Crafts, Enfield, Sandleheath, Fordingbridge,
Hants SP6 1PA. Tel./Fax: 01425 654663**

Cheshire Fayre

Feb 6/7	Trentham Gardens, North Staffs
Feb 20/21	Fenton Manor, Stoke-on-Trent, Staffs
Mar 6/7	Trentham Gardens, North Staffs
Mar 27/28	Fenton Manor, Stoke-on-Trent, Staffs
Apr 3-5	Gawsworth Hall, Macclesfield, Cheshire
Apr 17/18	Quarry Bank Mill, Styal, Cheshire
May 8/9	Trentham Gardens, North Staffs
May 29-31	Gawsworth Hall, Macclesfield, Cheshire
Jun 2/3	Staffordshire Show, Stafford
Aug 28-30	Gawsworth Hall, Macclesfield, Cheshire
Sep 11/12	Trentham Gardens, North Staffs
Sep 18/19	Quarry Bank Mill, Styal, Cheshire
Oct 9/10	Fenton Manor, Stoke-on-Trent, Staffs
Oct 30/31	Arley Hall, Near Knutsford
Nov 12-14	Trentham Gardens, North Staffs
Nov 27/28	Quarry Bank Mill, Styal, Cheshire
Dec 4/5	Fenton Manor, Stoke-on-Trent, Staffs

Samples or colour photographs required
SAE to Cheshire Fayre, P.O.Box 51,
Macclesfield, Cheshire, SK10 4EL
Tel: 01625 430519

April 17-18	**CRAFT FAIR/St William's College, York, North Yorks**
	Keld Craft Fairs
April 17-18	**STONEYHURST CRAFT WEEKEND/Stoneyhurst College, Clitheroe, Lancs**
	Living Heritage Craft Shows Ltd	*See display advertisement*
April 17-18	**CRAFT FAIR/Elton Hall, Elton, nr Peterborough, Cambs**
	MGA Fairs	*See display advertisement*
April 17-18	**LIVE CRAFTS SHOW/Boughton Monchelsea Place, nr Maidstone, Kent**
	The Exhibition Team Ltd	*See display advertisement*
April 17-18	**JUST ARTS & CRAFTS/Rosebery Suites, Epsom Racecourse, Epsom, Surrey**
	Traditional Crafts Ltd	*See display advertisement*
April 17-18	**YORKRAFT FAIR/Kilburn Village Hall, Kilburn, nr Thirsk, North Yorks**
	Yorkraft Fairs
April 18	**CRAFT FAIR/Whitchurch Leisure Centre, High Street, Whitchurch, Salop**
	Archer Promotions
April 18	**CRAFT FAIR/The Pemberton Centre, Rushden, Northants**
	Cambridge Craft Fairs
April 18	**CRAFT FAIR/Lacock Village Hall, Lacock, nr Chippenham, Wilts**
	Countrycraft
April 18	**DOLL FAIR/Elvaston Castle, M1 Junction 24/25, Derbys**
	East Midlands Doll Fairs
April 18	**ARTS & CRAFTS FAIR/Woburn Village Hall, Woburn, Beds**
	Falcon Fairs
April 18	**CRAFT & ANTIQUE FAIR/Ground Floor Centre, Hebden Bridge, West Yorks**
	Lancastrian Fairs
April 18	**CRAFT FAIR/Brockenhurst Masonic Hall, Brockenhurst, Hants**
	Oakleaf Craft Fairs	*See display advertisement*
April 20	**CRAFT FAIR/White Hart Inn, Hawes, North Yorks**
	Keld Craft Fairs
April 22-25	**THE 15TH SOUTHERN KNITTING, NEEDLECRAFT & HOBBYCRAFTS EXHIBITION/Bath & West Showground, Shepton Mallet, Somerset**
	Nationwide Exhibitions (UK) Ltd
April 22-25	**CRAFT MARQUEE AT THE HARROGATE SPRING FLOWER SHOW/Great Yorkshire Showground, Harrogate, North Yorks**
	Heart of England Craftworkers	*See display advertisement*
April 22-25	**THE HARROGATE SPRING FLOWER SHOW/Great Yorkshire Showground, Hookstone Oval, Harrogate (main organiser)**
	North of England Horticultural Society
April 23-25	**THE QUILT FAIR/York Racecourse, York, North Yorks**
	Quilt Events Ltd

THE LIVERPOOL SHOW
'IDEAL HOME MARQUEE'

approx 300-400 foot marquee
Stands 10' x 6' – £145.00

attendance 150,000

*Saturday, Sunday
Bank Hollday Monday
May 29th to 31st 1999
10am to 6pm each day*

For booking form send sae:
**The Liverpool Show
98 Victoria Road, Formby, Merseyside L37 1LP
Tel: 01704 833207**

MAURTRAID
CRAFT SHOWS

DATES FOR YOUR DIARY 1999

**CMK SHOPPING CENTRE MIDDLETON HALL
MILTON KEYNES MOTOR/BOAT/LEISURE/CRAFT SHOW
SLOUGH -THE CENTRE**

SLOUGH - THE CENTRE MAY 21/22/23
SLOUGH - THE CENTRE OCTOBER 8/9/10
CMK SHOPPING CENTRE MARCH 9-14
CMK SHOPPING CENTRE - Autumn SEPTEMBER 16-19
CMK SHOPPING CENTRE - Pre Christmas OCTOBER 26-31
MILTON KEYNES MOTOR/LEISURE/POWER BOAT SHOW JUNE 5-6

**MAURTRAID CRAFT SHOWS
202 Buckingham Road, Bletchley, Milton Keynes MK3 5JB
TEL.: 01908 271833 (9am-8pm Answerphone service)**

April 23-25	**JUST ARTS & CRAFTS MARQUEE EVENT/Hyde End, Great Missenden, Bucks** Traditional Crafts Ltd *See display advertisement*
April 24	**CRAFT MARKET/Fisher Hall, Guildhall Place, Cambridge, Cambs** Balthazar
April 24	**CRAFT FAIR/Corn Exchange, Haddington, East Lothian** Border Fairs
April 24	**DOLL FAIR/Civic Hall, Stratford-upon-Avon, Warks** East Midlands Doll Fairs
April 24	**CRAFT FAIR/Malden Centre, Blagdon Road, New Malden, Surrey** Eden Crafts
April 24	**ANTIQUES, CRAFTS & COLLECTABLES FAIR/The Parish Hall, Culcheth, nr Warrington, Cheshire** Gem Fairs
April 24-25	**CRAFT FAYRE/Blakemere Craft Centre, Chester Road, Sandiway, Northwich, Cheshire** Blakemere Craft Centre *See display advertisement*
April 24-25	**CRAFT, DESIGN & GIFT FAIR/Hurrans Garden Centre, Leigh Sinton, nr Malvern, Worcs** Cottage Industries Association *See display advertisement*
April 24-25	**CRAFT FAIR/Lowther Pavilion, West Beach, Lytham, Lancs** Creative Crafts Associaiton *See display advertisement*
April 24-25	**CRAFT FAIR/Victoria Hall, Bourton-on-the-Water, Glos** M&B Crafts
April 24-25	**CRAFT FAIR/Goodwood Racecourse, nr Chichester, West Sussex** Mascot Craft & Gift Fairs
April 24-25	**THE CRAFT MOVEMENT/Battersea Arts Centre, Battersea, London** The Craft Movement
April 24-25	**LIVE CRAFTS SHOW/Bath Racecourse, Bath** The Exhibition Team Ltd *See display advertisement*
April 24-25	**YORKRAFT FAIR/Kilburn Village Hall, Kilburn, nr Thirsk, North Yorks** Yorkraft Fairs
April 24-25 (provisional)	**CRAFT MARQUEE AT THE AINSWORTH VINTAGE SHOW/St Neots, nr Huntingdon, Cambs** The Craft Tent Company
April 25	**CRAFT FAIR/The Leisure Centre, Kinver, nr Stourbridge, West Midlands** Central Promotions *See display advertisement*
April 25	**CRAFT FAIR/Manorial Barn, Whiston, Rotherham, South Yorks** Cottage Creations Craft Fairs
April 25	**CRAFT FAIR/Lacock Village Hall, Lacock, nr Chippenham, Wilts** Countrycraft

| April 25 | **CRAFT FAIR/Hinchingbrooke House, Huntingdon, Cambs**
Kingfisher Promotions |

April 25   **CRAFT FAIR/Hinchingbrooke House, Huntingdon, Cambs**
Kingfisher Promotions

April 25   **CRAFT & ANTIQUE FAIR/Gargrave Village Hall, nr Skipton, North Yorks**
Lancastrian Fairs

April 25   **CRAFT & ANTIQUE FAIR/Ground Floor Centre, Hebden Bridge, West Yorks**
Lancastrian Fairs

April 27   **CRAFT FAIR/White Hart Inn, Hawes, North Yorks**
Keld Craft Fairs

April 28   **CRAFT FAYRE/Blakemere Craft Centre, Chester Road, Sandiway, Northwich, Cheshire**
Blakemere Craft Centre   *See display advertisement*

April 30-May 3 **CRAFT FAIR/Gatcombe Park, nr Stroud, Glos**
Rainbow Fair

May 1   **CRAFT MARKET/Fisher Hall, Guildhall Place, Cambridge, Cambs**
Balthazar

May 1   **CRAFT FAIR/Town Hall, Jedburgh, Roxburghshire**
Border Fairs

May 1   **TYNESIDE DOLL & TEDDY FAIR/Gateshead Civic Centre, Regent Street, Gateshead, Tyne & Wear**
Dolly Domain Fairs

May 1   **DULWICH CRAFT FAIR/St Barnabas Hall, Dulwich, London SE21**
Dulwich Craft Fairs   *See display advertisement*

May 1   **CRAFT FAIR/Guildhall, Sandwich, Kent**
East Kent Fairs   *See display advertisement*

May 1   **ARTS & CRAFTS FAIR/Town Hall, Towcester, Northants**
Falcon Fairs

May 1   **ART & CRAFT FAIR/The Arts Centre, Biddick Lane, Fatfield, Washington, Tyne & Wear**
The Arts Centre

May 1-2   **CRAFT FAIR/Hawkshead Market Hall, nr Ambleside, Cumbria**
Aphrodite

May 1-3   **GARDEN & CRAFT SHOW/Exbury Gardens, Exbury, nr Beaulieu, Hants**
Avocet Crafts

May 1-3   **CRAFT FAYRE/Blakemere Craft Centre, Chester Road, Sandiway, Northwich, Cheshire**
Blakemere Craft Centre   *See display advertisement*

May 1-3   **CRAFT FAIR/The Village Hall, Bolton Abbey, nr Skipton, North Yorks**
CFL Craft Shows

May 1-3   **CRAFT FAIR/Brigade Hall, Bakewell, Derbys**
Cottage Creations Craft Fairs

| May 1-3 | **CRAFT, DESIGN & GIFT FAIR/Percy Thrower's Gardening Centre, Shrewsbury, Salop** |
| | Cottage Industries Association *See display advertisement* |

May 1-3   **CRAFT, DESIGN & GIFT FAIR/Percy Thrower's Gardening Centre, Shrewsbury, Salop**
Cottage Industries Association   *See display advertisement*

May 1-3   **THE CRAFT SHOW FOR CALKE/Calke Abbey, Derbys**
Eastern Events Ltd   *See display advertisement*

May 1-3   **COUNTRYSIDE & CRAFTS COME TO TOWN/Morden Hall Park, Surrey**
Four Seasons (Events) Ltd

May 1-3   **WEALD OF KENT CRAFT SHOW/Penshurst Place, nr Tonbridge, Kent**
ICHF Ltd

May 1-3   **CRAFT FAIR/St William's College, York, North Yorks**
Keld Craft Fairs

May 1-3   **OXFORDSHIRE CRAFT SHOW/Blenheim Palace, Woodstock, Oxon**
Living Heritage Craft Shows Ltd   *See display advertisement*

May 1-3   **RINGWOOD CRAFT SHOW/Somerley Estate, Somerley, nr Ringwood, Hants**
Living Heritage Craft Shows Ltd   *See display advertisement*

May 1-3   **CRAFTS MARQUEE AT THE MILTON KEYNES GARDEN SHOW/Walton Hall, Open University, Milton Keynes, Bucks**
Romor Exhibitions Ltd   *See display advertisement*

May 1-3   **RURAL CRAFTS ASSOCIATION AT THE TONBRIDGE GARDENING SHOW/ Tonbridge, Kent**
Rural Crafts Association   *See display advertisement*

May 1-3   **CRAFT FAIR AT SPALDING FLOWER FESTIVAL/Springfields, Camelgate, Spalding, Lincs**
Springfields Exhibition Centre

May 1-3   **CRAFT MARQUEE AT THE RUSHDEN CALVACADE & COUNTRY SHOW/ Higham Ferrers, nr Wellingborough, Northants**
The Craft Tent Company

May 1-3   **LIVE CRAFTS SHOW/Chiltern Open Air Museum, Chalfont St Giles, Bucks**
The Exhibition Team Ltd   *See display advertisement*

May 1-3   **OLD MAY DAY FAIR/St Fagans, Cardiff**
Wales Craft Council

May 1-3   **CRAFT MARKET AT THE HEAVY HORSE SHOW/Castlefield, Southsea, Hants**
Woodland Crafts   *See display advertisement*

May 1-3   **YORKRAFT FAIR/Pickering Over Sixties Club, Pickering, North Yorks**
Yorkraft Fairs

May 2   **DOLLS HOUSE & MINIATURE FAIR/Hopetoun House, South Queensferry, Edinburgh**
Brentwood Fairs

May 2   **CRAFT FAYRE/The Belgrave Hotel, Torquay, Devon**
Cherrycraft Fayres & Festivals

| May 2 | **CRAFT FAIR/Exmouth Pavilion, Exmouth, Devon** |
| | J M Evans |

| May 2 | **CRAFT FAIR/Holiday Inn, Seaton Burn, Newcastle upon Tyne, Tyne & Wear** |
| | Quintet Promotions |

| May 2 | **CRAFT FAIR/Pavilion Theatre, Worthing, West Sussex** |
| | Worthing Leisure |

| May 2-3 | **CRAFT FAIR/The Ingestre Suite, County Showground, Weston Road, Stafford** |
| | Central Promotions | *See display advertisement* |

| May 2-3 | **CRAFT FAIR/Lacock Village Hall, Lacock, nr Chippenham, Wilts** |
| | Countrycraft |

| May 2-3 | **CRAFT, FOOD & GIFTS FAIR/Capesthorne Hall, nr Macclesfield, Cheshire** |
| | Countrywide Events |

| May 2-3 | **CRAFT FAIR/Dog & Fox Hotel, High Street Wimbledon, Wimbledon Village, London** |
| | Eden Crafts |

| May 2-3 | **CRAFT FAIR/Elvaston Castle, Borrowash, Derbys** |
| | Heathfield Craft Fairs |

| May 2-3 | **CRAFT FAIR/Gargrave Village Hall, Gargrave, nr Skipton, North Yorks** |
| | Heritage Fairs |

| May 2-3 | **COUNTRY CRAFTS WEEKEND/Eastnor Castle, Ledbury, Herefordshire** |
| | Hobby Horse Design & Craft Fairs |

| May 2-3 | **ARTS & CRAFTS FAIR/Town Hall, Grassington, nr Skipton, North Yorks** |
| | Jean Bryon |

| May 2-3 | **CRAFTS AT THE YORKSHIRE EAST RIDING GARDEN & KITE FESTIVAL/ Beverley Race Course, Beverley, East Yorks** |
| | Jean Welch Shows | *See display advertisement* |

| May 2-3 | **CRAFT FAIR/Ely Maltings, Ely, Cambs** |
| | Kingfisher Promotions |

| May 2-3 | **CRAFT & ANTIQUE FAIR/Ground Floor Centre, Hebden Bridge, West Yorks** |
| | Lancastrian Fairs |

| May 2-3 | **CRAFTS AT THE SHROPSHIRE GAME FAIR/Chetwynd Park, Newport, nr Telford, Salop** |
| | Laurel Crafts |

| May 2-3 | **CRAFT MARQUEE AT TRUCKFEST '99/Peterborough, Cambs** |
| | Live Promotions Ltd |

| May 2-3 | **KNEBWORTH COUNTRY SHOW/Knebworth House & Gardens, Junction 7 A1M, Stevenage, Herts** |
| | Living Heritage Craft Shows Ltd | *See display advertisement* |

| May 2-3 | **CRAFT FESTIVAL & GARDEN SHOW/Lamport Hall, Lamport, Northants** |
| | MGA Fairs | *See display advertisement* |

| May 2-3 | **CRAFT FAIR/Tatton Park, Knutsford, Cheshire** |
| | Oak Craft Fairs *See display advertisement* |

| May 2-3 | **CRAFT FAIR/Lyndhurst Community Centre, Lyndhurst, Hants** |
| | Oakleaf Craft Fairs *See display advertisement* |

| May 2-3 | **CRAFT & GIFT FAIR/St George Swallow Hotel, Harrogate, North Yorks** |
| | Quality Craft & Gift Fairs *See display advertisement* |

| May 2-3 | **CRAFTS AT THE 9TH SPRING SMALLHOLDERS SHOW/Kent County Showground, Detling, nr Maidstone, Kent** |
| | Smallholder Shows |

| May 2-3 | **CRAFT FAIR/Civic Hall, Ramsbottom, nr Bury, Lancs** |
| | West Pennine Promotions |

| May 2-3 | **CRAFT FAIR/Hollingworth Lake Rowing Club, Littleborough, Lancs** |
| | West Pennine Promotions |

| May 3 | **CRAFT FAIR/Wycombe Sports Centre (Handycross), Marlow Hill, High Wycombe, Bucks** |
| | Cottage Craft Fairs *See display advertisement* |

| May 3 | **CRAFTS AT BRERETON CARNIVAL DAY/Brereton, nr Rugeley, Staffs** |
| | Cottage Industries Association *See display advertisement* |

| May 3 | **CRAFT FAIR/Wilmslow Leisure Centre, Wilmslow, Cheshire** |
| | Creative Crafts Association *See display advertisement* |

| May 3 | **ARTS & CRAFTS SHOW/Lauderdale House, Highgate Hill, London N6** |
| | Lauderdale Arts & Crafts |

| May 3 | **ANTIQUE & CRAFT FAIR/Hedworth Hall, Westoe, South Shields, Tyne & Wear** |
| | Quintet Promotions |

| May 3 | **DOLLS HOUSE FAIR/Shuttleworth Centre, nr Biggleswade, Beds** |
| | R J Exhibitions |

| May 3 | **THE ROYAL LEAMINGTON SPA MAY DAY CRAFT FAIR/Royal Spa Centre, Leamington Spa, Warks** |
| | West Country Craft Fairs *See display advertisement* |

| May 3 | **ART, CRAFT & DESIGN MARQUEE AT THE NORTH SOMERSET SHOW/ Ashton Court Estate, Bristol** |
| | Creativity |

| May 3 | **RURAL CRAFTS ASSOCIATION AT THE NORTH SOMERSET SHOW/Ashton Court, Bristol** |
| | Rural Crafts Association *See display advertisement* |

| May 4 | **CRAFT FAIR/White Hart Inn, Hawes, North Yorks** |
| | Keld Craft Fairs |

| May 6-9 | **LIVING CRAFTS/Hatfield House, Hatfield, Herts** |
| | Living Crafts |

May 6-9	**HEART OF ENGLAND CRAFTWORKERS MARQUEE AT THE MITSUBISHI BADMINTON HORSE TRIALS/Badminton Village, Glos** Heart of England Craftworkers *See display advertisement*
May 6-9	**RURAL CRAFTS ASSOCIATION AT THE MITSUBISHI BADMINTON HORSE TRIALS/Badminton Village, Glos** Rural Crafts Association *See display advertisement*
May 7-8	**RURAL CRAFTS ASSOCIATION AT THE NOTTINGHAMSHIRE COUNTY SHOW/Winthrope, Newark, Notts** Rural Crafts Association *See display advertisement*
May 7-9	**ELTON HALL HOME DESIGN & INTERIORS EXHIBITION/Elton, nr Peterborough, Cambs** Buckingham Publicity *See display advertisement*
May 7-9	**CRAFTS MARQUEE AT THE MALVERN SPRING GARDENING SHOW/Three Counties Showground, Malvern, Worcs** Cotswold Craftsmen
May 7-9	**WELSH CRAFTS AT THE MALVERN SPRING GARDENING SHOW/Three Counties Showground, Malvern, Worcs** Wales Craft Council
May 8	**CRAFT & GIFT FAIR/The Harlington Centre, High Street, Fleet, Hants** Aquarius Fairs
May 8	**CRAFT MARKET/Fisher Hall, Guildhall Place, Cambridge, Cambs** Balthazar
May 8	**CRAFT FAIR/Corn Exchange, Haddington, East Lothian** Border Fairs
May 8	**CRAFT MARKET/Methodist Church Hall, Ashton Square, Dunstable, Beds** Dunstable Craft Market
May 8	**ARTS & CRAFTS FAIR/Town Hall, Brackley, Northants** Falcon Fairs
May 8	**CRAFT & GIFT FAIR/Barnet Library, Stapylton Road, Barnet, Herts** Marie Margaret Promotions
May 8	**CRAFT FAIR/Market Hall, Abergavenny, Monmouthshire** Monmouthshire County Council
May 8-9	**CRAFT FAIR/Hawkshead Market Hall, nr Ambleside, Cumbria** Aphrodite
May 8-9	**CRAFT FAYRE/Craft Centre, Chester Road, Sandlway, Northwich, Cheshire** Blakemere Craft Centre *See display advertisement*
May 8-9	**CRAFT FAYRE/Trentham Gardens, Stone Road (A34), Trentham, Stoke-on-Trent, Staffs** Cheshire Fayre *See display advertisement*
May 8-9	**CRAFT FAIR/Brigade Hall, Bakewell, Derbys** Cottage Creations Craft Fairs

| May 8-9 | **CRAFT, DESIGN & GIFT FAIR/Hurrans Garden Centre, West Hagley, nr Stourbridge, Worcs** |
| | Cottage Industries Association   *See display advertisement* |

May 8-9   **CRAFT, DESIGN & GIFT FAIR/Hurrans Garden Centre, West Hagley, nr Stourbridge, Worcs**
Cottage Industries Association   *See display advertisement*

May 8-9   **CRAFT FAIR/Victoria Hall, Bourton-on-the-Water, Glos**
M&B Crafts

May 8-9   **RURAL CRAFTS ASSOCIATION AT THE CHATSWORTH ANGLING FAIR/ Chatsworth House, Baslow, Derbys**
Rural Crafts Association   *See display advertisement*

May 8-9   **YORKRAFT FAIR/Parish Rooms, Thornton Dale, nr Pickering, North Yorks**
Yorkraft Fairs

May 8-15 (provisional)   **CARDIFF SPRING CRAFT FESTIVAL/St John's Square, Cardiff**
Craft*Folk

May 9   **CRAFT FAIR/Northwood Stadium, Keelings Road, Northwood, Hanley, Stoke-on-Trent, Staffs**
Archer Promotions

May 9   **DOLLSHOUSE, MINIATURES, DOLL & TEDDY FAIR/Shepherd's Inn, Rosehill, Carlisle, Cumbria**
Caile Fairs

May 9   **CRAFT FAIR/Lacock Village Hall, Lacock, nr Chippenham, Wilts**
Countrycraft

May 9   **RURAL CRAFTS AT THE COWPIE COUNTRY SHOW/Betchworth, Dorking, Surrey**
Cowpie Country Show

May 9   **CRAFT FAIR/Hoole Hall Hotel, Chester, Cheshire**
Creative Crafts Association   *See display advertisement*

May 9   **CRAFT & GIFT FAIR/Barton Village Hall, nr Preston, Lancs**
Golden Age Fairs

May 9   **CRAFT & ANTIQUE FAIR/Gargrave Village Hall, nr Skipton, North Yorks**
Lancastrian Fairs

May 9   **CRAFT & ANTIQUE FAIR/Ground Floor Centre, Hebden Bridge, West Yorks**
Lancastrian Fairs

May 9   **CRAFT FAIR/Downham Village Hall, Downham, nr Clitheroe, Lancs**
West Pennine Promotions

May 9-11   **IMAGE '99/RAI Exhibition Centre, Amsterdam, HOLLAND**
Trade Promotion Services Ltd

May 9-11   **THE BRITISH CRAFT TRADE FAIR/Harrogate Exhibition Centre, Harrogate, North Yorks (main organiser)**
Marathon Event Management Ltd   *See display advertisement*

May 9-11   **RURAL CRAFTS ASSOCIATION AT THE BRITISH CRAFT TRADE FAIR/ Harrogate Exhibition Centre, Harrogate, North Yorks**
Rural Crafts Association   *See display advertisement*

May 9-11	**WELSH CRAFTS AT THE BRITISH CRAFT TRADE FAIR/Harrogate Exhibition Centre, Harrogate, North Yorks** Wales Craft Council
May 13-16	**RURAL CRAFTS ASSOCIATION AT ROYAL WINDSOR HORSE SHOW/Berks** Rural Crafts Association *See display advertisement*
May 14-16	**LEIGH COURT HOME DESIGN & INTERIORS EXHIBITION/Abbots Leigh, Bristol** Buckingham Publicity *See display advertisement*
May 14-16	**CRAFTS AT THE TEESSIDE GARDEN FESTIVAL/Preston Park, Stockton-on-Tees, Cleveland** Jean Welch Shows *See display advertisement*
May 14-16	**LIVE CRAFTS SHOW/Mapledurham House, nr Reading, Oxon** The Exhibition Team Ltd *See display advertisement*
May 15	**CRAFT MARKET/Fisher Hall, Guildhall Place, Cambridge, Cambs** Balthazar
May 15	**CRAFT FAIR/Burgh Hall, Peebles** Border Fairs
May 15	**CRAFT FAYRE/St Mary's Centre, Grassmere Close, Felpham, nr Bognor Regis, West Sussex** Good Ideas Craft Fayres
May 15-16	**CRAFT FAYRE/Blakemere Craft Centre, Chester Road, Sandiway, Northwich, Cheshire** Blakemere Craft Centre *See display advertisement*
May 15-16	**CRAFT FAIR/Brigade Hall, Bakewell, Derbys** Cottage Creations Craft Fairs
May 15-16	**CRAFT, DESIGN & GIFT FAIR/Jardinerie Garden Place, Kenilworth Road (A452), Hampton-in-Arden, West Midlands** Cottage Industries Association *See display advertisement*
May 15-16	**CRAFT FAIR/Wood Green Animal Shelters, Godmanchester, Cambs** Kingfisher Promotions
May 15-16	**COUNTRYSIDE CRAFT SHOW/Langley Park, A412 Slough to Uxbridge Road, nr Slough, Berks** Living Heritage Craft Shows Ltd *See display advertisement*
May 15-16	**CRAFT MARQUEE AT THE ORMESBY SPRING GARDEN SHOW/Ormesby Hall, Middlesbrough, Cleveland** Quality Craft & Gift Fairs *See display advertisement*
May 15-16	**THE LONDON DOLLSHOUSE FESTIVAL/Kensington Town Hall, Hornton Street, Kensington, London W8** The London Dollshouse Festival
May 15-16	**CRAFT MARQUEE AT THE WILTSHIRE COUNTY SHOW 99/Lord's Hill Showground, A350, nr Warminster, Wilts** Wiltshire County Show

May 15-16	**YORKRAFT FAIR/Kilburn Village Hall, Kilburn, nr Thirsk, North Yorks** Yorkraft Fairs
May 16	**CRAFT FAIR/Biddulph Leisure Centre, Thames Drive, off Congleton Road, Biddulph, Staffs** Archer Promotions
May 16	**DOLL & TEDDY FAIR/The Marine Hall, The Esplanade, Fleetwood, Lancs** Brentwood Fairs
May 16	**CRAFT FAIR/Lacock Village Hall, Lacock, nr Chippenham, Wilts** Countrycraft
May 16	**DOLL FAIR/Aylestone Leisure Centre, Leicester, Leics** East Midlands Doll Fairs
May 16	**ARTS & CRAFTS FAIR/Woburn Village Hall, Woburn, Beds** Falcon Fairs
May 16	**CRAFT & ANTIQUE FAIR/Ground Floor Centre, Hebden Bridge, West Yorks** Lancastrian Fairs
May 20-22	**HEART OF ENGLAND CRAFTWORKERS MARQUEE AT DEVON COUNTY SHOW/ Devon County Showground, Westpoint, Clyst St Mary, Exeter** Heart of England Craftworkers *See display advertisement*
May 20-22	**RURAL CRAFTS ASSOCIATION AT THE DEVON COUNTY SHOW/Devon County Showground, Westpoint, Clyst St Mary, Exeter, Devon** Rural Crafts Association *See display advertisement*
May 21	**CRAFT FAIR/Community Centre, Leyburn, North Yorks** Keld Craft Fairs
May 21-22	**CRAFT SHOW/The Centre, Slough, Berks** Maurtraid Craft Shows *See display advertisement*
May 21-23	**CRAFT FAIR/The Leisure Centre, University of Keele, Keele, nr Newcastle-under-Lyme, Staffs** Mary Holland Craft Fairs Ltd *See display advertisement*
May 21-25	**CRAFT & ANTIQUE FAIR/The Guild Hall, York, North Yorks** Lancastrian Fairs
May 22	**CRAFT MARKET/Fisher Hall, Guildhall Place, Cambridge, Cambs** Balthazar
May 22-23	**CRAFT FAIR/Hawkshead Market Hall, nr Ambleside, Cumbria** Aphrodite
May 22-23	**CRAFT MARQUEE AT THE TALLINGTON STEAM & COUNTRY FESTIVAL/ Tallington, nr Stamford, Lincs** Arrow Management & Marketing Ltd
May 22-23	**CRAFT FAYRE/Blakemere Craft Centre, Chester Road, Sandiway, Northwich, Cheshire** Blakemere Craft Centre *See display advertisement*

| May 22-23 | **CRAFT FAIR/Brigade Hall, Bakewell, Derbys** |
| | Cottage Creations Craft Fairs |

| May 22-23 | **CRAFT, DESIGN & GIFT FAIR/William Wheat's Garden Centre, Old Chester Road (A452), Little Aston, West Midlands** |
| | Cottage Industries Association *See display advertisement* |

| May 22-23 | **CRAFT FAIR/White Hart Inn, Hawes, North Yorks** |
| | Keld Craft Fairs |

| May 22-23 | **RURAL CRAFTS ASSOCIATION AT THE BELMONT HORSE TRIALS & COUNTRY FAIR 1999/Mill Hill, London** |
| | Rural Crafts Association *See display advertisement* |

| May 22-23 | **THE FARNHAM MALTINGS FESTIVAL OF CRAFTS/Bridge Square, Farnham, Surrey** |
| | The Farnham Maltings |

| May 22-23 | **YORKRAFT FAIR/Thornton Dale Parish Rooms, Thornton Dale, nr Pickering, North Yorks** |
| | Yorkraft Fairs |

| May 23 | **CRAFT FAIR/Lordsbridge Arena, Barton, Cambs** |
| | Cambridge Craft Fairs |

| May 23 | **CRAFT FAIR/Lacock Village Hall, Lacock, nr Chippenham, Wilts** |
| | Countrycraft |

| May 23 | **DOLLS, DOLLSHOUSES & MINIATURES SHOW/Swallow Hotel, Old Shire Lane, Waltham Abbey (handmade British miniatures only)** |
| | Four Seasons Fairs |

| May 23 | **CRAFT & ANTIQUE FAIR/Ground Floor Centre, Hebden Bridge, West Yorks** |
| | Lancastrian Fairs |

| May 23 | **CRAFT FAIR/Brockenhurst Masonic Hall, Brockenhurst, Hants** |
| | Oakleaf Craft Fairs *See display advertisement* |

| May 23 | **CRAFT & GIFT FAIR/Pudsey Civic Hall, nr Leeds, West Yorks** |
| | Quality Craft & Gift Fairs *See display advertisement* |

| May 23 | **CRAFT & GIFT FAYRE AT THE FAIRTHORNE FAYRE/YMCA, Botley, Hants** |
| | Something Special Craft & Gift Fayres |

| May 23 | **SPRING CRAFT FAIR/Royal Shakespeare Theatre, Stratford-upon-Avon, Warks** |
| | West Country Craft Fairs *See display advertisement* |

| May 23-24 | **LTS RAIL SOUTHEND AIRSHOW/Southend-on-Sea, Essex** |
| | Special Events - Southend Borough Council |

| May 26 | **CRAFT FAYRE/Blakemere Craft Centre, Chester Road, Sandiway, Northwich, Cheshire** |
| | Blakemere Craft Centre *See display advertisement* |

| May 27 | **CRAFT FAIR/Market Hall, Hawes, North Yorks** |
| | Keld Craft Fairs |

May 28	**CRAFT FAIR/Community Centre, Leyburn, North Yorks** Keld Craft Fairs
May 28-30	**CRAFT FAIR/Hawkshead Market Hall, nr Ambleside, Cumbria** Aphrodite
May 28-31	**CRAFT, ART, FOOD & WINE SHOW/Exbury Gardens, nr Beaulieu, Hants** Avocet Crafts
May 28-31	**CRAFT & ANTIQUE FAIR/The Guild Hall, York, North Yorks** Lancastrian Fairs
May 29	**CRAFT MARKET/Fisher Hall, Guildhall Place, Cambridge, Cambs** Balthazar
May 29	**CRAFT FAIR/Village Hall, Ferring Street, Ferring, nr Worthing, West Sussex** Craft Developments
May 29	**CRAFTS IN ACTION AT THE HEATHFIELD AGRICULTURAL SHOW/ Heathfield, East Sussex** Crafts in Action
May 29	**ARTS & CRAFTS FAYRE/Winter Gardens, Weston-super-Mare, North Somerset** Fountain Fayres & Exhibitions
May 29	**CRAFTS AT THE WHISTON SUMMER FAIR/Whiston Higherside Community School, Cumber Lane, Whiston, Merseyside** Golden Age Fairs
May 29	**THE LYME REGIS SPRING BANK HOLIDAY CRAFT FAIR/Marine Theatre, Lyme Regis, Dorset** West Country Craft Fairs *See display advertisement*
May 29-30	**CRAFT FAIR/The Village Hall, Bolton Abbey, nr Skipton, North Yorks** CFL Craft Shows
May 29-30	**CRAFTS AT THE BERMONDSEY CARNIVAL/Bermondsey, London** Jets Quality Craft Fairs
May 29-30	**RURAL CRAFTS ASSOCIATION AT THE HERTFORDSHIRE COUNTY SHOW/St Albans, Herts** Rural Crafts Association *See display advertisement*
May 29-31	**CRAFT FAYRE/Blakemere Craft Centre, Chester Road, Sandiway, Northwich, Cheshire** Blakemere Craft Centre *See display advertisement*
May 29-31	**CRAFT FAYRE/Gawsworth Hall, Macclesfield, Cheshire** Cheshire Fayre *See display advertisement*
May 29-31	**CRAFT FAIR/Brigade Hall, Bakewell, Derbys** Cottage Creations Craft Fairs
May 29-31	**SPRING CRAFTS & GARDEN SHOW AT CHETTLE/Chettle House, nr Blandford, Dorset** Craft Carnival

May 29-31	**SPRING CRAFT, FASHION & DESIGN FESTIVAL/Harewood House, Leeds, West Yorks**
	Dalesway Festivals Ltd *See display advertisement*

May 29-31	**CRAFT MARQUEE AT THE GREAT EAST KENT GARDEN SHOW/Castle Community School, Hamilton Road, Deal, Kent**
	East Kent Fairs *See display advertisement*

May 29-31	**FELBRIGG COAST & COUNTRY SHOW/Felbrigg Hall, nr Cromer, Norfolk**
	Eastern Events Ltd *See display advertisement*

May 29-31	**ROBIN HOOD CRAFT FAYRE/Norbury Park, nr Leatherhead, Surrey**
	Four Seasons (Events) Ltd

May 29-31	**ALDEBURGH CRAFT FESTIVAL/Jubilee Hall, Aldeburgh, Suffolk**
	Four Seasons Fairs

May 29-31	**COUNTRY CRAFTS WEEKEND/Shugborough Estate, nr Stafford, Staffs**
	Hobby Horse Design & Craft Fairs

May 29-31	**SHOW OF EXCELLENCE/Stonor Park, Henley-on-Thames, Oxon**
	ICHF Ltd

May 29-31	**CRAFT FAIR/St William's College, York, North Yorks**
	Keld Craft Fairs

May 29-31	**THE IDEAL HOME MARQUEE AT THE LIVERPOOL SHOW/Wavertree Showground, Liverpool, Merseyside**
	Linda Powell *See display advertisement*

May 29-31	**BEDFORDSHIRE CRAFT SHOW/Woburn Abbey, M1 Junction 12/13, Beds**
	Living Heritage Craft Shows Ltd *See display advertisement*

May 29-31	**ESSEX CRAFT SHOW/Blake Hall, A414, Ongar, Essex**
	Living Heritage Craft Shows Ltd *See display advertisement*

May 29-31	**LUDLOW CASTLE FESTIVAL OF CRAFTS/Ludlow Castle, Ludlow, Salop**
	Ludlow Castle Festival of Crafts

May 29-31	**CHILLI GARDEN, HOME & LEISURE SHOW/Chilli Showground, A2 nr Dover, Kent**
	M B County Fairs

May 29-31	**CRAFT FAIR/The National Trust Petworth Park, Petworth, West Sussex**
	Mary Holland Craft Fairs Ltd *See display advertisement*

May 29-31	**CRAFT MARKET AT WINDOW ON THE WORLD INTERNATIONAL MUSIC FESTIVAL/The Fish Quay, North Shields, Tyne & Wear**
	North Tyneside Council

May 29-31	**CRAFT FAIR/Burghley House, Stamford, Lincs**
	Rainbow Fair

May 29-31	**CRAFTS MARQUEE AT THE WREST PARK GARDEN SHOW/Wrest Park, Silsoe (A6), Beds**
	Romor Exhibitions Ltd *See display advertisement*

| May 29-31 | **RURAL CRAFTS ASSOCIATION AT THE RICHMOND HORSE SHOW/ Richmond, Surrey** |
| | Rural Crafts Association *See display advertisement* |

| May 29-31 | **THE CRAFT MOVEMENT/Queen Charlotte Hall, Richmond, Surrey** |
| | The Craft Movement |

| May 29-31 | **LIVE CRAFTS SHOW/Breamore House, Fordingbridge, Hants** |
| | The Exhibition Team Ltd *See display advertisement* |

| May 29-31 | **FORT PURBROOK CRAFT FAYRE/Portsdown Hill, Cosham, nr Portsmouth, Hants** |
| | Woodland Crafts *See display advertisement* |

| May 29-31 | **YORKRAFT FAIR/Pickering Over Sixties Club, Pickering, North Yorks** |
| | Yorkraft Fairs |

| May 30 | **CRAFT FAIR/Lyndhurst Community Centre, Lyndhurst, Hants** |
| | Oakleaf Craft Fairs *See display advertisement* |

| May 30 | **ANTIQUE & CRAFT FAIR/Seaburn Centre, Seaburn, Sunderland, Tyne & Wear** |
| | Quintet Promotions |

| May 30 | **BT COUNTRY FAIR/Florence Court, Enniskillen, Co Fermanagh** |
| | The National Trust, Florence Court |

| May 30 | **THE STRATFORD-UPON-AVON SPRING BANK HOLIDAY CRAFT FAIR/ Royal Shakespeare Theatre, Stratford-upon-Avon, Warks** |
| | West Country Craft Fairs *See display advertisement* |

| May 30-31 | **CRAFT SHOW/Hatherley Manor, Down Hatherley Lane, Gloucester, Glos** |
| | CFL Craft Shows |

| May 30-31 | **CRAFT FAIR/Community Centre, Kinver, nr Stourbridge, West Midlands** |
| | Central Promotions *See display advertisement* |

| May 30-31 | **CRAFTS AT THE BIRMINGHAM LORD MAYOR'S SHOW/Cannon Hill Park, Birmingham, West Midlands** |
| | Cottage Industries Association *See display advertisement* |

| May 30-31 | **CRAFTS AT THE LICHFIELD SUMMER FLOWER SHOW/Beacon Park, Lichfield, Staffs** |
| | Cottage Industries Association *See display advertisement* |

| May 30-31 | **CRAFT FAIR/Lacock Village Hall, Lacock, nr Chippenham, Wilts** |
| | Countrycraft |

| May 30-31 | **SPRING FAIR (CRAFTS & GARDEN)/Finchcocks, Riseden, Goudhurst, Kent** |
| | Finchcocks |

| May 30-31 | **CRAFT MARQUEE/Rufford Abbey, Notts** |
| | Heathfield Craft Fairs |

| May 30-31 | **ARTS & CRAFTS FAIR/Grassington Town Hall, Grassington,nr Skipton, North Yorks** |
| | Jean Bryon |

| May 30-31 | **CRAFT FAIR/Ely Maltings, Ely, Cambs** |
| | Kingfisher Promotions |

| May 30-31 | **LAMPORT COUNTRY FESTIVAL/Lamport Hall, Lamport, Northants** |
| | Lamport Hall Trust |

| May 30-31 | **CRAFT & ANTIQUE FAIR/Gargrave Village Hall, nr Skipton, North Yorks** |
| | Lancastrian Fairs |

| May 30-31 | **CRAFT & ANTIQUE FAIR/Ground Floor Centre, Hebden Bridge, West Yorks** |
| | Lancastrian Fairs |

| May 30-31 | **ARTS & CRAFTS SHOW/Lauderdale House, Highgate Hill, London N6** |
| | Lauderdale Arts & Crafts |

| May 30-31 | **CRAFTS AT FALCONRY & RAPTOR FAIR/Offchurch, Leamington Spa, Warks** |
| | Laurel Crafts |

| May 30-31 | **HAMPSHIRE COUNTRY SHOW/Broadlands, nr Romsey, Hants** |
| | Living Heritage Craft Shows Ltd _See display advertisement_ |

| May 30-31 | **CRAFT MARQUEE AT THE POTWALLOPING FESTIVAL/Westward Ho, nr Bideford, Devon** |
| | Potwalloping Festival |

| May 30-31 | **CRAFT & GIFT FAIR/St George Swallow Hotel, Harrogate, North Yorks** |
| | Quality Craft & Gift Fairs _See display advertisement_ |

| May 30-31 | **CRAFTS IN ACTION AT ST DONAT'S CASTLE/St Donat's, nr Llantwit Major, South Glam** |
| | St Donats Arts Centre |

| May 30-31 | **CRAFT FAIR/The Pavilion, Buxton, Derbys** |
| | Town & Country Craft Fairs |

| May 30-31 | **WELSH CRAFTS AT THE CITY OF SWANSEA SHOW/Singleton Park, Swansea, West Glam** |
| | Wales Craft Council |

| May 30-31 | **CRAFT FAIR/Civic Hall, Ramsbottom, nr Bury, Lancs** |
| | West Pennine Promotions |

| May 30-31 | **CRAFT FAIR/Hollingworth Lake Rowing Club, Littleborough, Lancs** |
| | West Pennine Promotions |

| May 31 | **CRAFT FAIR/Rivermead Complex, Richfield Avenue, Caversham, nr Reading, Berks** |
| | Cottage Craft Fairs _See display advertisement_ |

| May 31 | **CRAFT FAIR/De Vere Hotel, East Park Drive, Blackpool, Lancs** |
| | Creative Crafts Association _See display advertisement_ |

| May 31 | **ARTS & CRAFTS FAIR/Woburn Village Hall, Woburn, Beds** |
| | Falcon Fairs |

| May 31 | **CRAFT FAIR/Much Hadham Village Hall, nr Ware, Herts** |
| | Isabel Hospice Craft Fairs |

| May 31 | **CRAFT FAIR/Exmouth Pavilion, Exmouth, Devon** |
| | J M Evans |

| May 31 | **CRAFT FAIR/Pavilion, Weymouth, Dorset** |
| | Kevin Murphy Craft Fairs |

| May 31 | **CRAFT MARQUEES & STANDS AT THE MELTON MOWBRAY SHOW/ Melton Mowbray, Leics** |
| | Melton Mowbray Show | *See display advertisement* |

| May 31 | **CRAFT FAIR/Market Hall, Abergavenny, Monmouthshire** |
| | Monmouthshire County Council |

| May 31 | **DOLLS HOUSE FAIR/The Priory Centre, St Neots, Cambs** |
| | R J Exhibitions |

| May 31 | **RURAL CRAFTS ASSOCIATION AT THE SURREY COUNTY SHOW/Stoke Park, Guildford, Surrey** |
| | Rural Crafts Association | *See display advertisement* |

| June 1 | **CRAFT FAIR/White Hart Inn, Hawes, North Yorks** |
| | Keld Craft Fairs |

| June 2-3 | **CRAFTS AT THE STAFFORDSHIRE COUNTY SHOW/Weston Road, Stafford** |
| | Cheshire Fayre | *See display advertisement* |

| June 2-3 | **RURAL CRAFTS ASSOCIATION AT THE SUFFOLK SHOW/Suffolk Showground, Bucklesham Road, Ipswich, Suffolk** |
| | Rural Crafts Association | *See display advertisement* |

| June 2-5 | **HEART OF ENGLAND CRAFTWORKERS MARQUEE AT THE ROYAL BATH & WEST SHOW/Bath & West Showground, Shepton Mallet, Somerset** |
| | Heart of England Craftworkers | *See display advertisement* |

| June 2-5 | **RURAL CRAFTS ASSOCIATION AT THE ROYAL BATH & WEST SHOW/Bath & West Showground, Shepton Mallet, Somerset** |
| | Rural Crafts Association | *See display advertisement* |

| June 3-4 | **CRAFT FAIR/Market Hall, Hawes, North Yorks** |
| | Keld Craft Fairs |

| June 3-5 | **CRAFT & ANTIQUE FAIR/The Guild Hall, York, North Yorks** |
| | Lancastrian Fairs |

| June 4-6 | **INGATESTONE HALL HOME DESIGN & INTERIORS EXHIBITION/ Ingatestone, nr Chelmsford, Essex** |
| | Buckingham Publicity | *See display advertisement* |

| June 4-6 | **CRAFT GUILD IN ACTION WEEKEND/Martin Mere Wildfowl & Wetlands Trust Centre, Burscough, nr Ormskirk, Lancs** |
| | The Craft Guild of West Lancashire |

| June 4-6 | **LIVE CRAFTS SHOW/Loseley House, Compton, nr Guildford, Surrey** |
| | The Exhibition Team Ltd | *See display advertisement* |

| June 5 | **ARTS & CRAFTS FAIR/Town Hall, Towcester, Northants** |
| | Falcon Fairs |

June 5	**CRAFT & GIFT FAIR/Barnet Library, Stapylton Road, Barnet, Herts**
	Marie Margaret Promotions

June 5   **ART & CRAFT FAIR/The Arts Centre, Biddick Lane, Fatfield, Washington, Tyne & Wear**
The Arts Centre

June 5-6   **CRAFT FAYRE/Craft Centre, Chester Road, Sandiway, Northwich, Cheshire**
Blakemere Craft Centre   *See display advertisement*

June 5-6   **CRAFTS MARQUEE AT THE LEICESTERSHIRE FLOWER FESTIVAL/Stanford Hall, Lutterworth, Leics**
CFL Craft Shows

June 5-6   **CRAFT MARQUEE AT GARDENERS WEEKEND/Castle Bromwich Hall, Chester Road, Castle Bromwich, Birmingham, West Midlands**
Castle Bromwich Hall Gardens Trust

June 5-6   **CRAFT FAIR/Brigade Hall, Bakewell, Derbys**
Cottage Creations Craft Fairs

June 5-6   **CRAFTS AT THE WALSALL SUMMER SHOW/Bosty Lane Airport, Aldridge, nr Walsall, West Midlands**
Cottage Industries Association   *See display advertisement*

June 5-6   **MILTON KEYNES MOTOR, BOAT, LEISURE & CRAFT SHOW/Willen Leisure, Milton Keynes, Bucks**
Maurtraid Craft Shows   *See display advertisement*

June 5-6   **CRAFTS MARQUEE AT THE WOBURN ABBEY GARDEN SHOW/Woburn Abbey, Woburn, Beds**
Romor Exhibitions Ltd   *See display advertisement*

June 5-6   **CRAFTS & GIFT FAYRE AT THE HMS SULTAN SHOW/Gosport, Hants**
Something Special Craft & Gift Fayres

June 5-6   **JUST ARTS & CRAFTS MARQUEE EVENT/Bowley Showground, Horspath, nr Oxford, Oxon**
Traditional Crafts Ltd   *See display advertisement*

June 5-6   **FORT BROCKHURST CRAFT FAYRE/nr Fareham, Hants**
Woodland Crafts   *See display advertisement*

June 6   **CRAFT FAIR/Whitchurch Leisure Centre, High Street, Whitchurch, Salop**
Archer Promotions

June 6   **CRAFT FAYRE/The Belgrave Hotel, Torquay, Devon**
Cherrycraft Fayres & Festivals

June 6   **CRAFT FAIR/Lacock Village Hall, Lacock, nr Chippenham, Wilts**
Countrycraft

June 6   **CRAFT FAIR/Village Hall, Lewes Road, Ditchling, nr Hassocks, West Sussex**
Craft Developments

June 6   **CRAFT FAIR/The Platform, Morecambe, Lancs**
Creative Crafts Association   *See display advertisement*

June 6	**CRAFT FAIR/Downham Village Hall, Downham, nr Clitheroe, Lancs** West Pennine Promotions
June 9	**CRAFT FAIR/Bridport Arts Centre, Bridport, Dorset** J M Evans
June 10-12	**CRAFTS IN ACTION AT THE SOUTH OF ENGLAND SHOW/South of England Showground, Ardingly, nr Haywards Heath, West Sussex** Crafts in Action
June 10-12	**HEART OF ENGLAND CRAFTWORKERS MARQUEE AT SOUTH OF ENGLAND SHOW/South of England Showground, Ardingly, Haywards Heath** Heart of England Craftworkers *See display advertisement*
June 10-12	**RURAL CRAFTS ASSOCIATION AT THE SOUTH OF ENGLAND SHOW/ South of England Showground, Ardingly, Haywards Heath, West Sussex** Rural Crafts Association *See display advertisement*
June 10-12	**CRAFT & ANTIQUE FAIR/The Guild Hall, York, North Yorks** Lancastrian Fairs
June 10-12	**RURAL CRAFTS ASSOCIATION AT THE ROYAL CORNWALL SHOW/ Wadebridge, Cornwall** Rural Crafts Association *See display advertisement*
June 10-13	**RURAL CRAFTS ASSOCIATION AT THE BRAMHAM HORSE TRIALS/ Bramham, North Yorks** Rural Crafts Association *See display advertisement*
June 11	**CRAFT FAIR/Community Centre, Leyburn, North Yorks** Keld Craft Fairs
June 11-13	**WESSEX FLOWER & CRAFT SHOW/Wilton House, Salisbury, Wilts** ICHF Ltd
June 11-13 (provisional)	**RURAL CRAFTS ASSOCIATION AT THE GOODWOOD FESTIVAL OF SPEED/Goodwood, nr Chichester, West Sussex** Rural Crafts Association *See display advertisement*
June 12	**CRAFT & GIFT FAIR/The Harlington Centre, High Street, Fleet, Hants** Aquarius Fairs
June 12	**CRAFT MARKET/Fisher Hall, Guildhall Place, Cambridge, Cambs** Balthazar
June 12	**CRAFT FAIR/Corn Exchange, Haddington, East Lothian** Border Fairs
June 12	**DUNSTABLE CRAFT MARKET/Methodist Church Hall, Ashton Square, Dunstable, Beds** Dunstable Craft Market
June 12	**CRAFT FAIR/Market Hall, Abergavenny, Monmouthshire** Monmouthshire County Council
June 12	**CRAFT GUILD SHOW/Platform Gallery, Clitheroe, Lancs** The Craft Guild of West Lancashire

| June 12-13 | **CRAFT FAYRE/Blakemere Craft Centre, Chester Road, Sandiway, Northwich, Cheshire** |
| | Blakemere Craft Centre *See display advertisement* |

| June 12-13 | **CRAFT FAIR/Brigade Hall, Bakewell, Derbys** |
| | Cottage Creations Craft Fairs |

June 12-13   **CRAFT FAYRE/Blakemere Craft Centre, Chester Road, Sandiway, Northwich, Cheshire**
Blakemere Craft Centre   *See display advertisement*

June 12-13   **CRAFT FAIR/Brigade Hall, Bakewell, Derbys**
Cottage Creations Craft Fairs

June 12-13   **CRAFT, DESIGN & GIFT FAIR/Dobbies Gardening World, A5, Penkridge, nr Cannock, Staffs**
Cottage Industries Association   *See display advertisement*

June 12-13   **CRAFT MARQUEE AT THE CHESHIRE GAME & ANGLING FAIR/Peover Hall, nr Knutsford, Cheshire**
Jean Welch Shows   *See display advertisement*

June 12-13   **CRAFTS AT THE NESS BOTANIC GARDENS GARDEN FESTIVAL/Ness, nr Chester, South Wirral, Cheshire**
Jean Welch Shows   *See display advertisement*

June 12-13   **CRAFTS AT THE DULWICH COUNTRY FAYRE/Dulwich, London**
Jets Quality Craft Fairs

June 12-13   **CRAFT FAIR/White Hart Inn, Hawes, North Yorks**
Keld Craft Fairs

June 12-13   **BUCKINGHAMSHIRE CRAFT SHOW/Hughenden Manor, High Wycombe, Bucks**
Living Heritage Craft Shows Ltd   *See display advertisement*

June 12-13   **THE REDBRIDGE SHOW CRAFT FAIR/Valentines Park, Ilford, Essex**
London Borough of Redbridge

June 12-13   **CRAFT FAIR/Newby Hall, nr Ripon, North Yorks**
Rainbow Fair

June 12-13   **CRAFTS AT THE TRUCK & MOTOR SHOW SOUTH WEST 99/Westpoint Showground, Clyst St Mary, Exeter, Devon**
South West Truckers

June 12-13   **CRAFTS MARQUEE AT THE STOKE ROW STEAM RALLY 1999/English Farm, off A1430, Nuffield, nr Henley-on-Thames, Oxon**
Stoke Row Steam Rally

June 12-13   **YORKRAFT FAIR/Kilburn Village Hall, Kilburn, nr Thirsk, North Yorks**
Yorkraft Fairs

June 13   **CRAFT FAIR/Hawkshead Market Hall, nr Ambleside, Cumbria**
Aphrodite

June 13   **CRAFT FAIR/Lacock Village Hall, Lacock, nr Chippenham, Wilts**
Countrycraft

June 13   **CRAFT FAIR/Village Hotel, Whiston, nr Prescot, Merseyside**
Creative Crafts Association   *See display advertisement*

June 13   **DOLL FAIR/Lamport Hall, Lamport, Northants**
East Midlands Doll Fairs

June 13	**CRAFT SECTION AT EUSTON PARK RURAL PASTIMES/Thetford, Norfolk** Euston Park Rural Pastimes
June 13	**CRAFT & GIFT FAIR/Barton Village Hall, nr Preston, Lancs** Golden Age Fairs
June 13	**CRAFT MARQUEE AT THE KNOWSLEY SHOW/Bridgefield Sports & Leisure Centre, Halewood, Liverpool, Merseyside** Golden Age Fairs
June 13	**CRAFT FAIR/Dunkenhalgh Hotel, Clayton-le-Moors, nr Accrington, Lancs** Heritage Fairs
June 13	**CRAFT FAIR/Victoria Hall, Bourton-on-the-Water, Glos** M&B Crafts
June 13	**CRAFT FAIR/Brockenhurst Masonic Hall, Brockenhurst, Hants** Oakleaf Craft Fairs *See display advertisement*
June 16-20	**HEART OF ENGLAND CRAFTWORKERS AT BBC GARDENERS WORLD LIVE/ National Exhibition Centre, Birmingham, West Midlands** Heart of England Craftworkers *See display advertisement*
June 17-20	**PATCHINGS ART & CRAFT CONVENTION/Oxton Road, Calverton, Notts** Patchings Art Centre
June 18-20	**RURAL CRAFTS ASSOCIATION AT THE EAST OF ENGLAND SHOW/East of England Showground, Peterborough, Cambs** Rural Crafts Association *See display advertisement*
June 18-20	**RURAL CRAFTS ASSOCIATION AT THE ESSEX COUNTY SHOW/Essex County Showground, Great Leighs, Chelmsford, Essex** Rural Crafts Association *See display advertisement*
June 18-20	**RURAL CRAFTS MARQUEE AT THE THREE COUNTIES SHOW/Three Counties Showground, Malvern, Worcs** Cotswold Craftsmen
June 18-20	**WELSH CRAFTS AT THE THREE COUNTIES SHOW/Three Counties Showground, Malvern, Worcs** Wales Craft Council
June 19	**CRAFT MARKET/Fisher Hall, Guildhall Place, Cambridge, Cambs** Balthazar
June 19	**CRAFT FAIR/Volunteer Hall, Galashiels, Selkirkshire** Border Fairs
June 19	**CRAFT FAIR/Guildhall, Salisbury, Wilts** Kevin Murphy Craft Fairs
June 19-20	**CRAFT FAIR/Hawkshead Market Hall, nr Ambleside, Cumbria** Aphrodite
June 19-20	**CRAFT FAYRE/Blakemere Craft Centre, Chester Road, Sandiway, Northwich, Cheshire** Blakemere Craft Centre *See display advertisement*

| June 19-20 | **CRAFT FAIR/Town Hall, Moffat, Dumfriesshire** |
| | Caile Fairs |

| June 19-20 | **CRAFT FAIR/Brigade Hall, Bakewell, Derbys** |
| | Cottage Creations Craft Fairs |

June 19-20   **CRAFT, DESIGN & GIFT FAIR/Wyndley Garden Centre, Lichfield Road, Sutton Coldfield, West Midlands**
Cottage Industries Association   *See display advertisement*

June 19-20   **THE CRAFT SHOW/Erddig Hall, nr Wrexham, Clwyd**
Eastern Events Ltd   *See display advertisement*

June 19-20   **CRAFT FAIR/St William's College, York, North Yorks**
Keld Craft Fairs

June 19-20   **THE 'ENGINEERING IN MINIATURE' SUMMER FESTIVAL/Warwickshire Exhibition Centre, The Fosse, Fosse Way, Leamington Spa**
Meridienne Exhibitions Ltd

June 19-20   **SCOTTISH MINIATURA - THE DOLLS' HOUSE SHOW/Scottish Exhibition & Conference Centre, Glasgow**
Miniatura Dolls House Shows

June 19-20   **CRAFT FAIR/Rockingham Castle, Corby, Northants**
Rainbow Fair

June 19-20   **YORKRAFT FAIR/Kilburn Village Hall, Kilburn, nr Thirsk, North Yorks**
Yorkraft Fairs

June 19-20   **CRAFT SECTION AT THE GRAVESEND TOWN REGATTA/Gravesend, Kent**
Goldfinch Crafts

June 19-20 (provisional)   **RURAL CRAFTS ASSOCIATION AT THE CHATSWORTH GARDEN SHOW/ Chatsworth House, Baslow, Derbys**
Rural Crafts Association   *See display advertisement*

June 20   **TEDDY BEAR FAIR/Cresta Court Hotel, Altrincham, Cheshire**
Brentwood Fairs

June 20   **CRAFT FAIR/Lacock Village Hall, Lacock, nr Chippenham, Wilts**
Countrycraft

June 20   **CRAFT FAIR/Dog & Fox Hotel, High Street Wimbledon, Wimbledon Village, London**
Eden Crafts

June 20   **ARTS & CRAFTS FAIR/Woburn Village Hall, Woburn, Beds**
Falcon Fairs

June 20   **CRAFT FAIR/Exmouth Pavilion, Exmouth, Devon**
J M Evans

June 20   **CRAFT & GIFT FAIR/Sun Pavilion, Valley Gardens, Cornwall Road, Harrogate, North Yorks**
Quality Craft & Gift Fairs   *See display advertisement*

| June 20 | **CRAFTS AT THE PRESTWICH CARNIVAL/Prestwich, Manchester** |
| | West Pennine Promotions |

| June 23 | **CRAFT FAIR/Bridport Arts Centre, Bridport, Dorset** |
| | J M Evans |

| June 23-24 | **HEART OF ENGLAND CRAFTWORKERS MARQUEE AT THE LINCOLN-SHIRE SHOW/Lincolnshire Showground, Grange-de-Lings, nr Lincoln** |
| | Heart of England Craftworkers | *See display advertisement* |

| June 23-24 | **RURAL CRAFTS ASSOCIATION AT THE LINCOLNSHIRE SHOW/Lincoln-shire Showground, Grange-de-Lings, nr Lincoln, Lincs** |
| | Rural Crafts Association | *See display advertisement* |

| June 24-25 | **CRAFT FAIR/Market Hall, Hawes, North Yorks** |
| | Keld Craft Fairs |

| June 24-27 | **RURAL CRAFTS ASSOCIATION AT THE ROYAL HIGHLAND SHOW/Royal Highland Showground, Ingliston, Edinburgh** |
| | Rural Crafts Association | *See display advertisement* |

| June 25-27 | **RURAL CRAFTS ASSOCIATION AT THE NORTHERN IRELAND GAME FAIR/ Shanes Castle Estate, Co Antrim** |
| | Rural Crafts Association | *See display advertisement* |

| June 25-27 | **LIVE CRAFTS SHOW/Great Missenden, Bucks** |
| | The Exhibition Team Ltd | *See display advertisement* |

| June 26 | **CRAFT MARKET/Fisher Hall, Guildhall Place, Cambridge, Cambs** |
| | Balthazar |

| June 26 | **CRAFT FAIR/Burgh Hall, Peebles** |
| | Border Fairs |

| June 26 | **CRAFTS AT THE HALTON SPECTACULAR/Halton Airfield, Aylesbury, Bucks** |
| | Cottage Craft Fairs | *See display advertisement* |

| June 26 | **ANTIQUES, CRAFTS & COLLECTABLES FAIR/The Parish Hall, Culcheth, nr Warrington, Cheshire** |
| | Gem Fairs |

| June 26-27 | **CRAFT FAYRE/Balmer Lawn Hotel, Brockenhurst, Hants** |
| | Avocet Crafts |

| June 26-27 | **CRAFT FAYRE/Blakemere Craft Centre, Chester Road, Sandiway, Northwich, Cheshire** |
| | Blakemere Craft Centre | *See display advertisement* |

| June 26-27 | **CRAFT FAIR/Brigade Hall, Bakewell, Derbys** |
| | Cottage Creations Craft Fairs |

| June 26-27 | **CRAFT, DESIGN & GIFT FAIR/Hurrans Garden Centre, Leigh Sinton, nr Malvern, Worcs** |
| | Cottage Industries Association | *See display advertisement* |

| June 26-27 | **CRAFT FAIR/Cressing Temple Barns, Cressing, nr Braintree, Essex** |
| | Hallmark Fairs |

| June 26-27 | **4TH ESSEX FLOWER SHOW/Blake Hall, A414, Ongar, Essex** |
| | Living Heritage Craft Shows Ltd _See display advertisement_ |

| June 26-27 | **WEST SUSSEX CRAFT SHOW/Leonardslee Gardens, Lower Beeding, nr Horsham, West Sussex** |
| | Living Heritage Craft Shows Ltd _See display advertisement_ |

| June 26-27 | **CRAFT FAIR/Victoria Hall, Bourton-on-the-Water, Glos** |
| | M&B Crafts |

| June 26-27 | **CRAFTS AT THE MIDDLESEX COUNTY SHOW/Uxbridge, Middx** |
| | Middlesex County Show |

| June 26-27 | **CRAFT FAIR/Haddon Hall, Bakewell, Derbys** |
| | Oak Craft Fairs _See display advertisement_ |

| June 26-27 | **CRAFT FAIR/Arbury Hall, Nuneaton, Warks** |
| | Rainbow Fair |

| June 26-27 | **CRAFT FAIR/The Pavilion, Buxton, Derbys** |
| | Town & Country Craft Fairs |

| June 26-27 | **YORKRAFT FAIR/Thornton Dale Parish Rooms, Thornton Dale, nr Pickering, North Yorks** |
| | Yorkraft Fairs |

| June 26-27 (provisional) | **CRAFT STALLS AT THE MARGAM PARK MODEL & CRAFT SHOW 1999/ Margam Country Park, Port Talbot, South Wales** |
| | Craft*Folk |

| June 27 | **CRAFT MARQUEE AT THE ULLSWATER COUNTRY FAIR/Patterdale, nr Penrith, Cumbria** |
| | Aphrodite |

| June 27 | **CRAFT FAIR/Kingfisher Hotel, Wall Heath (A44), nr Kingswinford, West Midlands** |
| | Central Promotions _See display advertisement_ |

| June 27 | **CRAFT FAIR/Lacock Village Hall, Lacock, nr Chippenham, Wilts** |
| | Countrycraft |

| June 27 | **THE HOLME VALLEY SHOW/Sands Recreation Ground, Holmfirth, nr Huddersfield, West Yorks** |
| | Holmfirth Round Table |

| June 27 | **CRAFT FAIR/Exmouth Pavilion, Exmouth, Devon** |
| | J M Evans |

| June 27 | **ARTS & CRAFTS SHOW/Lauderdale House, Highgate Hill, London N6** |
| | Lauderdale Arts & Crafts |

| June 27 | **CRAFT FAIR/Lyndhurst Community Centre, Lyndhurst, Hants** |
| | Oakleaf Craft Fairs _See display advertisement_ |

| June 27 | **CRAFT MARQUEE AT THE CHIGWELL CLASSIC CAR SHOW/High Road, Chigwell, Essex** |
| | Quality Craft Fairs |

| June 27 | **CRAFT FAIR/Royal Shakespeare Theatre, Stratford-upon-Avon, Warks** |
| | West Country Craft Fairs *See display advertisement* |

| June 30 | **CRAFT FAYRE/Blakemere Craft Centre, Chester Road, Sandiway, Northwich, Cheshire** |
| | Blakemere Craft Centre *See display advertisement* |

June 30-July 1 **ROYAL NORFOLK SHOW/Norfolk Showground, Dereham Road, New Costessey, nr Norwich, Norfolk (main organiser)**
Royal Norfolk Agricultural Association

June 30-July 1 **RURAL CRAFTS ASSOCIATION AT THE ROYAL NORFOLK SHOW/Norfolk Showground, Dereham Road, New Costessey, nr Norwich, Norfolk**
Rural Crafts Association *See display advertisement*

July 1
(provisional) **CRAFT FAIR/Pooley Bridge Memorial Hall, nr Penrith, Cumbria**
Aphrodite

July 3 **CRAFT MARKET/Fisher Hall, Guildhall Place, Cambridge, Cambs**
Balthazar

July 3 **CRAFT FAIR/Municipal Hall, Biggar, Lanarkshire**
Border Fairs

July 3 **ARTS & CRAFTS FAIR/Town Hall, Towcester, Northants**
Falcon Fairs

July 3 **CRAFT & GIFT FAIR/Barnet Library, Stapylton Road, Barnet, Herts**
Marie Margaret Promotions

July 3 **ART & CRAFT FAIR/The Arts Centre, Biddick Lane, Fatfield, Washington, Tyne & Wear**
The Arts Centre

July 3-4 **CRAFT FAYRE/Blakemere Craft Centre, Chester Road, Sandiway, Northwich, Cheshire**
Blakemere Craft Centre *See display advertisement*

July 3-4 **CRAFT MARQUEE AT THE BROOME PARK COUNTRY FAIR/Broome Park, Barham, nr Canterbury, Kent**
Broome Park Country & Craft Fair

July 3-4 **CRAFT FAIR/Brigade Hall, Bakewell, Derbys**
Cottage Creations Craft Fairs

July 3-4 **CRAFT, DESIGN & GIFT FAIR/William Wheat's Garden Centre, Old Chester Road (A452), Little Aston, West Midlands**
Cottage Industries Association *See display advertisement*

July 3-4 **CRAFT, DESIGN & GIFT FAIR/Wyevale Garden Centre & Farm Shop,Telford, Salop**
Cottage Industries Association *See display advertisement*

July 3-4 **SUMMER CRAFT, FASHION & DESIGN FESTIVAL/Dalkeith Place, nr Edinburgh**
Dalesway Festivals Ltd *See display advertisement*

July 3-4	**CRAFTS AT TOWER BRIDGE/London** Jets Quality Craft Fairs
July 3-4	**SAVERNAKE FOREST CRAFT SHOW/Tottenham House, nr Marlborough, Wilts** Living Heritage Craft Shows Ltd _See display advertisement_
July 3-4	**CRAFTS AT THE 14TH SUSSEX SMALLHOLDERS SHOW/South of England Centre, Ardingly, nr Haywards Heath, West Sussex** Smallholder Shows
July 3-4	**CRAFT TENT AT THE GREAT YORKSHIRE STEAM FAIR & RALLY/Duncombe Park, Helmsley, North Yorks** The Great Yorkshire Traction Engine Club
July 3-7	**YORKRAFT FAIR/ Parish Rooms, Thornton Dale, nr Pickering, North Yorks** Yorkraft Fairs
July 4	**CRAFT FAYRE/The Belgrave Hotel, Torquay, Devon** Cherrycraft Fayres & Festivals
July 4	**CRAFT FAIR/Lacock Village Hall, Lacock, nr Chippenham, Wilts** Countrycraft
July 4	**CRAFTS IN ACTION AT RMA SANDHURST/Sandhurst, Camberley, Surrey** Crafts in Action
July 4	**CRAFT MARQUEE AT THE FORD FAMILY FUN DAY/Ford Sports & Social Club, 77 Cronton Lane, Widnes, Cheshire** Golden Age Fairs
July 4	**CRAFT TENT AT THE HOOK NORTON RURAL FAYRE/Rural Fayre Field, Hook Norton, nr Banbury, Oxon** Hook Norton Rural Fayre
July 4	**24TH HOVENDEN GALA & CRAFT FAIR/Hovenden House, Spalding, Lincs** Hovenden Gala & Craft Fair
July 4	**CRAFT FAIR/Exmouth Pavilion, Exmouth, Devon** J M Evans
July 4	**CRAFT FAIR/Godshill Village Hall, Godshill, Hants** Oakleaf Craft Fairs _See display advertisement_
July 4	**CRAFT FAIR/Downham Village Hall, Downham, nr Clitheroe, Lancs** West Pennine Promotions
July 5-8	**HEART OF ENGLAND CRAFTWORKERS MARQUEE AT THE ROYAL SHOW/ National Agricultural Centre, Stoneleigh Park, Warks** Heart of England Craftworkers _See display advertisement_
July 5-8	**RURAL CRAFTS ASSOCIATION AT THE ROYAL SHOW/National Agricultural Centre, Stoneleigh Park, Warks** Rural Crafts Association _See display advertisement_
July 6-11	**WELSH CRAFTS AT THE INTERNATIONAL MUSICAL EISTEDDFOD/ Llangollen, Clwyd** Wales Craft Council

July 7-11   **CRAFTS IN ACTION AT THE ROYAL INTERNATIONAL HORSE SHOW/The All England Jumping Course, Hickstead, West Sussex**
Crafts in Action

July 8   **CRAFT FAIR/Market Hall, Hawes, North Yorks**
Keld Craft Fairs

July 8
(provisional)   **CRAFT FAIR/Pooley Bridge Memorial Hall, nr Penrith, Cumbria**
Aphrodite

July 9-11   **CRAFT FAIR/Hawkshead Market Hall, nr Ambleside, Cumbria**
Aphrodite

July 9-11   **LIVE CRAFTS SHOW/Firle Place, Lewes, East Sussex**
The Exhibition Team Ltd   *See display advertisement*

July 10   **CRAFT MARKET/Fisher Hall, Guildhall Place, Cambridge, Cambs**
Balthazar

July 10   **CRAFT FAIR/Village Hall, High Street, Henfield, West Sussex**
Craft Developments

July 10   **TYNESIDE DOLLS HOUSE & MINIATURES FAIR/Gateshead Civic Centre, Regent Street, Gateshead, Tyne & Wear**
Dolly Domain Fairs

July 10   **DUNSTABLE CRAFT MARKET/Methodist Church Hall, Ashton Square, Dunstable, Beds**
Dunstable Craft Market

July 10   **ARTS & CRAFTS FAIR/Town Hall, Brackley, Northants**
Falcon Fairs

July 10   **CRAFT FAIR/Market Hall, Abergavenny, Monmouthshire**
Monmouthshire County Council

July 10   **CRAFTS AT NEWTON LE WILLOWS TOWN SHOW/Newton le Willows, nr Bedale, North Yorks**
West Pennine Promotions

July 10-11   **CRAFT FAYRE/Blakemere Craft Centre, Chester Road, Sandiway, Northwich, Cheshire**
Blakemere Craft Centre   *See display advertisement*

July 10-11   **CRAFT FAIR/The Village Hall, Bolton Abbey, nr Skipton, North Yorks**
CFL Craft Shows

July 10-11   **CRAFT FAIR/Brigade Hall, Bakewell, Derbys**
Cottage Creations Craft Fairs

July 10-11   **CRAFT, DESIGN & GIFT FAIR/Byrkley Park Garden Centre, Rangemore, Burton-on-Trent, Staffs**
Cottage Industries Association   *See display advertisement*

July 10-11   **SUMMER CRAFT WEEKEND/Ditchling Garden Centre, Ditchling, West Sussex**
Jets Quality Craft Fairs

July 10-11	**CRAFT FAIR/St William's College, York, North Yorks** Keld Craft Fairs
July 10-11	**ASHRIDGE COUNTRY CRAFT SHOW/The Ashridge Estate, Berkhamsted, Herts** Living Heritage Craft Shows Ltd *See display advertisement*
July 10-11	**CRAFT FAIR/Victoria Hall, Bourton-on-the-Water, Glos** M&B Crafts
July 10-11	**CRAFT MARQUEE AT THE HORSHAM FESTIVAL WEEKEND/Horsham Park, Horsham, West Sussex** Southwater Promotions
July 10-11	**CRAFT MARQUEE AT THE WIRRAL SHOW/Wallasey, Merseyside** Wirral Show Craft Marquee
July 10-11	**CRAFT MARQUEE AT THE QUEEN ELIZABETH COUNTRY PARK SHOW/ nr Petersfield, Hants** Woodland Crafts *See display advertisement*
July 10-11	**YORKRAFT FAIR/Kilburn Village Hall, Kilburn, nr Thirsk, North Yorks** Yorkraft Fairs
July 11	**DOLL FAIR/Kelham Hall, Newark, Notts** East Midlands Doll Fairs
July 11	**CRAFT FAIR/Brockenhurst Masonic Hall, Brockenhurst, Hants** Oakleaf Craft Fairs *See display advertisement*
July 11	**CRAFT FAIR/Royal Shakespeare Theatre, Stratford-upon-Avon, Warks** West Country Craft Fairs *See display advertisement*
July 13	**CRAFT FAIR/White Hart Inn, Hawes, North Yorks** Keld Craft Fairs
July 13-15	**HEART OF ENGLAND CRAFTWORKERS MARQUEE AT THE GREAT YORKSHIRE SHOW/Great Yorkshire Showground, Harrogate, North Yorks** Heart of England Craftworkers *See display advertisement*
July 13-15	**RURAL CRAFTS ASSOCIATION AT THE GREAT YORKSHIRE SHOW/Great Yorkshire Showground, Hookstone Oval, Harrogate, North Yorks** Rural Crafts Association *See display advertisement*
July 14-15	**YORKRAFT FAIR/Town Hall, Helmsley, North Yorks** Yorkraft Fairs
July 15 (provisional)	**CRAFT FAIR/Pooley Bridge Memorial Hall, nr Penrith, Cumbria** Aphrodite
July 15-17	**RURAL CRAFTS ASSOCIATION AT THE KENT COUNTY SHOW/Kent County Showground, Detling, nr Maidstone, Kent** Rural Crafts Association *See display advertisement*
July 15-18	**ART IN ACTION/Waterperry House, Wheatley, Oxon** Art in Action

July 16-18	**ROBIN HOOD CRAFT FAYRE/Ealing Common, London W5** Four Seasons (Events) Ltd
July 17	**CRAFT & GIFT FAIR/The Harlington Centre, High Street, Fleet, Hants** Aquarius Fairs
July 17	**CRAFT MARKET/Fisher Hall, Guildhall Place, Cambridge, Cambs** Balthazar
July 17	**DOLL & TEDDY FAIR/Rivington Hall Barn, Horwich, nr Bolton, Lancs** Brentwood Fairs
July 17	**CRAFT FAYRE/St Mary's Centre, Grassmere Close, Felpham, nr Bognor Regis, West Sussex** Good Ideas Craft Fayres
July 17	**HEART OF ENGLAND CRAFTWORKERS MARQUEE AT THE NEWPORT & DISTRICT AGRICULTURAL SHOW/Newport, Salop** Heart of England Craftworkers *See display advertisement*
July 17	**CRAFTS AT TY MAWR COUNTRY FAYRE/Ty Mawr Country Park, Cefn Mawr, Wrexham, Clwyd** Ty Mawr Country Park
July 17-18	**CRAFT FAYRE/Craft Centre, Chester Road, Sandiway, Northwich, Cheshire** Blakemere Craft Centre *See display advertisement*
July 17-18	**CRAFTS MARQUEE AT THE DERBYSHIRE FLOWER FESTIVAL/Locko Park, Derby, Derbys** CFL Craft Shows
July 17-18	**CRAFT FAIR/Castle Bromwich Hall, Chester Road, Castle Bromwich, Birmingham, West Midlands** Castle Bromwich Hall Gardens Trust
July 17-18	**CRAFT FAIR/Brigade Hall, Bakewell, Derbys** Cottage Creations Craft Fairs
July 17-18	**CRAFT, DESIGN & GIFT FAIR/Jardinerie Garden Place, Kenilworth Road (A452), Hampton-in-Arden, West Midlands** Cottage Industries Association *See display advertisement*
July 17-18	**CRAFTS & GARDENS AT LARMER TREE/Larmer Tree, nr Shaftesbury, Wilts** Craft Carnival
July 17-18	**CRAFT SECTION AT THE GRAVESEND SUMMER REGATTA/Gravesend, Kent** Goldfinch Crafts
July 17-18	**THE HEART OF ENGLAND CRAFTWORKERS MARQUEE AT THE HOLKHAM COUNTRY SHOW/Holkham, nr Wells-next-the-Sea, Norfolk** Heart of England Craftworkers *See display advertisement*
July 17-18	**ARTS & CRAFTS FAIR Town Hall, Grassington, nr Skipton, North Yorks** Jean Bryon
July 17-18	**SUMMER CRAFT WEEKEND/Ashdown Forest Garden Centre, West Sussex** Jets Quality Craft Fairs

July 17-18	**CRAFT FAIR/St William's College, York, North Yorks** Keld Craft Fairs
July 17-18	**CRAFTS AT THE LAMBETH COUNTRY SHOW/Brockwell Park, Herne Hill, London SE23** Lambeth Country Show
July 17-18	**LANCASHIRE CRAFT SHOW/Stoneyhurst College, Clitheroe, Lancs** Living Heritage Craft Shows Ltd _See display advertisement_
July 17-18	**NOSTELL PRIORY COUNTRY SHOW/Nostell Priory, A638 Doncaster Road, nr Wakefield, West Yorks** Living Heritage Craft Shows Ltd _See display advertisement_
July 17-18	**CRAFT FAIR/Elton Hall, Elton, nr Peterborough, Cambs** Oak Craft Fairs _See display advertisement_
July 17-18	**CRAFT FAIR/Dalemain, nr Penrith, Cumbria** Rainbow Fair
July 17-18	**RURAL CRAFTS ASSOCIATION AT THE HOLKHAM COUNTRY FAIR/ Holkham, nr Wells-next-the-Sea, Norfolk** Rural Crafts Association _See display advertisement_
July 17-18	**TUDOR REVEL SHOW/Hatfield House, Hatfield, Herts** The Exhibition Team Ltd _See display advertisement_
July 17-21	**YORKRAFT FAIR/Thornton Dale Parish Rooms, Thornton Dale, nr Pickering, North Yorks** Yorkraft Fairs
July 18	**CRAFT FAIR/Whitchurch Leisure Centre, High Street, Whitchurch, Salop** Archer Promotions
July 18	**DOLLS HOUSE & MINIATURE FAIR/Cresta Court Hotel, Altrincham, Cheshire** Brentwood Fairs
July 18	**CRAFT FAIR/The Pemberton Centre, Rushden, Northants** Cambridge Craft Fairs
July 18	**CRAFT FAIR/Lacock Village Hall, Lacock, nr Chippenham, Wilts** Countrycraft
July 18	**ARTS & CRAFTS FAIR/Woburn Village Hall, Woburn, Beds** Falcon Fairs
July 18	**CRAFT & GIFT FAIR/Sun Pavilion, Valley Gardens, Cornwall Road, Harrogate, North Yorks** Quality Craft & Gift Fairs _See display advertisement_
July 18	**CRAFT FAIR AT THE VINTAGE VEHICLE SHOW/Springfields, Camelgate, Spalding, Lincs** Springfields Exhibition Centre
July 18	**CRAFT FAIR/Royal Shakespeare Theatre, Stratford-upon-Avon, Warks** West Country Craft Fairs _See display advertisement_

| July 18 | **CRAFT FAIR/Pavilion Theatre, Worthing, West Sussex** |
| | Worthing Leisure |

| July 18 | **CRAFT MARQUEE AT ROYAL MAIL SHOW/Walsall Arboretum, West Midlands** |
| (provisional) | The Craft Tent Company |

| July 18-21 | **HOME & GIFT 99/Harrogate Exhibition Centre, North Yorks** |
| | P&O Events Ltd |

| July 19-22 | **HEART OF ENGLAND CRAFTWORKERS MARQUEE AT THE ROYAL WELSH SHOW/Royal Welsh Showground, Llanelwedd, Builth Wells, Powys** |
| | Heart of England Craftworkers   *See display advertisement* |

| July 19-22 | **RURAL CRAFTS ASSOCIATION AT THE ROYAL WELSH SHOW/Royal Welsh Showground, Llanelwedd, Builth Wells, Powys** |
| | Rural Crafts Association   *See display advertisement* |

| July 19-22 | **WELSH CRAFTS AT THE ROYAL WELSH SHOW/Royal Welsh Showground, Llanelwedd, Builth Wells, Powys** |
| | Wales Craft Council |

| July 21 | **CRAFT FAIR/Bridport Arts Centre, Bridport, Dorset** |
| | J M Evans |

| July 22 | **CRAFT FAIR/Market Hall, Hawes, North Yorks** |
| | Keld Craft Fairs |

| July 22 | **CRAFT FAIR/Pooley Bridge Memorial Hall, nr Penrith, Cumbria** |
| (provisional) | Aphrodite |

| July 23 | **CRAFT FAIR/Community Centre, Leyburn, North Yorks** |
| | Keld Craft Fairs |

| July 23-24 | **CRAFT FAIR/Hawkshead Market Hall, nr Ambleside, Cumbria** |
| | Aphrodite |

| July 23-24 | **CRAFT STALLS AT CAERPHILLY CHEESE FESTIVAL/Caerphilly, South Wales** |
| (provisional) | Craft*Folk |

| July 23-25 | **BRANCEPETH CASTLE SUMMER CRAFT FAIR/Brancepeth Castle, 4 miles west of Durham City on A690** |
| | Brancepeth Castle Craft Fairs |

| July 23-25 | **MEDIEVAL CRAFT FAYRE/The Vyne, Basingstoke, Hants** |
| | Four Seasons (Events) Ltd |

| July 23-25 | **LIVE CRAFTS SHOW/Berkeley Castle, Berkeley, nr Gloucester, Glos** |
| | The Exhibition Team Ltd   *See display advertisement* |

| July 24 | **CRAFT MARKET/Fisher Hall, Guildhall Place, Cambridge, Cambs** |
| | Balthazar |

| July 24 | **CRAFT FAIR/Corn Exchange, Haddington, East Lothian** |
| | Border Fairs |

| July 24 | **ARTS & CRAFTS FAYRE/Winter Gardens, Weston-super-Mare, Somerset** |
| | Fountain Fayres & Exhibitions |

| July 24 | **LYME REGIS MID-SUMMER CRAFT FAIR/Marine Theatre, Lyme Regis, Dorset** |
| | West Country Craft Fairs *See display advertisement* |

| July 24-25 | **CRAFT FAYRE/Blakemere Craft Centre, Chester Road, Sandiway, Northwich, Cheshire** |
| | Blakemere Craft Centre *See display advertisement* |

| July 24-25 | **CRAFT FAIR/Brigade Hall, Bakewell, Derbys** |
| | Cottage Creations Craft Fairs |

| July 24-25 | **CRAFT, DESIGN & GIFT FAIR/Hurrans Garden Centre, Newport, Gwent** |
| | Cottage Industries Association *See display advertisement* |

| July 24-25 | **SUMMER CRAFT, FASHION & DESIGN FESTIVAL/Floors Castle, Kelso, Roxburghshire** |
| | Dalesway Festivals Ltd *See display advertisement* |

| July 24-25 | **KENT & SUSSEX CRAFT SHOW/Groombridge Place Gardens, B2110, nr Tunbridge Wells, Kent** |
| | Living Heritage Craft Shows Ltd *See display advertisement* |

| July 24-25 | **LIVING HERITAGE AT THE ROYAL INTERNATIONAL AIR TATTOO/RAF Fairford, Glos** |
| | Living Heritage Craft Shows Ltd *See display advertisement* |

| July 24-25 | **CRAFT FAIR/Sherborne Castle, Sherborne, Dorset** |
| | Rainbow Fair |

| July 24-25 | **CRAFTS AT THE ROYAL INTERNATIONAL AIR TATTOO/RAF Fairford, Glos** |
| | Royal International Air Tattoo *See display advertisement* |

| July 24-25 | **INTERNATIONAL RUBBER STAMP FAIR/Artstamps at the Corn Exchange, Newbury, Berks** |
| | Stamps Unlimited |

| July 24-25 | **THE CRAFT & CIDER COUNTRY FAYRE/Shepeys Cider Farm, Bradford On Tone, nr Taunton, Somerset** |
| | The Craft & Cider Country Fayre |

| July 24-25 | **YORKRAFT FAIR/Kilburn Village Hall, Kilburn, nr Thirsk, North Yorks** |
| | Yorkraft Fairs |

| July 24-Aug 8 | **CRAFT GUILD TWO-WEEK EXHIBITION/Samlesbury Hall, Samlesbury, nr Preston, Lancs** |
| | The Craft Guild of West Lancashire |

| July 25 | **CRAFT MARQUEE AT CONISTON COUNTRY FAIR/Coniston Hall, Cumbria** |
| | Aphrodite |

| July 25 | **CRAFT FAIR/Community Centre, Kinver, nr Stourbridge, West Midlands** |
| | Central Promotions *See display advertisement* |

| July 25 | **CRAFT FAIR/Lacock Village Hall, Lacock, nr Chippenham, Wilts** |
| | Countrycraft |

| July 25 | **CRAFT FAIR/Exmouth Pavilion, Exmouth, Devon** |
| | J M Evans |

July 25	**ARTS & CRAFTS SHOW/Lauderdale House, Highgate Hill, London N6**
	Lauderdale Arts & Crafts

July 25	**CRAFT FAIR/Lyndhurst Community Centre, Lyndhurst, Hants**
	Oakleaf Craft Fairs *See display advertisement*

July 25	**CRAFT FAIR/Hollingworth Lake Rowing Club, Littleborough, Lancs**
	West Pennine Promotions

July 25 (provisional)	**CRAFT MARQUEE AT THE ROLLING THUNDER AIR SHOW/Bruntingthorpe Aerodrome, nr Lutterworth, Leics**
	The Craft Tent Company

July 27	**CRAFT FAIR/White Hart Inn, Hawes, North Yorks**
	Keld Craft Fairs

July 28	**CRAFT FAYRE/Blakemere Craft Centre, Chester Road, Sandiway, Northwich, Cheshire**
	Blakemere Craft Centre *See display advertisement*

July 28	**CRAFT FAIR/Bridport Arts Centre, Bridport, Dorset**
	J M Evans

July 29 (provisional)	**CRAFT FAIR/Pooley Bridge Memorial Hall, nr Penrith, Cumbria**
	Aphrodite

July 29-Aug 1	**16TH SYON PARK ARTS & CRAFTS SHOW/Syon Park, Isleworth, West London**
	Orchard Events Ltd *See display advertisement*

July 30	**CRAFT FAIR/Community Centre, Leyburn, North Yorks**
	Keld Craft Fairs

July 30-31	**CRAFT FAIR/Hawkshead Market Hall, nr Ambleside, Cumbria**
	Aphrodite

July 30-Aug 1	**CRAFT, DESIGN & GIFT FAIR/Wyndley Garden Centre, Warwick Road, Knowle, Warks**
	Cottage Industries Association *See display advertisement*

July 30-Aug 1	**CRAFT & GIFT MARQUEE AT THE ST HELENS SHOW/Sherdley Park, St Helens, Merseyside**
	Creative Crafts Association *See display advertisement*

July 30-Aug 1	**ROBIN HOOD CRAFT FAYRE/Tabley House, Knutsford, Cheshire**
	Four Seasons (Events) Ltd

July 30-Aug 1	**HEART OF ENGLAND CRAFTWORKERS MARQUEE AT THE CLA GAME FAIR/ Harewood House, Leeds, West Yorks**
	Heart of England Craftworkers *See display advertisement*

July 30-Aug 1	**HAMPSHIRE CRAFT SHOW/Broadlands, nr Romsey, Hants**
	Living Heritage Craft Shows Ltd *See display advertisement*

July 30-Aug 1	**RURAL CRAFTS ASSOCIATION AT INTERNATIONAL HISTORIC FESTIVAL/ Silverstone, Northants**
	Rural Crafts Association *See display advertisement*

| July 30-Aug 1 | **RURAL CRAFTS ASSOCIATION AT THE CLA GAME FAIR/Harewood House, Leeds, West Yorks** |
| | Rural Crafts Association   *See display advertisement* |

July 30-Aug 1   **RURAL CRAFTS ASSOCIATION AT THE CLA GAME FAIR/Harewood House, Leeds, West Yorks**
Rural Crafts Association   *See display advertisement*

July 30-Aug 1   **CRAFT, GIFTS & COLLECTORS MARQUEE AT THE ST HELENS SHOW/ Sherdley Park, St Helens, Merseyside**
St Helens Show

July 30-Aug 1   **LIVE CRAFTS SHOW/Basildon Park, Lower Basildon, nr Reading, Berks**
The Exhibition Team Ltd   *See display advertisement*

July 30-Aug 2   **SUMMER CRAFT, FASHION & DESIGN FESTIVAL/St Andrews, Fife**
Dalesway Festivals Ltd   *See display advertisement*

July 31   **CRAFT FAIR/Burgh Hall, Peebles**
Border Fairs

July 31   **CRAFT FAYRE/The Scala Hall, Brixham, Devon**
Cherrycraft Fayres & Festivals

July 31-Aug 1   **CRAFT FAYRE/Blakemere Craft Centre, Chester Road, Sandiway, Northwich, Cheshire**
Blakemere Craft Centre   *See display advertisement*

July 31-Aug 1   **CRAFT FAIR/Town Hall, Moffat, Dumfriesshire**
Caile Fairs

July 31-Aug 1   **CRAFT FAIR/Brigade Hall, Bakewell, Derbys**
Cottage Creations Craft Fairs

July 31-Aug 1   **GATESHEAD CRAFTS AT THE FLOWER SHOW/Central Nursery, Whickham, Tyne & Wear**
Gateshead Fairs

July 31-Aug 1 (provisional)   **CRAFTS STALLS AT THE CAERPHILLY BIG CHEESE FESTIVAL 1999/ Caerphilly Castle, South Wales**
Craft*Folk

July 31-Aug 4   **YORKRAFT FAIR/Thornton Dale Parish Rooms, Thornton Dale, nr Pickering, North Yorks**
Yorkraft Fairs

July 31-Aug 7   **CRAFT FORUM (Y GREFFT) AT THE NATIONAL EISTEDDFOD OF WALES/ Llanbedrgoch, Anglesey, Gwynedd**
National Eisteddfod of Wales

July 31-Aug 21 (provisional)   **CARDIFF SUMMER CRAFT FESTIVAL/St John's Square, Cardiff**
Craft*Folk

Aug 1   **CRAFT FAIR/Hawkshead Market Hall, nr Ambleside, Cumbria**
Aphrodite

Aug 1   **CRAFT FAYRE/The Belgrave Hotel, Torquay, Devon**
Cherrycraft Fayres & Festivals

Aug 1   **CRAFT FAIR/Lacock Village Hall, Lacock, nr Chippenham, Wilts**
Countrycraft

| Aug 1 | **CRAFT FAIR/Exmouth Pavilion, Exmouth, Devon** |
| | J M Evans |

| Aug 1 | **CRAFT FAIR/Godshill Village Hall, Godshill, Hants** |
| | Oakleaf Craft Fairs *See display advertisement* |

| Aug 1 | **CRAFT FAIR/Ford Castle, Ford, nr Wooler, Northumberland** |
| | Quintet Promotions |

| Aug 1 | **CRAFT FAIR/Downham Village Hall, Downham, nr Clitheroe, Lancs** |
| | West Pennine Promotions |

| Aug 1 | **DOLLS HOUSE, DOLLS, TOYS & MINIATURES FAIR/Westpoint, Exeter, Devon** |
| | West of England Fairs |

| Aug 3 | **CRAFT FAIR/White Hart Inn, Hawes, North Yorks** |
| | Keld Craft Fairs |

| Aug 4-5 | **CRAFT EXHIBITION AT THE BLACK ISLE SHOW/Mannsfield, Muir of Ord, Ross-shire** |
| | Black Isle Farmers Society |

| Aug 4-5 | **HEART OF ENGLAND CRAFTWORKERS MARQUEE AT THE BAKEWELL SHOW/Bakewell, Derbys** |
| | Heart of England Craftworkers *See display advertisement* |

| Aug 5 (provisional) | **CRAFT FAIR/Pooley Bridge Memorial Hall, nr Penrith, Cumbria** |
| | Aphrodite |

| Aug 5-6 | **OXBURGH CHILDREN'S EXTRAVAGANZA/Oxburgh Hall, King's Lynn, Norfolk** |
| | Eastern Events Ltd *See display advertisement* |

| Aug 5-8 | **CRAFTS AT THE BRISTOL INTERNATIONAL BALLOON FIESTA/Ashton Court, Bristol** |
| | Cottage Industries Association *See display advertisement* |

| Aug 6 | **CRAFT FAIR/Community Centre, Leyburn, North Yorks** |
| | Keld Craft Fairs |

| Aug 6-8 | **AMBLESIDE GARDEN FESTIVAL & CRAFT FAIR/Ambleside, Cumbria** |
| | Ambleside Horticultural & Craft Society |

| Aug 6-8 | **CRAFT FAIR/Hawkshead Market Hall, nr Ambleside, Cumbria** |
| | Aphrodite |

| Aug 6-8 | **RUNNYMEDE PAGEANT & CRAFT FAYRE/Runnymede Riverside Meadows, Egham, Surrey** |
| | Four Seasons (Events) Ltd |

| Aug 6-8 | **RURAL CRAFTS ASSOCIATION AT THE LOWTHER DRIVING TRIALS/ Lowther, nr Penrith, Cumbria** |
| | Rural Crafts Association *See display advertisement* |

| Aug 6-8 | **ART IN CLAY SHOW/Hatfield House, Hatfield, Herts** |
| | The Exhibition Team Ltd *See display advertisement* |

Aug 6-8	**CRAFT MARQUEE AT THE PORTSMOUTH & SOUTHSEA SHOW/Southsea Common, Southsea, Hants**

Aug 6-8   **CRAFT MARQUEE AT THE PORTSMOUTH & SOUTHSEA SHOW/Southsea Common, Southsea, Hants**
Woodland Crafts   *See display advertisement*

Aug 6-21   **CRAFT MARQUEE AT THE PLYMOUTH STREET FAIR 1999/Armada Way, Plymouth, Devon**
Cherrycraft Fayres & Festivals

Aug 7   **CRAFT MARKET/Fisher Hall, Guildhall Place, Cambridge, Cambs**
Balthazar

Aug 7   **CRAFT FAIR/Corn Exchange, Melrose, Roxburghshire**
Border Fairs

Aug 7   **CRAFTS AT THE BRECON COUNTY SHOW/Brecon, Powys**
Brecknockshire Agricultural Society

Aug 7   **THE OSWESTRY & DISTRICT SHOW CRAFT MARQUEE/Park Halls, Oswestry, Salop**
Croesoswallt Crafts

Aug 7   **ART & CRAFT FAIR/The Arts Centre, Biddick Lane, Fatfield, Washington, Tyne & Wear**
The Arts Centre

Aug 7 (provisional)   **CRAFT MARQUEE AT RUSHDEN & DIAMONDS FC OPEN DAY/Rushden, Northants**
The Craft Tent Company

Aug 7-8   **CRAFT FAYRE/Blakemere Craft Centre, Chester Road, Sandiway, Northwich, Cheshire**
Blakemere Craft Centre   *See display advertisement*

Aug 7-8   **CRAFT FAIR/The Village Hall, Bolton Abbey, nr Skipton, North Yorks**
CFL Craft Shows

Aug 7-8   **CRAFTS AT THE CHERTSEY SHOW/Chertsey, Surrey**
Chertsey Agricultural Association

Aug 7-8   **CRAFT FAIR/Brigade Hall, Bakewell, Derbys**
Cottage Creations Craft Fairs

Aug 7-8   **HEART OF ENGLAND CRAFTWORKERS MARQUEE AT THE LULWORTH HORSE & COUNTRY FAIR/Lulworth Castle, Dorset**
Heart of England Craftworkers   *See display advertisement*

Aug 7-8   **CRAFT FAIR/St William's College, York, North Yorks**
Keld Craft Fairs

Aug 7-8   **CRAFT FAIR/Wood Green Animal Shelters, Godmanchester, Cambs**
Kingfisher Promotions

Aug 7-8   **CRAFTS AT THE DUDLEY SHOW/Himley Hall, Dudley, West Midlands**
Laurel Crafts

Aug 7-8   **MEDWAY CRAFT & FLOWER SHOW/Cobham Hall, nr Gravesend, Kent**
Living Heritage Craft Shows Ltd   *See display advertisement*

| Aug 7-8 | **CRAFT FAIR/Ingestre Hall, Weston Road, Stafford, Staffs** |
| | Oak Craft Fairs *See display advertisement* |

Aug 7-8   **CRAFT FAIR/Ingestre Hall, Weston Road, Stafford, Staffs**
Oak Craft Fairs   *See display advertisement*

Aug 7-8   **CRAFTS AT AIR SHOW/Seaburn Centre, Seaburn, Sunderland, Tyne & Wear**
Quintet Promotions

Aug 7-8   **CRAFT FAIR/Grimsthorpe Castle, Bourne, Lincs**
Rainbow Fair

Aug 7-8   **CRAFTS AT THE THURLOW STEAM RALLY & SHOW/Haverhill Showground, Haverhill, Suffolk**
Thurlow Steam Rally & Show

Aug 7-8   **CRAFT FAIR/The Pavilion, Buxton, Derbys**
Town & Country Craft Fairs

Aug 7-8   **CRAFT MARKET AT THE WORTHING VICTORIAN FESTIVAL/Worthing, West Sussex**
Woodland Crafts   *See display advertisement*

Aug 7-8   **YORKRAFT FAIR/Kilburn Village Hall, Kilburn, nr Thirsk, North Yorks**
Yorkraft Fairs

Aug 8   **CRAFT FAIR/Northwood Stadium, Keelings Road, Northwood, nr Hanley, Stoke-on-Trent, Staffs**
Archer Promotions

Aug 8   **CRAFT FAIR/Lacock Village Hall, Lacock, nr Chippenham, Wilts**
Countrycraft

Aug 8   **CRAFT & GIFTS MARQUEE AT LANCASHIRE EVENING POST'S GALA DAY/ Olivers Place, Eastway, Fulwood, Preston, Lancs**
Golden Age Fairs

Aug 8   **CRAFT FAIR/Royal Shakespeare Theatre, Stratford-upon-Avon, Warks**
West Country Craft Fairs   *See display advertisement*

Aug 10   **CRAFT FAIR/White Hart Inn, Hawes, North Yorks**
Keld Craft Fairs

Aug 10   **CRAFT MARQUEE AT THE TAUNTON AGRICULTURAL SHOW/The Showground, Netherday Farm, Thurlbear, Taunton, Somerset**
Taunton Agricultural Show Ltd

Aug 11   **CRAFT FAIR/Bridport Arts Centre, Bridport, Dorset**
J M Evans

Aug 11-21   **CRAFT & GIFT MARKET/Old Market Square, Nottingham, Notts**
(provisional)   Nottingham City Council

Aug 12   **CRAFT MARQUEE AT THE OKEHAMPTON AGRICULTURAL SHOW/Stoney Park Showground, Okehampton, Devon**
Okehampton Show

Aug 12-13   **HEART OF ENGLAND CRAFTWORKERS MARQUEE AT THE UNITED COUNTIES SHOW/The Showground, Nant-y-Ci, Carmarthen, Dyfed**
Heart of England Craftworkers   *See display advertisement*

| Aug 12-15 | **THE SUSSEX GUILD IN ACTION/Michelham Priory, Upper Dicker, nr Hailsham, East Sussex** |
| | The Sussex Guild |

| Aug 12-15 | **YORKRAFT FAIR/Thornton Dale Parish Rooms, Thornton Dale, nr Pickering, North Yorks** |
| | Yorkraft Fairs |

| Aug 13 | **CRAFT FAIR/Community Centre, Leyburn, North Yorks** |
| | Keld Craft Fairs |

| Aug 13-15 | **CRAFT FAIR/Hawkshead Market Hall, nr Ambleside, Cumbria** |
| | Aphrodite |

| Aug 13-15 | **HAMPSHIRE SHOW/Royal Victoria Country Park, Netley, Southampton** |
| | Buckingham Publicity   *See display advertisement* |

| Aug 13-15 | **MEDIEVAL CRAFT FAYRE/Kingston Lacy House, Wimborne, Dorset** |
| | Four Seasons (Events) Ltd |

| Aug 14 | **CRAFT & GIFT FAIR/The Harlington Centre, High Street, Fleet, Hants** |
| | Aquarius Fairs |

| Aug 14 | **CRAFT MARKET/Fisher Hall, Guildhall Place, Cambridge, Cambs** |
| | Balthazar |

| Aug 14 | **CRAFT FAIR/Burgh Hall, Peebles** |
| | Border Fairs |

| Aug 14 | **DUNSTABLE CRAFT MARKET/Methodist Church Hall, Ashton Square, Dunstable, Beds** |
| | Dunstable Craft Market |

| Aug 14 | **CRAFT FAIR AT THE WORLD PIPE BAND CHAMPIONSHIPS/Glasgow Green, Glasgow** |
| | Glasgow City Council |

| Aug 14 | **CRAFT FAIR/Guildhall, Salisbury, Wilts** |
| | Kevin Murphy Craft Fairs |

| Aug 14 | **CRAFT FAIR/Victoria Hall, Bourton-on-the-Water, Glos** |
| | M&B Crafts |

| Aug 14 | **CRAFT FAIR/Market Hall, Abergavenny, Monmouthshire** |
| | Monmouthshire County Council |

| Aug 14 | **RURAL CRAFTS ASSOCIATION AT THE CHEPSTOW AGRICULTURAL SHOW/ Howick Farm, Chepstow, Gwent** |
| | Rural Crafts Association   *See display advertisement* |

| Aug 14-15 | **CRAFT FAYRE/Blakemere Craft Centre, Chester Road, Sandiway, Northwich, Cheshire** |
| | Blakemere Craft Centre   *See display advertisement* |

| Aug 14-15 | **CRAFTS AT THE CADEBY STEAM & COUNTRY FAYRE/Cadeby, nr Hinckley, Leics** |
| | Cadeby Steam & Country Fayre |

| Aug 14-15 | **CRAFT FAIR/Brigade Hall, Bakewell, Derbys** |
| | Cottage Creations Craft Fairs |

| Aug 14-15 | **CRAFT, DESIGN & GIFT FAIR/Hurrans Garden Centre, West Hagley, nr Stourbridge, Worcs** |
| | Cottage Industries Association | *See display advertisement* |

| Aug 14-15 | **CRAFT FAIR/White Hart Inn, Hawes, North Yorks** |
| | Keld Craft Fairs |

| Aug 14-15 | **HAMPSHIRE FLOWER SHOW/Broadlands, nr Romsey, Hants** |
| | Living Heritage Craft Shows Ltd | *See display advertisement* |

| Aug 14-15 | **THE RIVER THAMES CRAFT SHOW/Beale Park, Pangbourne, nr Reading, Berks** |
| | Living Heritage Craft Shows Ltd | *See display advertisement* |

| Aug 15 | **ARTS & CRAFTS FAIR/Woburn Village Hall, Woburn, Beds** |
| | Falcon Fairs |

| Aug 15 | **CRAFT FAIR/Exmouth Pavilion, Exmouth, Devon** |
| | J M Evans |

| Aug 15 | **CRAFT FAIR/Brockenhurst Masonic Hall, Brockenhurst, Hants** |
| | Oakleaf Craft Fairs | *See display advertisement* |

| Aug 15 | **CRAFT & GIFT FAIR/Sun Pavilion, Valley Gardens, Cornwall Road, Harrogate, North Yorks** |
| | Quality Craft & Gift Fairs | *See display advertisement* |

| Aug 17-19 | **HEART OF ENGLAND CRAFTWORKERS CRAFT MARQUEE AT THE PEMBROKESHIRE SHOW/Haverfordwest, Pembrokeshire** |
| | Heart of England Craftworkers | *See display advertisement* |

| Aug 18 | **CRAFT FAIR/Bridport Arts Centre, Bridport, Dorset** |
| | J M Evans |

| Aug 18 | **RURAL CRAFTS ASSOCIATION AT THE GILLINGHAM & SHAFTESBURY SHOW/Gillingham & Shaftesbury Showground, Motcombe, Dorset** |
| | Rural Crafts Association | *See display advertisement* |

| Aug 18-22 | **ARTISAN - EDINBURGH CONTEMPORARY CRAFT FESTIVAL/Edinburgh International Conference Centre, Morrison Street, Edinburgh** |
| | Artisan |

| Aug 19 (provisional) | **CRAFT FAIR/Pooley Bridge Memorial Hall, nr Penrith, Cumbria** |
| | Aphrodite |

| Aug 19-20 | **CRAFT FAIR/Market Hall, Hawes, North Yorks** |
| | Keld Craft Fairs |

| Aug 19-21 | **RURAL CRAFTS ASSOCIATION AT THE SOUTHPORT FLOWER SHOW/ Southport, Merseyside** |
| | Rural Crafts Association | *See display advertisement* |

| Aug 20-22 | **CRAFT FAIR/Hawkshead Market Hall, nr Ambleside, Cumbria** |
| | Aphrodite |

Aug 20-22	**CRAFT FAIR/Town Hall, Moffat, Dumfriesshire**
	Caile Fairs

Aug 20-22	**ROBIN HOOD CRAFT FAYRE/Aldenham Country Park, nr Elstree, Herts**
	Four Seasons (Events) Ltd

Aug 20-22	**NORTHAMPTON BALLOON FESTIVAL/Racecourse Park, Northampton**
	Northampton Borough Council

Aug 20-22   **LIVE CRAFTS SHOW/Parham Park, Parham, nr Pulborough, West Sussex**
The Exhibition Team Ltd   *See display advertisement*

Aug 21   **CRAFT MARKET/Fisher Hall, Guildhall Place, Cambridge, Cambs**
Balthazar

Aug 21   **CRAFT FAIR/Corn Exchange, Haddington, East Lothian**
Border Fairs

Aug 21   **CRAFT FAIR/Victoria Hall, Bourton-on-the-Water, Glos**
M&B Crafts

Aug 21   **CRAFTS AT THE SKELTON SHOW/Hutton-in-the-Forest, B5305, nr Penrith, Cumbria**
Skelton Show

Aug 21-22   **CRAFT FAYRE/Blakemere Craft Centre, Chester Road, Sandiway, Northwich, Cheshire**
Blakemere Craft Centre   *See display advertisement*

Aug 21-22   **CRAFT MARQUEE AT THE BOLTON SHOW/Leverhulme Park, Bolton, Lancs**
Bolton Metropolitan Borough

Aug 21-22   **CRAFT FAIR/Brigade Hall, Bakewell, Derbys**
Cottage Creations Craft Fairs

Aug 21-22   **CRAFT, DESIGN & GIFT FAIR/Dobbies Gardening World, A5, Penkridge, nr Cannock, Staffs**
Cottage Industries Association   *See display advertisement*

Aug 21-22   **CRAFT TENT AT THE DOWNS STEAM SHOW/Weald & Downland Open Air Museum, Singleton, nr Chichester, West Sussex**
Dean Management

Aug 21-22   **CRAFTS AT THE WARWICKSHIRE & WEST MIDLANDS GAME FAIR/Ragley Hall, Alcester, Warks**
Laurel Crafts

Aug 21-22   **HERTFORDSHIRE CRAFT SHOW/Knebworth House & Gardens, Junction 7 A1M, Stevenage, Herts**
Living Heritage Craft Shows Ltd   *See display advertisement*

Aug 21-22   **CRAFT FAIR/Coughton Court, Alcester, Warks**
Oak Craft Fairs   *See display advertisement*

Aug 22   **CRAFT FAIR/Lacock Village Hall, Lacock, nr Chippenham, Wilts**
Countrycraft

Aug 22	**CRAFT FAIR/Exmouth Pavilion, Exmouth, Devon** J M Evans
Aug 22	**SUMMER CRAFT FAIR/Florence Court, Enniskillen, Co Fermanagh** The National Trust, Florence Court
Aug 22	**CRAFT FAIR/Royal Shakespeare Theatre, Stratford-upon-Avon, Warks** West Country Craft Fairs *See display advertisement*
Aug 22	**CRAFT FAIR/Pavilion Theatre, Worthing, West Sussex** Worthing Leisure
Aug 24	**CRAFT FAIR/White Hart Inn, Hawes, North Yorks** Keld Craft Fairs
Aug 25	**CRAFT FAYRE/Craft Centre, Chester Road, Sandiway, Northwich, Cheshire** Blakemere Craft Centre *See display advertisement*
Aug 25	**CRAFT FAIR/Bridport Arts Centre, Bridport, Dorset** J M Evans
Aug 25-27	**ART, CRAFT & DESIGN MARQUEE AT THE BRISTOL FLOWER SHOW/ Durdham Downs, Bristol** Creativity
Aug 25-30	**CRAFTS IN ACTION AT THE EUROPEAN SHOW JUMPING CHAMPION- SHIPS/ The All England Jumping Course, Hickstead, West Sussex** Crafts in Action
Aug 26 (provisional)	**CRAFT FAIR/Pooley Bridge Memorial Hall, nr Penrith, Cumbria** Aphrodite
Aug 26-29	**RURAL CRAFTS ASSOCIATION AT THE BOWMORE BLAIR CASTLE HORSE TRIALS/Blair Atholl, Perthshire** Rural Crafts Association *See display advertisement*
Aug 27	**CRAFT FAIR/Community Centre, Leyburn, North Yorks** Keld Craft Fairs
Aug 27-29	**CRAFT FAIR/Hawkshead Market Hall, nr Ambleside, Cumbria** Aphrodite
Aug 27-30	**CRAFT FAIR/Norfolk Showground, Dereham Road, New Costessey, nr Norwich, Norfolk** Country Cottage Crafts
Aug 27-30	**CHILTERNS CRAFT SHOW/Stonor Park, Henley-on-Thames, Oxon** ICHF Ltd
Aug 27-30	**CRAFT FAIR/Sandringham Park, Norfolk** Rainbow Fair
Aug 27-30	**THE CRAFT MOVEMENT/The Guildhall, Winchester, Hants** The Craft Movement
Aug 28	**CRAFT MARKET/Fisher Hall, Guildhall Place, Cambridge, Cambs** Balthazar

Aug 28	**ANTIQUES, CRAFTS & COLLECTABLES FAIR/The Parish Hall, Culcheth, nr Warrington, Cheshire** Gem Fairs

Aug 28   **THE LYME REGIS AUGUST BANK HOLIDAY CRAFT FAIR/Marine Theatre, Lyme Regis, Dorset**
West Country Craft Fairs   *See display advertisement*

Aug 28-29   **CRAFTS AT THE NATIONAL FISHING CHAMPIONSHIPS/Crown Meadow, River Avon, Evesham, Worcs**
Cottage Industries Association   *See display advertisement*

Aug 28-29   **CRAFT FAIR/Lyndhurst Community Centre, Lyndhurst, Hants**
Oakleaf Craft Fairs   *See display advertisement*

Aug 28-30   **CRAFT FAYRE/Blakemere Craft Centre, Chester Road, Sandiway, Northwich, Cheshire**
Blakemere Craft Centre   *See display advertisement*

Aug 28-30   **CRAFT FAIR/The Village Hall, Bolton Abbey, nr Skipton, North Yorks**
CFL Craft Shows

Aug 28-30   **WORKING CRAFTS SHOW/Kedleston Hall, Kedleston, nr Derby, Derbys**
CFL Craft Shows

Aug 28-30   **CRAFT FAYRE/Gawsworth Hall, Macclesfield, Cheshire**
Cheshire Fayre   *See display advertisement*

Aug 28-30   **CRAFT FAIR/Brigade Hall, Bakewell, Derbys**
Cottage Creations Craft Fairs

Aug 28-30   **SUMMER CRAFTS AT MONTACUTE/Montacute Park, nr Yeovil, Somerset**
Craft Carnival

Aug 28-30   **ROBIN HOOD CRAFT FAYRE/Wakehurst Place, Ardingly, nr Haywards Heath, West Sussex**
Four Seasons (Events) Ltd

Aug 28-30   **SUMMER CRAFTS FESTIVAL/Shugborough Estate, Shugborough, nr Stafford, Staffs**
Hobby Horse Design & Craft Fairs

Aug 28-30   **CRAFT FAIR/St William's College, York, North Yorks**
Keld Craft Fairs

Aug 28-30   **ESSEX CRAFT SHOW/Blake Hall, A414, Ongar, Essex**
Living Heritage Craft Shows Ltd   *See display advertisement*

Aug 28-30   **OXFORDSHIRE CRAFT SHOW/Blenheim Palace, Woodstock, Oxon**
Living Heritage Craft Shows Ltd   *See display advertisement*

Aug 28-30   **RINGWOOD CRAFT SHOW/Somerley Estate, Somerley, nr Ringwood, Hants**
Living Heritage Craft Shows Ltd   *See display advertisement*

Aug 28-30   **MENIMORE CRAFT & DESIGN SHOW/Mentmore, nr Leighton Buzzard, Beds**
Mary Holland Craft Fairs Ltd   *See display advertisement*

Aug 28-30   **THE WREST PARK CRAFTS FESTIVAL/Wrest Park, Silsoe (A6), Beds**
Romor Exhibitions Ltd   *See display advertisement*

Aug 28-30   **CRAFTS AT THE RUDGWICK STEAM & COUNTRY SHOW/Rudgwick, nr Horsham, West Sussex**
Rudgwick Steam & Country Show

Aug 28-30   **LIVE CRAFTS SHOW/Highclere Castle, nr Newbury, Berks**
The Exhibition Team Ltd   *See display advertisement*

Aug 28-30   **CRAFTS AT THE HERSTMONCEUX CASTLE MEDIEVAL FESTIVAL/ Herstmonceux, nr Hailsham, East Sussex**
The Malcolm Group Events Ltd

Aug 28-30   **CRAFT STANDS AT THE TOWN & COUNTRY FESTIVAL/National Agricultural Centre, Stoneleigh Park, Warks**
Town & Country Festival

Aug 28-30   **CRAFT MARQUEE AT THE INTERNATIONAL KITE FESTIVAL/Southsea Common, Southsea, Hants**
Woodland Crafts   *See display advertisement*

Aug 28-30   **FORT PURBROOK CRAFT FAYRE/Portsdown Hill, Cosham, Hants**
Woodland Crafts   *See display advertisement*

Aug 28-30   **YORKRAFT FAIR/Pickering Over Sixties Club, Pickering, North Yorks**
Yorkraft Fairs

Aug 29   **CRAFT FAIR/Exmouth Pavilion, Exmouth, Devon**
J M Evans

Aug 29   **THE STRATFORD-UPON-AVON AUGUST BANK HOLIDAY CRAFT FAIR/ Royal Shakespeare Theatre, Stratford-upon-Avon, Warks**
West Country Craft Fairs   *See display advertisement*

Aug 29 (provisional)   **DOLLS HOUSE & MINIATURE FAIR/Town Hall, Falkirk**
Brentwood Fairs

Aug 29-30   **CRAFT MARQUEE AT THE SOUTH STAFFS TOWN & COUNTRY FESTIVAL/ Weston Park, Shifnal, nr Telford, Salop**
Arrow Management & Marketing Ltd

Aug 29-30   **CRAFT FAYRE/Balmer Lawn Hotel, Brockenhurst, Hants**
Avocet Crafts

Aug 29-30   **CRAFT STALLS AT STREET FESTIVAL 1999/Market Street, Colne, Lancashire**
Borough of Pendle E.D.U.

Aug 29-30   **CRAFT FAIR/Lacock Village Hall, Lacock, nr Chippenham, Wilts**
Countrycraft

Aug 29-30   **CRAFTS IN ACTION AT EDENBRIDGE & OXTED AGRICULTURAL SHOW/ Lingfield, Surrey**
Crafts in Action

Aug 29-30   **CRAFT FAIR/Lowther Pavilion, West Beach, Lytham, Lancs**
Creative Crafts Association   *See display advertisement*

Aug 29-30	**CRAFT MARQUEE/Rufford Abbey, Notts** Heathfield Craft Fairs
Aug 29-30	**ARTS & CRAFTS FAIR/Grassington Town Hall, Grassington, nr Skipton, North Yorks** Jean Bryon
Aug 29-30	**CRAFT FAIR/Ely Maltings, Ely, Cambs** Kingfisher Promotions
Aug 29-30	**ARTS & CRAFTS SHOW/Lauderdale House, Highgate Hill, London N6** Lauderdale Arts & Crafts
Aug 29-30	**CRAFTS AT THE TOWN & COUNTY FAIR/Weston Park, Shifnal, Telford, Salop** Laurel Crafts
Aug 29-30	**CRAFT MARQUEE AT THE TEESSIDE FESTIVAL OF TRANSPORT/Ormesby Hall, Middlesbrough, Cleveland** Quality Craft & Gift Fairs *See display advertisement*
Aug 29-30	**CRAFT FAIR/Civic Hall, Ramsbottom, nr Bury, Lancs** West Pennine Promotions
Aug 29-30	**CRAFT FAIR/Hollingworth Lake Rowing Club, Littleborough, Lancs** West Pennine Promotions
Aug 29-30 (provisional)	**CRAFT STALLS AT THE MARGAM PARK COUNTRY SHOW 1999/Margam Country Park, Port Talbot, South Wales** Craft*Folk
Aug 30	**CRAFT MARQUEE AT THE MUNCASTER COUNTRY FAIR/Muncaster Castle, nr Ravenglass, Cumbria** Aphrodite
Aug 30	**CRAFT FAIR/Wycombe Sports Centre (Handycross), Marlow Hill, High Wycombe, Bucks** Cottage Craft Fairs *See display advertisement*
Aug 30	**CRAFT & GIFTS MARQUEE AT FLOWER FAIR & FAMILY FUN DAY/Moor Park, Preston, Lancs** Golden Age Fairs
Aug 30	**CRAFT FAIR/Pavilion, Weymouth, Dorset** Kevin Murphy Craft Fairs
Aug 30	**CRAFT FAIR/Market Hall, Abergavenny, Monmouthshire** Monmouthshire County Council
Aug 30	**ANTIQUE & CRAFT FAIR/Hedworth Hall, Westoe, South Shields, Tyne & Wear** Quintet Promotions
Aug 30	**DOLLS HOUSE FAIR/Silsoe Conference Centre, Silsoe, Beds** R J Exhibitions
Aug 30	**RURAL CRAFTS ASSOCIATION AT THE BERKELEY SHOW/Castle Meadows, Berkeley, Glos** Rural Crafts Association *See display advertisement*

Aug 30	**CRAFT FAIR/The Argory, Derrycaw Road, Moy, Dungannon, Co Armagh** The National Trust, The Argory
Aug 31	**CRAFT FAIR/Otford Village Memorial Hall, nr Sevenoaks, Kent** Goldfinch Crafts
Aug 31	**CRAFT FAIR/White Hart Inn, Hawes, North Yorks** Keld Craft Fairs
Sept 1	**CRAFT MARQUEE AT THE MUKER SHOW/Muker, nr Richmond, North Yorks** Keld Craft Fairs
Sept 2 (provisional)	**CRAFT FAIR/Pooley Bridge Memorial Hall, nr Penrith, Cumbria** Aphrodite
Sept 2-5	**RURAL CRAFTS ASSOCIATION AT THE BURGHLEY HORSE TRIALS/ Stamford, Lincs** Rural Crafts Association *See display advertisement*
Sept 3	**CRAFT FAIR/Community Centre, Leyburn, North Yorks** Keld Craft Fairs
Sept 3-5	**CRAFTS AT THE BIRMINGHAM NATIONAL DOG SHOW/Perry Park (A34), Birmingham, West Midlands** Cottage Industries Association *See display advertisement*
Sept 3-5	**DESIGNER CRAFT MARQUEE AT AUTUMN GOLD GARDEN FESTIVAL/ Whalley Abbey, nr Clitheroe, Lancs** Jean Welch Shows *See display advertisement*
Sept 3-5	**THE 13TH SCOTTISH KNITTING, NEEDLECRAFT & HOBBYCRAFTS EXHIBITION/Royal Highland Centre, Ingliston, Edinburgh** Nationwide Exhibitions (UK) Ltd
Sept 3-5	**LIVE CRAFTS SHOW/Boughton Monchelsea Place, nr Maidstone, Kent** The Exhibition Team Ltd *See display advertisement*
Sept 4	**CRAFT MARKET/Fisher Hall, Guildhall Place, Cambridge, Cambs** Balthazar
Sept 4	**TYNESIDE DOLL & TEDDY FAIR/Gateshead Civic Centre, Regent Street, Gateshead, Tyne & Wear** Dolly Domain Fairs
Sept 4	**ARTS & CRAFTS FAIR/Town Hall, Towcester, Northants** Falcon Fairs
Sept 4	**ARTS & CRAFTS FAYRE/Winter Gardens, Weston-super-Mare, North Somerset** Fountain Fayres & Exhibitions
Sept 4	**CRAFT FAIR/Agricultural Hall, Maidstone, Kent** M B County Fairs
Sept 4	**CRAFT & GIFT FAIR/Barnet Library, Stapylton Road, Barnet, Herts** Marie Margaret Promotions

Sept 4	**ART & CRAFT FAIR/The Arts Centre, Biddick Lane, Fatfield, Washington, Tyne & Wear** The Arts Centre
Sept 4-5	**CRAFT MARQUEE AT THE 51ST WYCOMBE SHOW/The Rye, London Road, High Wycombe, Bucks** Bernard Dimmelow
Sept 4-5	**CRAFT FAYRE/Blakemere Craft Centre, Chester Road, Sandiway, Northwich, Cheshire** Blakemere Craft Centre *See display advertisement*
Sept 4-5	**HOBBIES, MODELS & CRAFT FESTIVAL/Spa Royal Hall, Bridlington, East Yorks** Bridlington Model Boat Society
Sept 4-5	**CRAFT FAIR/Brigade Hall, Bakewell, Derbys** Cottage Creations Craft Fairs
Sept 4-5	**ART, CRAFT & DESIGN MARQUEE AT INTERNATIONAL KITE FESTIVAL/ Ashton Court Estate, Bristol** Creativity
Sept 4-5	**HEART OF ENGLAND CRAFTWORKERS MARQUEE AT THE CHATSWORTH COUNTRY SHOW/Chatsworth House, Baslow, Derbys** Heart of England Craftworkers *See display advertisement*
Sept 4-5	**CRAFTS AT DITCHLING GARDEN CENTRE/Ditchling, West Sussex** Jets Quality Craft Fairs
Sept 4-5	**CRAFT FAIR/White Hart Inn, Hawes, North Yorks** Keld Craft Fairs
Sept 4-5	**BEDFORDSHIRE CRAFT SHOW/Woburn Abbey, M1 Junction 12/13, Woburn, Beds** Living Heritage Craft Shows Ltd *See display advertisement*
Sept 4-5	**CRAFT FAIR/Newby Hall, nr Ripon, North Yorks** Rainbow Fair
Sept 4-5	**RURAL CRAFTS ASSOCIATION AT THE CHATSWORTH COUNTRY FAIR/ Chatsworth House, Baslow, Derbys** Rural Crafts Association *See display advertisement*
Sept 4-5	**CRAFTS AT THE HEAVY HORSE SHOW & COUNTRY FAIR/Wimpole Hall, Arrington, nr Royston, Cambs** The National Trust, Wimpole Hall
Sept 4-5	**CRAFT MARQUEE AT THE SHOREHAM AIR SHOW/Shoreham Airport, Shoreham-by-Sea, West Sussex** Woodland Crafts *See display advertisement*
Sept 4-7	**YORKRAFT FAIR/Thornton Dale Parish Rooms, Thornton Dale, nr Pickering, North Yorks** Yorkraft Fairs
Sept 5	**TEDDY BEAR FAIR/Cresta Court Hotel, Altrincham, Cheshire** Brentwood Fairs

Sept 5	**CRAFT FAIR/Lacock Village Hall, Lacock, nr Chippenham, Wilts** Countrycraft
Sept 5	**CRAFT & GIFT FAIR/Barton Village Hall, nr Preston, Lancs** Golden Age Fairs
Sept 5	**CRAFT FAIR/Gargrave Village Hall, Gargrave, nr Skipton, North Yorks** Heritage Fairs
Sept 5	**CRAFT FAIR/Exmouth Pavilion, Exmouth, Devon** J M Evans
Sept 5	**CRAFT FAIR/Passage House Hotel, Newton Abbot, Devon** Kevin Murphy Craft Fairs
Sept 5	**CRAFT FAIR/Tenterden Leisure Centre, Recreation Ground Road, Tenterden, Kent** M B County Fairs
Sept 5	**CRAFT FAIR/Godshill Village Hall, Godshill, Hants** Oakleaf Craft Fairs *See display advertisement*
Sept 5	**CRAFT FAIR/Tait Hall, Edenside Road, Kelso, Roxburghshire** Quintet Promotions
Sept 5	**CRAFT FAIR/Downham Village Hall, Downham, nr Clitheroe, Lancs** West Pennine Promotions
Sept 5-8	**AUTUMN FAIR BIRMINGHAM/National Exhibition Centre, Birmingham, West Midlands (main organiser)** Trade Promotion Services Ltd
Sept 5-8	**WELSH CRAFTS AT THE AUTUMN FAIR BIRMINGHAM/National Exhibition Centre, Birmingham, West Midlands** Wales Craft Council
Sept 6	**CRAFT FAYRE/The Belgrave Hotel, Torquay, Devon** Cherrycraft Fayres & Festivals
Sept 8	**CRAFT FAIR/Bridport Arts Centre, Bridport, Dorset** J M Evans
Sept 9	**CRAFT FAIR/Market Hall, Hawes, North Yorks** Keld Craft Fairs
Sept 9-12	**ANNUAL EXHIBITION & SALE OF COTSWOLD CRAFTS/Southam Tithe Barn, nr Cheltenham, Glos** Cotswold Craftsmen
Sept 9-12	**NATIONAL NEEDLECRAFT SHOW/Olympia 2, Hammersmith Road, Kensington, London W14** Future Publishing
Sept 9-12	**RURAL CRAFTS ASSOCIATION AT THE BLENHEIM HORSE TRIALS/ Blenheim Palace, Woodstock, Oxon** Rural Crafts Association *See display advertisement*

Sept 10-11   **WELSH CRAFTS AT THE RARE BREEDS SHOW/National Agricultural Centre, Stoneleigh Park, Warks**
Wales Craft Council

Sept 10-12   **WEALD OF KENT CRAFT SHOW/Penshurst Place, nr Tonbridge, Kent**
ICHF Ltd

Sept 11   **CRAFT & GIFT FAIR/The Harlington Centre, High Street, Fleet, Hants**
Aquarius Fairs

Sept 11   **CRAFT MARKET/Fisher Hall, Guildhall Place, Cambridge, Cambs**
Balthazar

Sept 11   **CRAFT FAIR/Municipal Hall, Biggar, Lanarkshire**
Border Fairs

Sept 11   **DOLLSHOUSE, MINIATURES, TEDDY & DOLL FAIR/Arts Centre, Vane Terrace, Darlington, Co Durham**
Caile Fairs

Sept 11   **DUNSTABLE CRAFT MARKET/Methodist Church Hall, Ashton Square, Dunstable, Beds**
Dunstable Craft Market

Sept 11   **ARTS & CRAFTS FAIR/Town Hall, Brackley, Northants**
Falcon Fairs

Sept 11   **CRAFT TENT AT THE HENLEY SHOW/Hambleden, nr Henley-on-Thames, Oxon**
Henley & District Agricultural Association Ltd

Sept 11   **CRAFT FAIR/Market Hall, Abergavenny, Monmouthshire**
Monmouthshire County Council

Sept 11   **DOLLS HOUSE & MINIATURES FAIR/Somerset Hall, Portishead, Somerset**
Rita Daniels/Posset Fundraisers

Sept 11-12   **CRAFT FAYRE/Blakemere Craft Centre, Chester Road, Sandiway, Northwich, Cheshire**
Blakemere Craft Centre   *See display advertisement*

Sept 11-12   **CRAFT FAYRE/Trentham Gardens, Stone Road (A34), Trentham, Stoke-on-Trent, Staffs**
Cheshire Fayre   *See display advertisement*

Sept 11-12   **CRAFT FAIR/Brigade Hall, Bakewell, Derbys**
Cottage Creations Craft Fairs

Sept 11-12   **CRAFT, DESIGN & GIFT FAIR/Hurrans Garden Centre, Newport, Gwent**
Cottage Industries Association   *See display advertisement*

Sept 11-12   **CRAFT FAIR/Haydock Park Racecourse Exhibition Centre, St Helens, Merseyside**
Creative Crafts Association   *See display advertisement*

Sept 11-12   **CRAFT FAIR/Leas Cliff Hall, Folkestone, Kent**
East Kent Fairs   *See display advertisement*

Sept 11-12	**ESSEX STEAM RALLY & COUNTRY SHOW/Barleylands Farm Museum & Visitor Centre, Barleylands Road, Billericay, Essex**
	Essex Steam Rally & Country Show
Sept 11-12	**CRAFT FAIR/St William's College, York, North Yorks**
	Keld Craft Fairs
Sept 11-12	**EDWARDIAN CRAFT SHOW/Cliveden, Taplow, nr Maidenhead, Berks**
	Living Heritage Craft Shows Ltd
Sept 11-12	**MIDDLESBROUGH CRAFT SHOW/Ormsby Hall, Middlesbrough, Cleveland**
	Living Heritage Craft Shows Ltd
Sept 11-12	**CRAFT FAIR/Kings Hall, Herne Bay, Kent**
	M B County Fairs
Sept 11-12	**CRAFT FAIR/Victoria Hall, Bourton-on-the-Water, Glos**
	M&B Crafts
Sept 11-12	**AUTUMN CRAFT FESTIVAL/Lamport Hall, Lamport, Northants**
	MGA Fairs
Sept 11-12	**CRAFT FAIR/Leighton Hall, Carnforth, Lancs**
	Rainbow Fair
Sept 11-12	**CRAFTS AT THE 4TH PARHAM COUNTRY SHOW/Parham Park, Parham, Pulborough, West Sussex**
	Smallholder Shows
Sept 11-12	**THE CRAFT MOVEMENT/Kensington Town Hall, London**
	The Craft Movement
Sept 11-14	**YORKRAFT FAIR/Town Hall, Helmsley, North Yorks**
	Yorkraft Fairs
Sept 12	**CRAFT FAIR/Biddulph Leisure Centre, Thames Drive, Biddulph, Staffs**
	Archer Promotions
Sept 12	**DOLLS HOUSE & MINIATURE FAIR/The Marine Hall, The Esplanade, Fleetwood, Lancs**
	Brentwood Fairs
Sept 12	**CRAFT FAIR/Community Centre, Kinver, nr Stourbridge, West Midlands**
	Central Promotions
Sept 12	**CRAFT FAIR/Lacock Village Hall, Lacock, nr Chippenham, Wilts**
	Countrycraft
Sept 12	**CRAFT FAIR/The Heath Hotel, Bewdley, Worcs**
	Laurel Crafts
Sept 12	**CRAFTS AT THE PESTALOZZI INTERNATIONAL FESTIVAL/Pestalozzi Children's Village Trust, Sedlescombe, Battle, East Sussex**
	Pestalozzi Children's Village Trust
Sept 12	**DOLLS HOUSES, DOLLS & MINIATURES FAIR/Castle Hall, Hertford, Herts**
	Quality Craft Fairs

See display advertisement (Sept 11-12 EDWARDIAN CRAFT SHOW)

See display advertisement (Sept 11-12 MIDDLESBROUGH CRAFT SHOW)

See display advertisement (Sept 11-12 AUTUMN CRAFT FESTIVAL)

See display advertisement (Sept 12 CRAFT FAIR/Community Centre, Kinver)

Sept 12 **AUTUMN CRAFT FAIR/Royal Shakespeare Theatre, Stratford-upon-Avon, Warks**
West Country Craft Fairs *See display advertisement*

Sept 12 **CRAFT MARQUEE AT TRAX 99, XR OWNERS CLUB RALLY/Silverstone,**
(provisional) **Northants**
The Craft Tent Company

Sept 12-15 **THE NORTH-EASTERN AUTUMN GIFTS TRADE FAIR/North-Eastern Exhibition Centre, Newcastle upon Tyne, Tyne & Wear**
Northern Exhibitions

Sept 14 **CRAFT FAIR/White Hart Inn, Hawes, North Yorks**
Keld Craft Fairs

Sept 16 **CRAFT MARQUEE AT THE 132ND THAME SHOW/Thame Show Ground (A4129), Thame, Oxon**
Bernard Dimmelow

Sept 17 **CRAFT FAIR/Community Centre, Leyburn, North Yorks**
Keld Craft Fairs

Sept 17-19 **CRAFT FAIR/Hawkshead Market Hall, nr Ambleside, Cumbria**
Aphrodite

Sept 17-19 **GARDEN CRAFT FAIR/RHS Rosemoor Garden, Torrington, Devon**
Creativity

Sept 17-19 **BRITISH CRAFT SHOW/Stockwood Park, Luton, Beds**
ICHF Ltd

Sept 17-19 **STITCHCRAFT '99/G-Mex Centre, Manchester**
Nationwide Exhibitions (UK) Ltd

Sept 17-19 **RURAL CRAFTS ASSOCIATION AT THE NATIONAL DRESSAGE CHAMPIONSHIPS/National Agricultural Centre, Stoneleigh Park, Warks**
Rural Crafts Association *See display advertisement*

Sept 17-19 **LIVE CRAFTS SHOW/Osterley Park, Isleworth, Middx**
The Exhibition Team Ltd *See display advertisement*

Sept 17-19 **HEART OF ENGLAND CRAFTWORKERS MARQUEE AT THE HARROGATE AUTUMN FLOWER SHOW/Great Yorkshire Showground, Harrogate**
Heart of England Craftworkers *See display advertisement*

Sept 17-19 **THE HARROGATE AUTUMN FLOWER SHOW/Great Yorkshire Showground, Hookstone Oval, Harrogate, North Yorks (main organiser)**
North of England Horticultural Society

Sept 18 **CRAFT MARKET/Fisher Hall, Guildhall Place, Cambridge, Cambs**
Balthazar

Sept 18 **CRAFT FAIR/Corn Exchange, Haddington, East Lothian**
Border Fairs

Sept 18 **ARTS & CRAFTS FAIR/Buckingham Community Centre, Bucks**
Falcon Fairs

Sept 18	**CRAFT FAYRE/St Mary's Centre, Grassmere Close, Felpham, nr Bognor Regis, West Sussex** Good Ideas Craft Fayres
Sept 18	**CRAFT GUILD SHOW/Platform Gallery, Clitheroe, Lancs** The Craft Guild of West Lancashire
Sept 18-19	**CRAFT FAYRE/Blakemere Craft Centre, Chester Road, Sandiway, Northwich, Cheshire** Blakemere Craft Centre *See display advertisement*
Sept 18-19	**CRAFT FAIR/Town Hall, Moffat, Dumfriesshire** Caile Fairs
Sept 18-19	**CRAFT FAIR/The Ingestre Suite, County Showground, Weston Road, Stafford, Staffs** Central Promotions *See display advertisement*
Sept 18-19	**CRAFT FAYRE/Quarry Bank Mill, Styal, Cheshire** Cheshire Fayre *See display advertisement*
Sept 18-19	**CRAFT FAIR/Brigade Hall, Bakewell, Derbys** Cottage Creations Craft Fairs
Sept 18-19	**MEDIEVAL CRAFT FAYRE/Lloyd Park, Coombe Road, Croydon, Surrey** Four Seasons (Events) Ltd
Sept 18-19	**ARTS & CRAFTS FAIR/Grassington Town Hall, Grassington,nr Skipton, North Yorks** Jean Bryon
Sept 18-19	**COOMBE ABBEY CRAFT SHOW/Coombe Abbey, Coventry, Warks** Living Heritage Craft Shows Ltd *See display advertisement*
Sept 18-19	**CRAFT FAIR/Sevenoaks Community Centre, Otford Road, Sevenoaks, Kent** M B County Fairs
Sept 18-19	**CRAFT FAIR/Elton Hall, Elton, nr Peterborough, Cambs** MGA Fairs *See display advertisement*
Sept 18-19	**CRAFT FAIR/Hanbury Hall, Droitwich, Worcs** Oak Craft Fairs *See display advertisement*
Sept 18-19	**CRAFT FAIR/Capesthorne Hall, Macclesfield, Cheshire** Rainbow Fair
Sept 18-19	**YORKRAFT FAIR/Thornton Dale Parish Rooms, Thornton Dale, nr Pickering, North Yorks** Yorkraft Fairs
Sept 18-19	**HEART OF ENGLAND CRAFTWORKERS MARQUEE AT THE MIDLAND GAME & COUNTRY FAIR/Weston Park, Shifnal, nr Telford, Salop** Heart of England Craftworkers *See display advertisement*
Sept 18-19	**CRAFT & FOOD MARQUEES AT THE MIDLAND GAME & COUNTRY FAIR/ Weston Park, Shifnal, nr Telford, Salop** Town & Country Craft Fairs

Sept 19	**CRAFT FAIR/Rivermead Complex, Richfield Avenue, Caversham, nr Reading, Berks** Cottage Craft Fairs *See display advertisement*
Sept 19	**CRAFT, DESIGN & GIFT FAIR/Bromsgrove Market Hall, Worcs** Cottage Industries Association *See display advertisement*
Sept 19	**CRAFT FAIR/Lacock Village Hall, Lacock, nr Chippenham, Wilts** Countrycraft
Sept 19	**CRAFT FAIR/The Platform, Morecambe, Lancs** Creative Crafts *See display advertisement*
Sept 19	**ARTS & CRAFTS FAIR/Woburn Village Hall, Woburn, Beds** Falcon Fairs
Sept 19	**CRAFT FAIR/The Jarvis International Hotel, Willerby, nr Hull, East Yorks** Holland Fairs
Sept 19	**CRAFT FAIR/Exmouth Pavilion, Exmouth, Devon** J M Evans
Sept 19	**CRAFT FAIR/Chase Hotel, Ross-on-Wye, Herefordshire** Kevin Murphy Craft Fairs
Sept 19-21	**INTERNATIONAL GARDEN & LEISURE EXHIBITION/National Exhibition Centre, Birmingham, West Midlands** Trade Promotion Services Ltd
Sept 22	**CRAFT FAIR/Town Hall, Northallerton, North Yorks** Keld Craft Fairs
Sept 23	**YORKRAFT FAIR/Wetherby Town Hall, Wetherby, West Yorks** Yorkraft Fairs
Sept 23-24	**CRAFT FAIR/Market Hall, Hawes, North Yorks** Keld Craft Fairs
Sept 24-26	**AVINGTON PARK HOME DESIGN & INTERIORS EXHIBITION/Avington, nr Winchester, Hants** Buckingham Publicity *See display advertisement*
Sept 24-26	**THE CRAFT SHOW/Chilford Halls, Linton, Cambs** Eastern Events Ltd *See display advertisement*
Sept 24-26	**SANDOWN NATIONAL WOODWORKING EXHIBITION/Sandown Park, Esher, Surrey** Meridienne Exhibitions Ltd
Sept 25	**CRAFT MARKET/Fisher Hall, Guildhall Place, Cambridge, Cambs** Balthazar
Sept 25	**CRAFT FAIR/Corn Exchange, Melrose, Roxburghshire** Border Fairs
Sept 25	**CRAFT FAYRE/The Scala Hall, Brixham, Devon** Cherrycraft Fayres & Festivals

Sept 25	**CRAFT FAIR/Town Hall, Dover, Kent** East Kent Fairs	*See display advertisement*
Sept 25	**ARTS & CRAFTS FAYRE/Somerset Hall, Portishead, nr Bristol** Fountain Fayres & Exhibitions	
Sept 25	**CRAFT FAIR/Victoria Hall, Bourton-on-the-Water, Glos** M&B Crafts	
Sept 25	**CRAFT FAIR/Lyndhurst Community Centre, Lyndhurst, Hants** Oakleaf Craft Fairs	*See display advertisement*
Sept 25-26	**CRAFT FAIR/Hawkshead Market Hall, nr Ambleside, Cumbria** Aphrodite	
Sept 25-26	**CRAFT FAYRE/Craft Centre, Chester Road, Sandiway, Northwich, Cheshire** Blakemere Craft Centre	*See display advertisement*
Sept 25-26	**CRAFT FAIR/Brigade Hall, Bakewell, Derbys** Cottage Creations Craft Fairs	
Sept 25-26	**CRAFT, DESIGN & GIFT FAIR/Percy Thrower's Gardening Centre, Shrewsbury, Salop** Cottage Industries Association	*See display advertisement*
Sept 25-26	**ART, CRAFTS & COUNTRY SHOPPING FAIR/Beaumanor Hall, Loughborough** Countrywide Events	
Sept 25-26	**CRAFT FAIR/St William's College, York, North Yorks** Keld Craft Fairs	
Sept 25-26	**LANGLEY PARK CRAFT SHOW/Langley Park, A412 Slough-Uxbridge Road, nr Slough, Berks** Living Heritage Craft Shows Ltd	*See display advertisement*
Sept 25-26	**NOSTELL PRIORY CRAFT SHOW/Nostell Priory, A638 Doncaster Road, nr Wakefield, West Yorks** Living Heritage Craft Shows Ltd	*See display advertisement*
Sept 25-26	**RURAL CRAFTS ASSOCIATION AT THE COTSWOLD SHOW & COUNTRY FAIR/Cirencester Park, Cirencester, Glos** Rural Crafts Association	*See display advertisement*
Sept 25-26	**THE CRAFT MOVEMENT/Camden Centre, Camden, London** The Craft Movement	
Sept 25-26	**LIVE CRAFTS SHOW/Oaklands College, St Albans, Herts** The Exhibition Team Ltd	*See display advertisement*
Sept 25-26	**WELSH CRAFTS AT THE MALVERN AUTUMN SHOW/Malvern, Worcs** Wales Craft Council	
Sept 26	**CRAFT FAIR/Public Hall, Appleby-in-Westmorland, Cumbria** Caile Fairs	
Sept 26	**CRAFT FAIR/Lordsbridge Arena, Barton, Cambs** Cambridge Craft Fairs	

| Sept 26 | **CRAFT FAIR/Royal International Pavilion, Ruthin Road, Llangollen, Clwyd** | |
| | Central Promotions | *See display advertisement* |

| Sept 26 | **CRAFT FAIR/Spelthorne Leisure Centre, Knowle Green, Staines, Middx** | |
| | Cottage Craft Fairs | *See display advertisement* |

Sept 26   **CRAFT FAIR/Lacock Village Hall, Lacock, nr Chippenham, Wilts**
Countrycraft

| Sept 26 | **CRAFT FAIR/Lowther Pavilion, West Beach, Lytham, Lancs** | |
| | Creative Crafts Association | *See display advertisement* |

Sept 26   **CRAFT FAIR/Dunkenhalgh Hotel, Clayton-le-Moors, nr Accrington, Lancs**
Heritage Fairs

Sept 26   **CRAFT FAIR/The Country Park Inn, Hessle Foreshore, nr Hull, East Yorks**
Holland Fairs

Sept 26   **CRAFT FAIR/Castle Sports Centre, Taunton, Somerset**
Kevin Murphy Craft Fairs

Sept 26   **ARTS & CRAFTS SHOW/Lauderdale House, Highgate Hill, London N6**
Lauderdale Arts & Crafts

Sept 26   **CRAFT FAIR/The Inn on the Lake, Shorne, nr Gravesend, Kent**
M B County Fairs

Sept 26   **CRAFT FAIR/Goodwood Racecourse, nr Chichester, West Sussex**
Mascot Craft & Gift Fairs

Sept 26   **CRAFT FAIR/Highfield Hotel, Middlesbrough, Cleveland**
Quintet Promotions

Sept 26   **CRAFT MARQUEE & STANDS AT THE RED ROSE FOREST WORKING WOODLANDS FESTIVAL/Moses Gate Country Park, Farnworth, Bolton**
Red Rose Forest

| Sept 27-Oct 3 | **NATIONAL CRAFTS FAIR/Fort Regent Leisure Centre, St Helier, Jersey, Channel Islands** | |
| | National Crafts Fair | *See display advertisement* |

Sept 28   **CRAFT FAIR/White Hart Inn, Hawes, North Yorks**
Keld Craft Fairs

| Sept 28-30 | **RURAL CRAFTS ASSOCIATION AT THE NATIONAL PLOUGHING MATCH/ Castletownroche, Mallow, Co Cork, EIRE** | |
| | Rural Crafts Association | *See display advertisement* |

| Sept 29 | **CRAFT FAYRE/Blakemere Craft Centre, Chester Road, Sandiway, Northwich, Cheshire** | |
| | Blakemere Craft Centre | *See display advertisement* |

Sept 30-Oct 3   **CRAFTS ALIVE & CREATIVE STITCHES/Westpoint, Clyst St Mary, Exeter, Devon**
ICHF Ltd

| Sept 30-Oct 3 | **THE 16TH NATIONAL KNITTING, NEEDLECRAFT & HOBBYCRAFTS EXHIBITION/National Exhibition Centre, Birmingham** |
| | Nationwide Exhibitions (UK) Ltd |

Oct 1-3   **KNEBWORTH HOUSE HOME DESIGN & INTERIORS EXHIBITION/ Knebworth, nr Stevenage, Herts**
Buckingham Publicity   *See display advertisement*

Oct 1-3   **CRAFT FAIR/Suffolk Showground, Bucklesham Road, Ipswich, Suffolk**
Country Cottage Crafts

Oct 1-3   **CRAFT FAIR/The Leisure Centre, University of Keele, Keele, nr Newcastle-under-Lyme, Staffs**
Mary Holland Craft Fairs Ltd   *See display advertisement*

Oct 1-3   **JUST ARTS & CRAFTS MARQUEE EVENT/Hyde End, Great Missenden, Bucks**
Traditional Crafts Ltd   *See display advertisement*

Oct 1-Nov 13   **SDC CRAFT EXHIBITION/Shire Hall Gallery, Stafford, Staffs**
Society of Designer Craftsmen

Oct 2   **CRAFT MARKET/Fisher Hall, Guildhall Place, Cambridge, Cambs**
Balthazar

Oct 2   **CRAFT FAIR/Town Hall, Jedburgh, Roxburghshire**
Border Fairs

Oct 2   **CRAFT FAIR/Steyning Centre, Fletchers Croft, Steyning, West Sussex**
Craft Developments

Oct 2   **ARTS & CRAFTS FAIR/Town Hall, Brackley, Northants**
Falcon Fairs

Oct 2   **CRAFT FAIR/Guildhall, Plymouth, Devon**
Kevin Murphy Craft Fairs

Oct 2   **CRAFT & GIFT FAIR/Barnet Library, Stapylton Road, Barnet, Herts**
Marie Margaret Promotions

Oct 2   **ART & CRAFT FAIR/The Arts Centre, Biddick Lane, Fatfield, Washington, Tyne & Wear**
The Arts Centre

Oct 2-3   **CRAFT FAIR/Hawkshead Market Hall, nr Ambleside, Cumbria**
Aphrodite

Oct 2-3   **CRAFT FAYRE/Blakemere Craft Centre, Chester Road, Sandiway, Northwich, Cheshire**
Blakemere Craft Centre   *See display advertisement*

Oct 2-3   **CRAFT, DESIGN & GIFT FAIR/Dobbies Gardening World, A5, Penkridge, nr Cannock, Staffs**
Cottage Industries Association   *See display advertisement*

Oct 2-3   **THE CRAFTS & DESIGN FAIR/Hagley Hall, nr Stourbridge, West Midlands**
Countrywide Events

Oct 2-3   **CRAFT FAIR/Cressing Temple Barns, Cressing, nr Braintree, Essex**
Hallmark Fairs

Oct 2-3   **CRAFT FAIR/Eastnor Castle, Ledbury, Herefordshire**
Hobby Horse Design & Craft Fairs

Oct 2-3   **CRAFT FAIR/St William's College, York, North Yorks**
Keld Craft Fairs

Oct 2-3   **CRAFT FAIR/Ely Maltings, Ely, Cambs**
Kingfisher Promotions

Oct 2-3   **REDDITCH CRAFT SHOW/Arrow Valley Country Park, Battens Drive, off Coventry Highway, Redditch, Worcs**
Living Heritage Craft Shows Ltd   *See display advertisement*

Oct 2-3   **CRAFT FAIR/Wyvern Hall, Swallows Leisure Centre, Central Avenue, Sittingbourne, Kent**
M B County Fairs

Oct 2-3   **'LADY FAIR' CRAFT FESTIVAL/Stanford Hall, Lutterworth, Leics**
MGA Fairs   *See display advertisement*

Oct 2-3   **CRAFT FAIR/Fritton Lake, Norfolk**
Rainbow Fair

Oct 2-3   **LIVE CRAFTS SHOW/Hoghton Tower, nr Preston, Lancs**
The Exhibition Team Ltd   *See display advertisement*

Oct 2-3   **OUT OF THE FOREST WOODCRAFT EVENT/Airedale Barn, East Riddlesden Hall, Bradford Road, Keighley, West Yorks**
The National Trust, East Riddlesden

Oct 3   **CRAFT FAIR/Northwood Stadium, Keelings Road, Northwood, nr Hanley, Stoke-on-Trent, Staffs**
Archer Promotions

Oct 3   **10TH ANNUAL BEADWORK & BEAD FAIR/Byron Hall, Leisure Centre, Harrow**
Bead Society of Great Britain

Oct 3   **CRAFT FAIR/The Manor Hotel, Hartlebury Road, Stourport, Worcs**
Central Promotions   *See display advertisement*

Oct 3   **CRAFT FAIR/Aston Hall, Aston, Sheffield, South Yorks**
Cottage Creations Craft Fairs

Oct 3   **CRAFT FAIR/Lacock Village Hall, Lacock, nr Chippenham, Wilts**
Countrycraft

Oct 3   **CRAFT FAIR/Village Hotel, Whiston, nr Prescot, Merseyside**
Creative Crafts Association   *See display advertisement*

Oct 3   **DOLL FAIR/Lamport Hall, Lamport, Northants**
East Midlands Doll Fairs

Oct 3   **CRAFT & GIFT FAIR/Barton Village Hall, nr Preston, Lancs**
Golden Age Fairs

Oct 3   **CRAFT FAIR/Newstead Abbey, Notts**
Heathfield Craft Fairs

Oct 3   **CRAFT FAIR/Gargrave Village Hall, Gargrave, nr Skipton, North Yorks**
Heritage Fairs

Oct 3   **CRAFT FAIR/Beverley Leisure Centre, Flemingate (opposite Army Museum), Beverley, East Yorks**
Holland Fairs

Oct 3   **CRAFT FAIR/Racecourse, Newton Abbot, Devon**
Kevin Murphy Craft Fairs

Oct 3   **CRAFT SELLING EXHIBITION/Aughton Village Hall, Winifred Lane, Aughton, Lancs**
The Craft Guild of West Lancashire

Oct 3   **CRAFT FAIR/Pavilion Theatre, Worthing, West Sussex**
Worthing Leisure

Oct 3   **YORKRAFT FAIR/Thornton Dale Parish Rooms, Thornton Dale, nr Pickering, North Yorks**
Yorkraft Fairs

Oct 3-5 **THE WALES FAIR/Royal Welsh Showground, Llanelwedd, BuilthWells, Powys**
Wales Craft Council

Oct 4   **CRAFT FAIR/St Herberts Parish Hall**
West Pennine Promotions

Oct 6-9 **NATIONAL CRAFTS FAIR/Beau Séjour Leisure Centre, St Peter Port, Guernsey, Channel Islands**
National Crafts Fair   *See display advertisement*

Oct 7   **CRAFT FAIR/Market Hall, Hawes, North Yorks**
Keld Craft Fairs

Oct 8-10 **CRAFTS FAIR/Finchcocks, Riseden, Goudhurst, Kent**
Finchcocks

Oct 8-10 **CRAFT FAIR/Thoresby Park, nr Newark, Notts**
Rainbow Fair

Oct 8-10 **ART IN WOOD SHOW/Chiltern Open Air Museum, Chalfont St Giles, Bucks**
The Exhibition Team Ltd   *See display advertisement*

Oct 9   **CRAFT & GIFT FAIR/The Harlington Centre, High Street, Fleet, Hants**
Aquarius Fairs

Oct 9   **CRAFT MARKET/Fisher Hall, Guildhall Place, Cambridge, Cambs**
Balthazar

Oct 9   **CRAFT FAIR/Burgh Hall, Peebles**
Border Fairs

Oct 9   **CRAFT FAYRE/The Town Hall, Torquay, Devon**
Cherrycraft Fayres & Festivals

Oct 9   **CRAFT FAIR/Village Hall, Trinity Road, Hurstpierpoint, nr Hassocks, West Sussex**
Craft Developments

Oct 9   **DUNSTABLE CRAFT MARKET/Methodist Church Hall, Ashton Square, Dunstable, Beds**
Dunstable Craft Market

Oct 9   **CRAFT FAIR/Malden Centre, Blagdon Road, New Malden, Surrey**
Eden Crafts

Oct 9   **ARTS & CRAFTS FAIR/Town Hall, Towcester, Northants**
Falcon Fairs

Oct 9   **CRAFT FAIR/Guildhall, Winchester, Hants**
Kevin Murphy Craft Fairs

Oct 9   **CRAFT FAIR/Market Hall, Abergavenny, Monmouthshire**
Monmouthshire County Council

Oct 9   **POSSET CRAFT FAYRE/Somerset Hall, Portishead, North Somerset**
Portishead Supporters

Oct 9   **CRAFT & GIFT FAYRE/Ferneham Hall, Fareham, Hants**
Something Special Craft & Gift Fayres

Oct 9-10   **CRAFT FAIR/Hawkshead Market Hall, nr Ambleside, Cumbria**
Aphrodite

Oct 9-10   **CRAFT FAYRE/Blakemere Craft Centre, Chester Road, Sandiway, Northwich, Cheshire**
Blakemere Craft Centre   *See display advertisement*

Oct 9-10   **CRAFT FAYRE/Fenton Manor, Fenton, Stoke-on-Trent, Staffs**
Cheshire Fayre   *See display advertisement*

Oct 9-10   **CRAFT, DESIGN & GIFT FAIR/Hurrans Garden Centre, West Hagley, nr Stourbridge, Worcs**
Cottage Industries Association   *See display advertisement*

Oct 9-10   **CRAFT, DESIGN & GIFT FAIR/William Wheat's Garden Centre, Old Chester Road (A452), Little Aston, West Midlands**
Cottage Industries Association   *See display advertisement*

Oct 9-10   **THE AUTUMN CRAFTS FAIR/Himley Hall, Dudley, West Midlands**
Countrywide Events

Oct 9-10   **CRAFT FAIR/Shugborough Estate, Shugborough, nr Stafford, Staffs**
Hobby Horse Design & Craft Fairs

Oct 9-10   **AUTUMN CRAFT WEEKEND/Ditchling Garden Centre, Ditchling, West Sussex**
Jets Quality Craft Fairs

Oct 9-10   **HOP FARM CRAFT SHOW/Hop Farm Country Park, Beltring, Paddock Wood, nr Tonbridge, Kent**
Living Heritage Craft Shows Ltd   *See display advertisement*

| Oct 9-10 | **TELFORD CRAFT SHOW/Telford International Exhibition Centre, Telford, Salop** |
| | Living Heritage Craft Shows Ltd *See display advertisement* |

| Oct 9-10 | **CRAFT FAIR/Sandwich Leisure Centre, Sandwich, Kent** |
| | M B County Fairs |

| Oct 9-10 | **AUTUMN CRAFT FESTIVAL/Ragley Hall, Alcester, Warks** |
| | MGA Fairs *See display advertisement* |

| Oct 9-10 | **CRAFT SHOW/The Centre, Slough, Berks** |
| | Maurtraid Craft Shows *See display advertisement* |

| Oct 9-10 | **LIVE CRAFTS SHOW/Bletchley Park, Bletchley, Bucks** |
| | The Exhibition Team Ltd *See display advertisement* |

| Oct 9-10 | **FORT PURBROOK CRAFT FAYRE/Portsdown Hill, Cosham, nr Portsmouth, Hants** |
| | Woodland Crafts *See display advertisement* |

| Oct 10 | **CRAFT FAIR/Congleton Town Hall, High Street, Congleton, Cheshire** |
| | Archer Promotions |

| Oct 10 | **DOLLS HOUSE & MINIATURE FAIR/Knights Hill Village Conference Centre, King's Lynn, Norfolk** |
| | Brentwood Fairs |

| Oct 10 | **CRAFT FAIR/The Pemberton Centre, Rushden, Northants** |
| | Cambridge Craft Fairs |

| Oct 10 | **CRAFT FAIR/The Moat House Hotel, M54 Junction 5, Telford, Salop** |
| | Central Promotions *See display advertisement* |

| Oct 10 | **CRAFT FAIR/Oasis Leisure Centre, North Star Avenue, Swindon, Wilts** |
| | Cottage Craft Fairs *See display advertisement* |

| Oct 10 | **CRAFT FAIR/Olde House Trading Post, Chesterfield, Derbys** |
| | Cottage Creations Craft Fairs |

| Oct 10 | **CRAFT FAIR/Floral Hall, The Promenade, Southport, Merseyside** |
| | Creative Crafts Association *See display advertisement* |

| Oct 10 | **DOLL FAIR/Nostell Priory, nr Wakefield, West Yorks** |
| | East Midlands Doll Fairs |

| Oct 10 | **CRAFT FAIR/Beaumanor Hall, Woodhouse Eaves, nr Loughborough, Leics** |
| | Heathfield Craft Fairs |

| Oct 10 | **CRAFT FAIR/Edgehill College, Bideford, Devon** |
| | Kevin Murphy Craft Fairs |

| Oct 10 | **CRAFT FAIR/Paxton House, Paxton, nr Berwick, Selkirkshire** |
| | Quintet Promotions |

| Oct 10 | **RURAL CRAFTS ASSOCIATION AT THE EAST OF ENGLAND AUTUMN EXHIBITION/East of England Showground, Peterborough, Cambs** |
| | Rural Crafts Association *See display advertisement* |

Oct 10 **YORKRAFT FAIR/Thornton Dale Parish Rooms, Thornton Dale, nr Pickering, North Yorks**
Yorkraft Fairs

Oct 11 **CRAFT FAIR/Nazareth House, Prestwich, Manchester**
West Pennine Promotions

Oct 12 **CRAFT FAIR/White Hart Inn, Hawes, North Yorks**
Keld Craft Fairs

Oct 12-24 **CHELSEA CRAFTS FAIR/Chelsea Old Town Hall, Kings Road, London SW3**
(closed Oct 18) Crafts Council

Oct 13 **CRAFT FAIR/Town Hall, Northallerton, North Yorks**
Keld Craft Fairs

Oct 14 **YORKRAFT FAIR/Wetherby Town Hall, Wetherby, West Yorks**
Yorkraft Fairs

Oct 14-24 **ABINGDON CRAFTS FESTIVAL/Medieval Abbey Buildings, Abingdon, Oxon**
(closed Oct 19) Mary Holland Craft Fairs Ltd *See display advertisement*

Oct 16 **CRAFT MARKET/Fisher Hall, Guildhall Place, Cambridge, Cambs**
Balthazar

Oct 16 **CRAFT FAIR/Volunteer Hall, Galashiels, Selkirkshire**
Border Fairs

Oct 16 **LEEDS DOLL & TEDDY FAIR/Civic Hall, New Pudsey, nr Leeds, West Yorks**
Dolly Domain Fairs

Oct 16 **ARTS & CRAFTS FAIR/Buckingham Community Centre, Bucks**
Falcon Fairs

Oct 16 **ARTS & CRAFTS FAYRE/Winter Gardens, Weston-super-Mare, North Somerset**
Fountain Fayres & Exhibitions

Oct 16 **CRAFT FAIR/Guildhall, Salisbury, Wilts**
Kevin Murphy Craft Fairs

Oct 16 **CRAFT FAIR/Lyndhurst Community Centre, Lyndhurst, Hants**
Oakleaf Craft Fairs *See display advertisement*

Oct 16-17 **CRAFT FAYRE/Blakemere Craft Centre, Chester Road, Sandiway, Northwich, Cheshire**
Blakemere Craft Centre *See display advertisement*

Oct 16-17 **CRAFT SHOW/Kelham Hall, Newark, Notts**
CFL Craft Shows

Oct 16-17 **CRAFT FAIR/Warwick Hall, National Agricultural Centre, Stoneleigh Park, Warks**
Central Promotions *See display advertisement*

Oct 16-17 **CRAFT FAIR/Brigade Hall, Bakewell, Derbys**
Cottage Creations Craft Fairs

Oct 16-17	**CRAFT, DESIGN & GIFT FAIR/Hurrans Garden Centre, Leigh Sinton, nr Malvern, Worcs** Cottage Industries Association *See display advertisement*
Oct 16-17	**CHESHIRE CRAFTS & DESIGN FAIR/Tatton Park, Knutsford, Cheshire** Countrywide Events
Oct 16-17	**CRAFT FAIR/Audley End House, Saffron Walden, Essex** Hobby Horse Design & Craft Fairs
Oct 16-17	**ARTS & CRAFTS FAIR/Town Hall, Grassington, nr Skipton, North Yorks** Jean Bryon
Oct 16-17	**SOUTH LONDON CRAFT SHOW/Dulwich College, Dulwich, London** Jets Quality Craft Fairs
Oct 16-17	**CRAFT FAIR/St William's College, York, North Yorks** Keld Craft Fairs
Oct 16-17	**AYLESBURY CRAFT WEEKEND/Civic Centre, Aylesbury, Bucks** Living Heritage Craft Shows Ltd *See display advertisement*
Oct 16-17	**CRAFTS AT THE MANOR HOUSE/The Manor House, Aldermaston, Berks** Living Heritage Craft Shows Ltd *See display advertisement*
Oct 16-17	**CRAFT FAIR/Chatham Grammar School for Girls, Rainham Road, Chatham, Kent** M B County Fairs
Oct 16-17	**CRAFT FAIR/Victoria Hall, Bourton-on-the-Water, Glos** M&B Crafts
Oct 16-17	**CRAFT FAIR/Rockingham Castle, Corby, Northants** Rainbow Fair
Oct 16-17	**LIVE CRAFTS SHOW/Ascot Exhibition Centre, Ascot, Berks** The Exhibition Team Ltd *See display advertisement*
Oct 16-17	**JUST ARTS & CRAFTS/Rosebery Suites, Epsom Racecourse, Epsom, Surrey** Traditional Crafts Ltd *See display advertisement*
Oct 16-17	**SWANSEA CRAFT & STITCHING/Swansea, West Glam** Wales Craft Council
Oct 16-21	**MIDLANDS MODEL ENGINEERING EXHIBITION/International Exhibition Centre, Donington, nr Derby, Derbys** Meridienne Exhibitions Ltd
Oct 17	**CRAFT FAIR/Whitchurch Leisure Centre, High Street, Whitchurch, Salop** Archer Promotions
Oct 17	**DOLLS HOUSE & MINIATURE FAIR/Leighton Hall, Carnforth, Lancs** Brentwood Fairs
Oct 17	**CRAFT FAIR/Loddon Valley Leisure Centre, Chalfont Way, Lower Earley, nr Reading, Berks** Cottage Craft Fairs *See display advertisement*

Oct 17	**CRAFT, DESIGN & GIFT FAIR/Bromsgrove Market Hall, Worcs**
	Cottage Industries Association *See display advertisement*
Oct 17	**CRAFT FAIR/Lacock Village Hall, Lacock, nr Chippenham, Wilts**
	Countrycraft
Oct 17	**CRAFT FAIR/Hoole Hall Hotel, Chester, Cheshire**
	Creative Crafts Association *See display advertisement*
Oct 17	**DOLL FAIR/Woburn Abbey, M1 Junction 13, Beds**
	East Midlands Doll Fairs
Oct 17	**ARTS & CRAFTS FAIR/Woburn Village Hall, Woburn, Beds**
	Falcon Fairs
Oct 17	**CRAFT FAIR/Ipswich County Hotel, (A12), Copdock, Suffolk**
	Hallmark Fairs
Oct 17	**CRAFT FAIR/Elvaston Castle, Borrowash, Derbys**
	Heathfield Craft Fairs
Oct 17	**CRAFT FAIR/Hinchingbrooke House, Huntingdon, Cambs**
	Kingfisher Promotions
Oct 17	**CRAFT & GIFT FAIR/Hilton National, Garforth, Leeds, West Yorks**
	Quality Craft & Gift Fairs *See display advertisement*
Oct 17	**CRAFT FAIR/Royal Chace Hotel, The Ridgeway, Enfield, Middx**
	Quality Craft Fairs
Oct 17	**CRAFT FAIR/Lumley Castle, Chester-le-Street, Co Durham**
	Quintet Promotions
Oct 17	**THE ST IVES TEDDY BEAR FAIR/St Ivo Recreation Centre, St Ives, Cambs**
	Romor Exhibitions Ltd *See display advertisement*
Oct 18 19	**CRAFT, DESIGN & GIFT FAIR/Jardinerie Garden Place, Kenilworth Road (A452), Hampton-in-Arden, West Midlands**
	Cottage Industries Association *See display advertisement*
Oct 22-24	**CRAFT FAIR/Gatcombe Park, nr Stroud, Glos**
	Rainbow Fair
Oct 23	**CRAFT MARKET/Fisher Hall, Guildhall Place, Cambridge, Cambs**
	Balthazar
Oct 23	**CRAFT FAIR/Municipal Hall, Biggar, Lanarkshire**
	Border Fairs
Oct 23	**CRAFT FAIR/Village Hall, Ferring Street, Ferring, nr Worthing, West Sussex**
	Craft Developments
Oct 23	**DOLL FAIR/Civic Hall, Stratford-upon-Avon, Warks**
	East Midlands Doll Fairs
Oct 23	**CRAFTS & COLLECTABLES FAIR/Parish Hall, Culcheth, Warrington, Cheshire**
	Gem Fairs

Oct 23   **CRAFT FAIR/Assembly Hall, Warminster, Wilts**
Kevin Murphy Craft Fairs

Oct 23   **ANTIQUE & CRAFT FAIR/Hedworth Hall, Westoe, South Shields, Tyne & Wear**
Quintet Promotions

Oct 23-24   **CRAFT FAYRE/Balmer Lawn Hotel, Brockenhurst, Hants**
Avocet Crafts

Oct 23-24   **CRAFT FAYRE/Blakemere Craft Centre, Chester Road, Sandiway, Northwich, Cheshire**
Blakemere Craft Centre   *See display advertisement*

Oct 23-24   **CRAFT, DESIGN & GIFT FAIR/Wyevale Garden Centre & Farm Shop,Telford, Salop**
Cottage Industries Association   *See display advertisement*

Oct 23-24   **CHRISTMAS GIFT FAIR/Tatton Park, Knutsford, Cheshire**
Countrywide Events

Oct 23-24   **CRAFT FAIR/Haydock Park Racecourse Exhibition Centre, St Helens, Merseyside**
Creative Crafts Association   *See display advertisement*

Oct 23-24   **CHRISTMAS CRAFT FAIR/Winter Gardens, Margate, Kent**
East Kent Fairs   *See display advertisement*

Oct 23-24   **HALLOWE'EN CRAFT FAYRE/Sandown Park, Esher, Surrey**
Four Seasons (Events) Ltd

Oct 23-24   **CRAFT FAIR/St William's College, York, North Yorks**
Keld Craft Fairs

Oct 23-24   **GIFTS & CRAFT FAIR/Lamport Hall, Lamport, Northants**
Lamport Hall Trust

Oct 23-24   **CHRISTMAS CRAFTS AT GROOMBRIDGE/Groombridge Place Gardens, B2110, nr Tunbridge Wells, Kent**
Living Heritage Craft Shows Ltd   *See display advertisement*

Oct 23-24   **GRIMSBY CRAFT WEEKEND/The Grimsby Auditorium, Cromwell Road, Grimsby, North East Lincs**
Living Heritage Craft Shows Ltd   *See display advertisement*

Oct 23-24   **LIVE CRAFTS SHOW/Surrey**
The Exhibition Team Ltd   *See display advertisement*

Oct 23-24   **THE FARNHAM MALTINGS FESTIVAL OF CRAFTS/Bridge Square, Farnham, Surrey**
The Farnham Maltings

Oct 23-24   **CRAFT FAIR/The Pavilion, Buxton, Derbys**
Town & Country Craft Fairs

Oct 23-26   **CRAFT FAIR/Hawkshead Market Hall, nr Ambleside, Cumbria**
Aphrodite

Oct 23-Nov 7 (provisional)	**CARDIFF RUGBY WORLD CUP CRAFT FESTIVAL/St John's Square, Cardiff** Craft*Folk
Oct 24	**CRAFT SHOW/The Belfry, Wishaw, Sutton Coldfield, West Midlands** CFL Craft Shows
Oct 24	**DOLLSHOUSE, MINIATURES, DOLL & TEDDY FAIR/Shepherd's Inn, Rosehill, Carlisle, Cumbria** Caile Fairs
Oct 24	**CRAFT FAIR/The Leisure Centre, Kinver, nr Stourbridge, West Midlands** Central Promotions *See display advertisement*
Oct 24	**CRAFT FAIR/Leisure Centre, Clewer Mead, Stovell Road, Windsor, Berks** Cottage Craft Fairs *See display advertisement*
Oct 24	**CRAFT FAIR/Keresforth Hall, Barnsley, South Yorks** Cottage Creations Craft Fairs
Oct 24	**CRAFT FAIR/Lacock Village Hall, Lacock, nr Chippenham, Wilts** Countrycraft
Oct 24	**CRAFT FAIR/Dog & Fox Hotel, High Street, Wimbledon Village, London** Eden Crafts
Oct 24	**CRAFT FAIR/Dunkenhalgh Hotel, Clayton-le-Moors, nr Accrington, Lancs** Heritage Fairs
Oct 24	**CRAFT FAIR/Yate Leisure Centre, Bristol** Kevin Murphy Craft Fairs
Oct 24	**CRAFT FAIR/Knights Barn, King's Lynn, Norfolk** Kingfisher Promotions
Oct 24	**ARTS & CRAFTS SHOW/Lauderdale House, Highgate Hill, London N6** Lauderdale Arts & Crafts
Oct 24	**CRAFT FAIR/Oatlands Park Hotel, Oatlands, Weybridge, Surrey** Mascot Craft & Gift Fairs
Oct 24	**CRAFT FAIR/The Bellhouse Hotel, Oxford Road (A40), Beaconsfield, Bucks** Midas Fairs
Oct 24	**CRAFT & GIFT FAIR/St George Swallow Hotel, Harrogate, North Yorks** Quality Craft & Gift Fairs *See display advertisement*
Oct 24	**CRAFT FAIR/The Post House, Brentwood, Essex** Quality Craft Fairs
Oct 24	**CRAFT FAIR/Gateshead International Stadium, Tyne & Wear** Quintet Promotions
Oct 24	**DOLLS HOUSE FAIR/Moat House Hotel, Borehamwood, Herts** R J Exhibitions
Oct 24	**CRAFT & GIFT FAYRE/Hilton National, Portsmouth, Hants** Something Special Craft & Gift Fayres

Oct 24   **AUTUMN CRAFT FAIR/Florence Court, Enniskillen, Co Fermanagh**
The National Trust, Florence Court

Oct 24   **DOLLS HOUSE, DOLLS, TOYS & MINIATURES FAIR/Exmouth Pavilion, Exmouth, Devon**
West of England Fairs

Oct 24-27   **THE HIGHLAND TRADE FAIR/Aviemore Centre, Aviemore, Inverness-shire**
Made in Scotland Ltd   *See display advertisement*

Oct 24-27   **AVIEMORE MERCURY TRADEX '99/Mercury Hotel, Aviemore Mountain Resort, Inverness-shire**
Northern Exhibitions

Oct 26   **CRAFT FAIR/White Hart Inn, Hawes, North Yorks**
Keld Craft Fairs

Oct 27   **CRAFT FAYRE/Blakemere Craft Centre, Chester Road, Sandiway, Northwich, Cheshire**
Blakemere Craft Centre   *See display advertisement*

Oct 28-29   **CRAFT FAIR/Market Hall, Hawes, North Yorks**
Keld Craft Fairs

Oct 29-30   **SHERBORNE CRAFT MARKET/Digby Hall, Hound Street, Sherborne, Dorset**
Sherborne Craft Market

Oct 29-31   **CRAFT FAIR/Hawkshead Market Hall, nr Ambleside, Cumbria**
Aphrodite

Oct 29-31   **CRAFTS ALIVE FOR SCOTLAND/Scottish Exhibition and Conference Centre, Glasgow**
ICHF Ltd

Oct 29-31   **CHRISTMAS FESTIVAL OF DESIGNER CRAFTS & FINE FOODS/Beverley Race Course, Beverley, East Yorks**
Jean Welch Shows   *See display advertisement*

Oct 29-31   **CRAFTS FOR CHRISTMAS - SUFFOLK/Suffolk Showground, Bucklesham Road, Ipswich, Suffolk**
Rural Crafts Association   *See display advertisement*

Oct 29-31   **CRAFT MATERIALS SHOW/Kempton Park Racecourse, Sunbury-on-Thames, Middx**
The Exhibition Team Ltd   *See display advertisement*

Oct 30   **CRAFT MARKET/Fisher Hall, Guildhall Place, Cambridge, Cambs**
Balthazar

Oct 30   **TEDDY BEAR & DOLL FAIR/Ellersly House Hotel, Edinburgh**
Brentwood Fairs

Oct 30   **CRAFT FAYRE/The Scala Hall, Brixham, Devon**
Cherrycraft Fayres & Festivals

Oct 30   **CRAFT FAIR/Leconfield Hall, Market Square, Petworth, West Sussex**
Craft Developments

Oct 30	**CHRISTMAS CRAFT FAIR/Astor Theatre, Deal, Kent**
	East Kent Fairs *See display advertisement*

Oct 30 — **CHRISTMAS CRAFT FAIR/Astor Theatre, Deal, Kent**
East Kent Fairs *See display advertisement*

Oct 30 — **CRAFT FAIR/Victoria Hall, Bourton-on-the-Water, Glos**
M&B Crafts

Oct 30 — **CRAFTS BUSINESS SEMINAR/The Art Workers' Guild, London**
Society of Designer Craftsmen

Oct 30-31 — **CRAFT FAYRE/Blakemere Craft Centre, Chester Road, Sandiway, Northwich, Cheshire**
Blakemere Craft Centre *See display advertisement*

Oct 30-31 — **CRAFT FAYRE/Arley Hall, nr Knutsford, Cheshire**
Cheshire Fayre *See display advertisement*

Oct 30-31 — **CRAFT, DESIGN & GIFT FAIR/Byrkley Park Garden Centre, Rangemore, Burton-on-Trent, Staffs**
Cottage Industries Association *See display advertisement*

Oct 30-31 — **CRAFT FAIR/Cliffs Pavilion, Station Road, Westcliff-on-Sea, Southend, Essex**
Hallmark Fairs

Oct 30-31 — **SOUTH EAST ENGLAND CRAFT SHOW/Leisure Centre, Crawley, West Sussex**
Jets Quality Craft Fairs

Oct 30-31 — **CRAFT FAIR/St William's College, York, North Yorks**
Keld Craft Fairs

Oct 30-31 — **CHRISTMAS CRAFTS AT BLAKE HALL/Blake Hall, A414, Ongar, Essex**
Living Heritage Craft Shows Ltd *See display advertisement*

Oct 30-31 — **MAIDENHEAD CRAFT WEEKEND/Magnet Leisure Centre, A4 Town Centre, Maidenhead, Berks**
Living Heritage Craft Shows Ltd *See display advertisement*

Oct 30-31 — **CRAFT FAIR/Leisure World, Cowdray Avenue, Colchester, Essex**
R&S Fairs

Oct 30-31 — **AUTUMN CRAFT FAIR/Stapehill Abbey, Crafts & Gardens, 276 Wimborne Road West, Stapehill, nr Wimborne, Dorset**
Stapehill Abbey, Crafts & Gardens

Oct 31 — **CRAFT FAIR/Biddulph Leisure Centre, Thames Drive, off Congleton Road, Biddulph, Staffs**
Archer Promotions

Oct 31 — **DOLLS HOUSE & MINIATURE FAIR/Hopetoun House, South Queensferry, Edinburgh**
Brentwood Fairs

Oct 31 — **CRAFT FAIR/Lordsbridge Arena, Barton, Cambs**
Cambridge Craft Fairs

Oct 31 — **CRAFT FAIR/Albrighton Hall Hotel, Ellesmere Road (A528), Shrewsbury, Salop**
Central Promotions *See display advertisement*

| Oct 31 | **CRAFT FAIR/Lacock Village Hall, Lacock, nr Chippenham, Wilts** |
| | Countrycraft |

Oct 31   **CRAFT FAIR/De Vere Hotel, East Park Drive, Blackpool, Lancs**
Creative Crafts Association   *See display advertisement*

Oct 31   **DOLL FAIR/Kelham Hall, Newark, Notts**
East Midlands Doll Fairs

Oct 31   **CRAFT FAIR/Great Hall, Worksop College, Manton, Worksop, Notts**
Heathfield Craft Fairs

Oct 31   **CRAFT FAIR/Mayflower Centre, Plymouth, Devon**
Kevin Murphy Craft Fairs

Oct 31   **CRAFT FAIR/Goodwood Racecourse, nr Chichester, West Sussex**
Mascot Craft & Gift Fairs

Oct 31   **CRAFT & GIFT FAIR/Marton Hotel & Country Club, Middlesbrough, Cleveland**
Quality Craft & Gift Fairs   *See display advertisement*

Oct 31   **CRAFT FAIR/The Rhodes Centre, Bishop's Stortford, Herts**
Quality Craft Fairs

Oct 31   **CRAFT FAIR/Royal Derwent Hotel, Allensford, Co Durham**
Quintet Promotions

Oct 31   **CRAFT FAIR/Hollingworth Lake Rowing Club, Littleborough, Lancs**
West Pennine Promotions

Oct 31
(provisional)   **CUMBRIA CRAFT GUILD ANNUAL EXHIBITION/Gallery in the Forest, Grizedale, nr Ambleside, Cumbria**
Cumbria Craft Guild

Nov 4   **CRAFT FAIR/Mercury Motel, Manchester Road, Westhoughton, Bolton, Lancs**
West Pennine Promotions

Nov 4-7   **THE SYON PARK CHRISTMAS GIFT & CRAFT FAIR/Syon Park, Isleworth, West London**
Orchard Events Ltd   *See display advertisement*

Nov 5-7   **COUGHTON COURT HOME DESIGN & INTERIORS EXHIBITION/ Coughton, nr Alcester, Warks**
Buckingham Publicity   *See display advertisement*

Nov 5-7   **CRAFT FAIR/Norfolk Showground, Dereham Road, New Costessey, nr Norwich, Norfolk**
Country Cottage Crafts

Nov 5-7   **CRAFTS AT CHRISTMAS/Aberdeen Exhibition & Conference Centre**
Dalesway Festivals Ltd   *See display advertisement*

Nov 5-7   **THE CRAFT SHOW/Marks Hall, nr Coggeshall, Essex**
Eastern Events Ltd   *See display advertisement*

Nov 5-7   **CHRISTMAS CRAFT FAIR/Brighton Centre, Kings Road, Brighton, East Sussex**
Marathon Event Management Ltd   *See display advertisement*

| Nov 5-7 | **CRAFTS FOR CHRISTMAS - KENT/Kent County Showground, Detling, nr Maidstone, Kent** |
| | Rural Crafts Association | *See display advertisement* |

| Nov 6 | **CRAFT MARKET/Fisher Hall, Guildhall Place, Cambridge, Cambs** |
| | Balthazar |

| Nov 6 | **CRAFT FAIR/Town Hall, Jedburgh, Roxburghshire** |
| | Border Fairs |

| Nov 6 | **CRAFT FAIR/Guildhall, Plymouth, Devon** |
| | Kevin Murphy Craft Fairs |

| Nov 6 | **CRAFT & GIFT FAIR/Barnet Library, Stapylton Road, Barnet, Herts** |
| | Marie Margaret Promotions |

| Nov 6 | **CRAFT FAIR/The Castle Hall, Hertford, Herts** |
| | Quality Craft Fairs |

| Nov 6 | **ANTIQUE & CRAFT FAIR/Memorial Hall, Darras Road, Ponteland, Northumberland** |
| | Quintet Promotions |

| Nov 6 | **ART & CRAFT FAIR/The Arts Centre, Biddick Lane, Fatfield, Washington, Tyne & Wear** |
| | The Arts Centre |

| Nov 6-7 | **CRAFT FAYRE/Blakemere Craft Centre, Chester Road, Sandiway, Northwich, Cheshire** |
| | Blakemere Craft Centre | *See display advertisement* |

| Nov 6-7 | **CRAFT SHOW/Hatherley Manor, Down Hatherley Lane, Gloucester, Glos** |
| | CFL Craft Shows |

| Nov 6-7 | **CRAFT, DESIGN & GIFT FAIR/Jardinerie Garden Place, Kenilworth Road (A452), Hampton-in-Arden, West Midlands** |
| | Cottage Industries Association | *See display advertisement* |

| Nov 6-7 | **CHRISTMAS CRAFT FAIR/Leas Cliff Hall, Folkstone, Kent** |
| | East Kent Fairs | *See display advertisement* |

| Nov 6-7 | **CRAFT FAIR/Guildford Civic Centre, London Road, Guildford, Surrey** |
| | Eden Crafts |

| Nov 6-7 | **CHRISTMAS CRAFTS/Warwickshire County Cricket Ground, Edgbaston, Birmingham, West Midlands** |
| | Hobby Horse Design & Craft Fairs |

| Nov 6-7 | **TEESSIDE CHRISTMAS FESTIVAL OF CRAFTS & FINE FOODS/Tall Trees, Yarm, Cleveland** |
| | Jean Welch Shows | *See display advertisement* |

| Nov 6-7 | **CRAFT FAIR/St William's College, York, North Yorks** |
| | Keld Craft Fairs |

| Nov 6-7 | **CRAFT FAIR/Ely Maltings, Ely, Cambs** |
| | Kingfisher Promotions |

| Nov 6-7 | **BEDFORDSHIRE CHRISTMAS CRAFT SHOW/Woburn Safari Park, Woburn, Beds** |
| | Living Heritage Craft Shows Ltd *See display advertisement* |

Nov 6-7   **BEDFORDSHIRE CHRISTMAS CRAFT SHOW/Woburn Safari Park, Woburn, Beds**
Living Heritage Craft Shows Ltd   *See display advertisement*

Nov 6-7   **CLACTON CRAFT WEEKEND/Highfields Holiday Park, London Road, Clacton-on-Sea, Essex**
Living Heritage Craft Shows Ltd   *See display advertisement*

Nov 6-7   **CRAFT FAIR/Black Lion Leisure Centre, Mill Road, Gillingham, Kent**
M B County Fairs

Nov 6-7   **CRAFT FAIR/Beaumanor Hall, Loughborough, Leics**
Oak Craft Fairs   *See display advertisement*

Nov 6-7   **CRAFT FAIR/Castle Combe, Wilts**
Rainbow Fair

Nov 6-7   **THE CRAFT MOVEMENT/The Concert Halls, Blackheath, London**
The Craft Movement

Nov 6-7   **LIVE CRAFTS SHOW/Bath Racecourse, Bath**
The Exhibition Team Ltd   *See display advertisement*

Nov 6-7   **FESTIVAL OF CRAFTS/Airedale Barn, East Riddlesden Hall, Bradford Road, Keighley, West Yorks**
The National Trust, East Riddlesden

Nov 6-7   **FORT PURBROOK CRAFT FAYRE/Portsdown Hill, Cosham, nr Portsmouth, Hants**
Woodland Crafts   *See display advertisement*

Nov 7   **CRAFT FAIR/Northwood Stadium, Keelings Road, Northwood, nr Hanley, Stoke-on-Trent, Staffs**
Archer Promotions

Nov 7   **CRAFT FAIR/The Leisure Centre, Ounsdale Road, Wombourne, West Midlands**
Central Promotions   *See display advertisement*

Nov 7   **CRAFT FAYRE/The Belgrave Hotel, Torquay, Devon**
Cherrycraft Fayres & Festivals

Nov 7   **CRAFT FAIR/Manorial Barn, Whiston, Rotherham, South Yorks**
Cottage Creations Craft Fairs

Nov 7   **COUNTRY LIVING STYLE, HOME, FASHION, GIFT, CRAFT & DESIGN SHOW/Savill Court, Savill Gardens, Englefield Green, Surrey**
Cottage Industry Shows

Nov 7   **CRAFT FAIR/Lacock Village Hall, Lacock, nr Chippenham, Wilts**
Countrycraft

Nov 7   **CRAFT FAIR/Village Hall, Lewes Road, Ditchling, nr Hassocks, West Sussex**
Craft Developments

Nov 7   **CRAFT FAIR/Village Hotel, Whiston, nr Prescot, Merseyside**
Creative Crafts Association   *See display advertisement*

Nov 7	**DOLLS, DOLLSHOUSES & MINIATURES SHOW/Hilton National Hotel, Grove Way, Milton Keynes (handmade British miniatures only)** Four Seasons Fairs
Nov 7	**CRAFT FAIR/Otford Village Memorial Hall, nr Sevenoaks, Kent** Goldfinch Crafts
Nov 7	**CRAFT FAIR/Mansfield Civic Centre, Chesterfield Road, Mansfield, Notts** Heathfield Craft Fairs
Nov 7	**CRAFT FAIR/The Jarvis International Hotel, Willerby, nr Hull, East Yorks** Holland Fairs
Nov 7	**CRAFT FAIR/Westland S&SC, Yeovil, Somerset** Kevin Murphy Craft Fairs
Nov 7	**CRAFT FAIR/Stone Manor Hotel, Stone, nr Kidderminster, Worcs** Laurel Crafts
Nov 7	**DOLLS HOUSES, DOLLS & MINIATURES FAIR/Royal Chace Hotel, The Ridgeway, Enfield, Middx** Quality Craft Fairs
Nov 7	**CRAFT FAIR/Durham County Cricket Club, Chester-le-Street, Co Durham** Quintet Promotions
Nov 7	**CRAFT FAIR/Southwater Village Centre, Southwater, Horsham, West Sussex** Southwater Promotions
Nov 7	**CRAFT FAIR/Pittville Pump Rooms, Cheltenham, Glos** Town & Country Craft Fairs
Nov 10-14 (provisional)	**THE 4TH COUNTRY LIVING CHRISTMAS FAIR/Business Design Centre, 52 Upper Street, Islington, London N1** The Country Living Fairs
Nov 11	**YORKRAFT FAIR/Wetherby Town Hall, Wetherby, West Yorks** Yorkraft Fairs
Nov 11-14	**CRAFTS ALIVE AT CHRISTMAS/National Exhibition Centre, Birmingham, West Midlands** ICHF Ltd
Nov 11-14	**CRAFTS FOR CHRISTMAS - YORKSHIRE/Great Yorkshire Showground, Hookstone Oval, Wetherby Road, Harrogate, North Yorks** Rural Crafts Association *See display advertisement*
Nov 11-14	**CRAFT FAIR/Garson Farm, West End Village, nr Esher, Surrey** VBR Crafts
Nov 12-14	**CRAFT FAYRE/Trentham Gardens, Stone Road (A34), Trentham, Stoke-on-Trent, Staffs** Cheshire Fayre *See display advertisement*
Nov 12-14	**GREAT THORPE PARK CHRISTMAS CRAFT FESTIVAL/Thorpe Park, nr Chertsey, Surrey** Four Seasons (Events) Ltd

Nov 12-14   **THE 2ND INTERNATIONAL MODEL BOAT SHOW/Warwickshire Exhibition Centre, The Fosse, Fosse Way, Leamington Spa**
Meridienne Exhibitions Ltd

Nov 13   **CRAFT & GIFT FAIR/The Harlington Centre, High Street, Fleet, Hants**
Aquarius Fairs

Nov 13   **CRAFT MARKET/Fisher Hall, Guildhall Place, Cambridge, Cambs**
Balthazar

Nov 13   **CRAFT FAIR/Corn Exchange, Melrose, Roxburghshire**
Border Fairs

Nov 13   **DOLL & TEDDY FAIR/Rivington Hall Barn, Horwich, nr Bolton, Lancs**
Brentwood Fairs

Nov 13   **CRAFT FAIR/Village Hall, Pagham Road, Pagham, nr Bognor Regis, West Sussex**
Craft Developments

Nov 13   **DUNSTABLE CRAFT MARKET/Methodist Church Hall, Ashton Square, Dunstable, Beds**
Dunstable Craft Market

Nov 13   **MOLE VALLEY CHRISTMAS CRAFT SHOW/Dorking Halls, Dorking, Surrey**
Jets Quality Craft Fairs

Nov 13   **CRAFT FAIR/Guildhall, Salisbury, Wilts**
Kevin Murphy Craft Fairs

Nov 13   **CRAFT FAIR/Market Hall, Abergavenny, Monmouthshire**
Monmouthshire County Council

Nov 13   **THE CITY OF WELLS 6TH ANNUAL CHRISTMAS CRAFT FAIR/Wells Town Hall, Wells, Somerset**
West Country Craft Fairs   *See display advertisement*

Nov 13-14   **CRAFT FAYRE/Blakemere Craft Centre, Chester Road, Sandiway, Northwich, Cheshire**
Blakemere Craft Centre   *See display advertisement*

Nov 13-14   **CRAFT FAIR/Brigade Hall, Bakewell, Derbys**
Cottage Creations Craft Fairs

Nov 13-14   **CRAFT, DESIGN & GIFT FAIR/Wyndley Garden Centre, Lichfield Road, Sutton Coldfield, West Midlands**
Cottage Industries Association   *See display advertisement*

Nov 13-14   **CHRISTMAS CRAFTS, GIFTS & FOOD FAIR/Tatton Park, Knutsford, Cheshire**
Countrywide Events

Nov 13-14   **CHRISTMAS CRAFTS AT POOLE ARTS CENTRE/Poole Arts Centre, Poole, Dorset**
Craft Carnival

Nov 13-14   **CRAFT FAIR/Lowther Pavilion, West Beach, Lytham, Lancs**
Creative Crafts Association   *See display advertisement*

Nov 13-14   **CRAFTS AT CHRISTMAS/Floors Castle, Kelso, Roxburghshire**
Dalesway Festivals Ltd   *See display advertisement*

Nov 13-14   **CHRISTMAS CRAFT FAIR/Kings Hall, Herne Bay, Kent**
East Kent Fairs   *See display advertisement*

Nov 13-14   **WHALLEY ABBEY CHRISTMAS FESTIVAL OF CRAFTS & FINE FOODS/**
Whalley, nr Clitheroe, Lancs
Jean Welch Shows   *See display advertisement*

Nov 13-14   **CRAFT FAIR/Racecourse, Newton Abbot, Devon**
Kevin Murphy Craft Fairs

Nov 13-14   **CHRISTMAS AT BROADLANDS/Broadlands, nr Romsey, Hants**
Living Heritage Craft Shows Ltd   *See display advertisement*

Nov 13-14   **CROYDON CRAFT WEEKEND/John Ruskin College, Selsdon Park Road,**
Selsdon, South Croydon, Surrey
Living Heritage Craft Shows Ltd   *See display advertisement*

Nov 13-14   **CRAFT FAIR/Newark Showground, Newark, Notts**
Rainbow Fair

Nov 13-14   **LIVE CRAFTS SHOW/Buckinghamshire College, Chalfont St Giles, Bucks**
The Exhibition Team Ltd   *See display advertisement*

Nov 13-14   **BUMPER CHRISTMAS FAIR/Towerlands Centre, Panfield Road, Braintree, Essex**
Towerlands Centre

Nov 14   **CRAFT FAIR/Congleton Town Hall, High Street, Congleton, Cheshire**
Archer Promotions

Nov 14   **DOLLS HOUSE & MINIATURE FAIR/Cresta Court Hotel, Altrincham, Cheshire**
Brentwood Fairs

Nov 14   **CRAFT SHOW/Morley Hayes, Morley, Derbys**
CFL Craft Shows

Nov 14   **CRAFT FAIR/The Arts Centre, Warwick University, Coventry, Warks**
Central Promotions   *See display advertisement*

Nov 14   **CRAFT, DESIGN & GIFT FAIR/Bromsgrove Market Hall, Worcs**
Cottage Industries Association   *See display advertisement*

Nov 14   **CRAFT FAIR/Lacock Village Hall, Lacock, nr Chippenham, Wilts**
Countrycraft

Nov 14   **DOLLS, DOLLSHOUSES & MINIATURES SHOW/Swallow Hotel, Old Shire**
Lane, Waltham Abbey (handmade British miniatures only)
Four Seasons Fairs

Nov 14   **CRAFT & GIFT FAIR/Barton Village Hall, nr Preston, Lancs**
Golden Age Fairs

Nov 14   **THE HORNCHURCH CRAFT FAIR/Harrow Lodge Park, Hornchurch Road,**
Hornchurch, Essex
Hallmark Fairs

Nov 14	**CHRISTMAS CRAFT FAIR/Jarvis International Hotel, Blackrod, nr Bolton, Lancs** Heritage Fairs
Nov 14	**ARTS & CRAFTS FAIR/Grassington Town Hall, Grassington, nr Skipton, North Yorks** Jean Bryon
Nov 14	**CRAFT & GIFT FAIR/Village Hotel, Otley Road, Leeds, West Yorks** Quality Craft & Gift Fairs *See display advertisement*
Nov 14	**CRAFT FAIR/The Library, Traps Hill, Loughton, Essex** Quality Craft Fairs
Nov 14	**CRAFT FAIR/Stakis Hotel, Coast Road, Wallsend, Tyne & Wear** Quintet Promotions
Nov 14	**THE ROYAL LEAMINGTON SPA CHRISTMAS CRAFT FAIR/Royal Spa Centre, Leamington Spa, Warks** West Country Craft Fairs *See display advertisement*
Nov 17	**CRAFT FAIR/Town Hall, Northallerton, North Yorks** Keld Craft Fairs
Nov 17	**CRAFT GUILD CHRISTMAS SHOPPING EVENT/Martin Mere Wildfowl & Wetlands Trust Centre, Burscough, nr Ormskirk, Lancs** The Craft Guild of West Lancashire
Nov 18-21	**THE COUNTRY STYLE FESTIVE FAIR/National Exhibition Centre, Birmingham, West Midlands** Orchard Events Ltd *See display advertisement*
Nov 18-21	**CRAFTS FOR CHRISTMAS - SOUTH OF ENGLAND/South of England Showground, Ardingly, nr Haywards Heath, West Sussex** Rural Crafts Association *See display advertisement*
Nov 18-Dec 6	**PLYMOUTH CHRISTMAS CRAFTS FESTIVAL/Armada Way, Plymouth, Devon (marquee)** Cherrycraft Fayres & Festivals
Nov 19-20	**ARTS & CRAFTS FAYRE/Winter Gardens, Weston-super-Mare, North Somerset** Fountain Fayres & Exhibitions
Nov 19-20	**CRAFT FAIR/Gateshead Central Library, Prince Consort Road, Gateshead, Tyne & Wear (evening only on Nov 19)** Gateshead Fairs
Nov 19-21	**STANSTED HOUSE HOME DESIGN & INTERIORS EXHIBITION/Rowland's Castle, Hants** Buckingham Publicity *See display advertisement*
Nov 19-21	**CRAFTS AT CHRISTMAS/Eastwood House, Giffnock, Glasgow** Dalesway Festivals Ltd *See display advertisement*
Nov 19-21	**DICKENSIAN CHRISTMAS CRAFT FAYRE/Transport Research Lab, Crowthorne, Berks** Four Seasons (Events) Ltd

Nov 19-21	**CRAFT IN ACTION SHOW/Lincolnshire Showground, Grange-de-Lings, nr Lincoln, Lincs** The Exhibition Team Ltd　　　*See display advertisement*
Nov 20	**CRAFT MARKET/Fisher Hall, Guildhall Place, Cambridge, Cambs** Balthazar
Nov 20	**CRAFT FAIR/Burgh Hall, Peebles** Border Fairs
Nov 20	**CRAFT FAIR/Village Hall, High Street, Henfield, West Sussex** Craft Developments
Nov 20	**ARTS & CRAFTS FAIR/Town Hall, Brackley, Northants** Falcon Fairs
Nov 20	**CRAFT FAIR/Bridport Arts Centre, Bridport, Dorset** J M Evans
Nov 20	**CRAFT FAIR/Lyndhurst Community Centre, Lyndhurst, Hants** Oakleaf Craft Fairs　　　*See display advertisement*
Nov 20	**DORCHESTER'S 5TH ANNUAL CHRISTMAS CRAFT FAIR/The Corn Exchange, Dorchester, Dorset** West Country Craft Fairs　　　*See display advertisement*
Nov 20-21	**CRAFT FAYRE/Balmer Lawn Hotel, Brockenhurst, Hants** Avocet Crafts
Nov 20-21	**CRAFT FAYRE/Blakemere Craft Centre, Chester Road, Sandiway, Northwich, Cheshire** Blakemere Craft Centre　　　*See display advertisement*
Nov 20-21	**CRAFT FAIR/Rivermead Complex, Richfield Avenue, Caversham, nr Reading, Berks** Cottage Craft Fairs　　　*See display advertisement*
Nov 20-21	**CRAFT, DESIGN & GIFT FAIR/Hurrans Garden Centre, West Hagley, nr Stourbridge, Worcs** Cottage Industries Association　　　*See display advertisement*
Nov 20-21	**THE CHRISTMAS GIFTS FAIR/Hagley Hall, nr Stourbridge, West Midlands** Countrywide Events
Nov 20-21	**CHRISTMAS CRAFT FAIR/Leisure Centre Sports Hall, Tenterden, Kent** East Kent Fairs　　　*See display advertisement*
Nov 20-21	**GORING CHRISTMAS CRAFT FAIR/Goring Village Hall, Bridge Approach, Goring-on-Thames, Oxon** Goring Christmas Craft Fair
Nov 20-21	**CHRISTMAS CRAFT WEEKEND/Ditchling Garden Centre, Ditchling, West Sussex** Jets Quality Craft Fairs
Nov 20-21	**CRAFT FAIR/St William's College, York, North Yorks** Keld Craft Fairs

Nov 20-21 **CRAFT FAIR/Wood Green Animal Shelters, Godmanchester, Cambs**
Kingfisher Promotions

Nov 20-21 **BRENTWOOD CRAFT WEEKEND/Shenfield Sports Centre, BrentwoodGreen, Essex**
Living Heritage Craft Shows Ltd   *See display advertisement*

Nov 20-21 **CHRISTMAS CRAFTS BY THE THAMES/Beale Park, Pangbourne, nr Reading, Berks**
Living Heritage Craft Shows Ltd   *See display advertisement*

Nov 20-21 **CRAFT FAIR/Victoria Hall, Bourton-on-the-Water, Glos**
M&B Crafts

Nov 20-21 **CRAFT FAIR/Tatton Park, Knutsford, Cheshire**
Oak Craft Fairs   *See display advertisement*

Nov 20-21 **CRAFT FAIR/Windsor Racecourse, Windsor, Berks**
Rainbow Fair

Nov 20-21 **ST IVES CHRISTMAS CRAFT FAIR/St Ivo Recreation Centre, St Ives, Cambs**
Romor Exhibitions Ltd   *See display advertisement*

Nov 20-21 **CHRISTMAS CRAFT FAIR/Springfields, Camelgate, Spalding, Lincs**
Springfields Exhibition Centre

Nov 20-21 **THE CRAFT MOVEMENT/Battersea Arts Centre, Battersea, London**
The Craft Movement

Nov 20-21 **ART IN CLAY SHOW/Farnham Maltings, Farnham, Surrey**
The Exhibition Team Ltd   *See display advertisement*

Nov 20-21 **LIVE CRAFTS SHOW/Buckinghamshire College, Chalfont St Giles, Bucks**
The Exhibition Team Ltd   *See display advertisement*

Nov 20-21 **CHRISTMAS CRAFT FAIR/Wimpole Hall, Arrington, nr Royston, Cambs**
The National Trust, Wimpole Hall

Nov 20-21 **THE SUSSEX GUILD CHRISTMAS CRAFT SHOW/Ditchling Village Hall, Lewes Road, Ditchling, West Sussex**
The Sussex Guild

Nov 20-21 **CRAFT FAIR/The Pavilion, Buxton, Derbys**
Town & Country Craft Fairs

Nov 20-21 **JUST ARTS & CRAFTS/Great Hall, Kempton Park Racecourse, Sunbury-on-Thames, Middx**
Traditional Crafts Ltd   *See display advertisement*

Nov 20-21 **FORT BROCKHURST CRAFT FAYRE/nr Fareham, Hants**
Woodland Crafts   *See display advertisement*

Nov 20-21 **CRAFT FAIR/Pavilion Theatre, Worthing, West Sussex**
Worthing Leisure

Nov 21 **CRAFT FAIR/Manor House Hotel, Audley Road, Alsager, Staffs**
Archer Promotions

Nov 21	**CRAFT FAIR/The Pemberton Centre, Rushden, Northants** Cambridge Craft Fairs
Nov 21	**CRAFT FAIR/The Tower Suite, Drayton Manor Park, Tamworth, Staffs** Central Promotions *See display advertisement*
Nov 21	**CRAFT FAIR/Aston Hall, Aston, Sheffield, South Yorks** Cottage Creations Craft Fairs
Nov 21	**CRAFT & DESIGN SHOW/Manor Country House Hotel, Newlands Corner, Surrey** Cottage Industry Shows
Nov 21	**CRAFT FAIR/Lacock Village Hall, Lacock, nr Chippenham, Wilts** Countrycraft
Nov 21	**CRAFT FAIR/Park Royal International Hotel, Stretton, Warrington, Cheshire** Creative Crafts Association *See display advertisement*
Nov 21	**DOLL FAIR/Aylestone Leisure Centre, Leicester, Leics** East Midlands Doll Fairs
Nov 21	**CRAFT FAIR/Chelsea Town Hall, Kings Road, Chelsea, London** Eden Crafts
Nov 21	**ARTS & CRAFTS FAIR/Woburn Village Hall, Woburn, Beds** Falcon Fairs
Nov 21	**ANTIQUES, CRAFTS & COLLECTABLES FAIR/The Parish Hall, Culcheth, nr Warrington, Cheshire** Gem Fairs
Nov 21	**CRAFT FAIR/Great Danes Hotel, Hollingbourne, nr Leeds, West Yorks** Goldfinch Crafts
Nov 21	**CHRISTMAS CRAFT FAIR/Norton Grange, Castleton, nr Rochdale, Lancs** Heritage Fairs
Nov 21	**CHRISTMAS CRAFTS/Jarvis Penns Hall Hotel, Sutton Coldfield, West Midlands** Hobby Horse Design & Craft Fairs
Nov 21	**CRAFT FAIR/The Country Park Inn, Hessle Foreshore, nr Hull, East Yorks** Holland Fairs
Nov 21	**CRAFT FAIR/Much Hadham Village Hall, nr Ware, Herts** Isabel Hospice Craft Fairs
Nov 21	**CRAFT FAIR/Exmouth Pavilion, Exmouth, Devon** J M Evans
Nov 21	**CRAFT FAIR/Scotch Horn Centre, Nailsea, Bristol** Kevin Murphy Craft Fairs
Nov 21	**CRAFT FAIR/Village Hall, Lane End, nr High Wycombe, Bucks** Lane End Craft Fair
Nov 21	**ARTS & CRAFTS SHOW/Lauderdale House, Highgate Hill, London N6** Lauderdale Arts & Crafts

| Nov 21 | **CRAFT FAIR/The Heath Hotel, Bewdley, Worcs** |
| | Laurel Crafts |

| Nov 21 | **CRAFT & GIFT FAIR/Ramside Hall Hotel, Carrville, Co Durham** |
| | Quality Craft & Gift Fairs | *See display advertisement* |

| Nov 21 | **CRAFT FAIR/Royal Chace Hotel, The Ridgeway, Enfield, Middx** |
| | Quality Craft Fairs |

| Nov 21 | **CRAFT FAIR/Hallgarth Manor, Pittington, Co Durham** |
| | Quintet Promotions |

| Nov 21 | **DOLLS HOUSE FAIR/Plinston Hall, Letchworth, Herts** |
| | R J Exhibitions |

| Nov 21 | **CRAFT & GIFT FAYRE/Hilton National, Portsmouth, Hants** |
| | Something Special Craft & Gift Fayres |

| Nov 24 | **CRAFT FAYRE/Craft Centre, Chester Road, Sandiway, Northwich, Cheshire** |
| | Blakemere Craft Centre | *See display advertisement* |

| Nov 25-28 | **LIVE CRAFTS SHOW/Loseley House, Compton, nr Guildford, Surrey** |
| | The Exhibition Team Ltd | *See display advertisement* |

| Nov 26-28 | **BRANCEPETH CASTLE CHRISTMAS CRAFT FAIR/Brancepeth Castle, 4 miles west of Durham City on A690** |
| | Brancepeth Castle Craft Fairs |

| Nov 26-28 | **FAWLEY COURT HOME DESIGN & INTERIORS EXHIBITION/Fawley, nr Henley-on-Thames, Oxon** |
| | Buckingham Publicity | *See display advertisement* |

| Nov 26-28 | **CRAFTS AT CHRISTMAS/Harewood House, Leeds, West Yorks** |
| | Dalesway Festivals Ltd | *See display advertisement* |

| Nov 26-28 | **DICKENSIAN CHRISTMAS CRAFT FAYRE/Alton Towers, Staffs** |
| | Four Seasons (Events) Ltd |

| Nov 26-28 | **CRAFTS ALIVE & CREATIVE STITCHES/Cardiff International Arena** |
| | ICHF Ltd |

| Nov 26-28 | **CRAFT FAIR/St William's College, York, North Yorks** |
| | Keld Craft Fairs |

| Nov 26-28 | **DERBY CRAFT WEEKEND/Assembly Rooms, Market Place, Derby, Derbys** |
| | Living Heritage Craft Shows Ltd | *See display advertisement* |

| Nov 26-28 | **CRAFTS FOR CHRISTMAS - THREE COUNTIES/Three Counties Showground, Malvern, Worcs** |
| | Rural Crafts Association | *See display advertisement* |

| Nov 26-28 (provisional) | **THE HEREFORD CONTEMPORARY CRAFT FAIR/The Courtyard, Centre for the Arts, Edgar Street, Hereford HR4 9JR** |
| | Herefordshire Council |

| Nov 27 | **CRAFT MARKET/Fisher Hall, Guildhall Place, Cambridge, Cambs** |
| | Balthazar |

Nov 27   **DOLLSHOUSE, MINIATURES, TEDDY & DOLL FAIR/Arts Centre, Vane Terrace, Darlington, Co Durham**
Caile Fairs

Nov 27   **CRAFT FAIR/Adastra Hall, Keymer Road, Hassocks, West Sussex**
Craft Developments

Nov 27   **DULWICH CRAFT FAIR/St Barnabas Hall, Dulwich, London SE21**
Dulwich Craft Fairs   *See display advertisement*

Nov 27   **CRAFT FAYRE/St Mary's Centre, Grassmere Close, Felpham, nr Bognor Regis, West Sussex**
Good Ideas Craft Fayres

Nov 27   **CRAFT FAIR/Pavilion, Weymouth, Dorset**
Kevin Murphy Craft Fairs

Nov 27   **CHRISTMAS CRAFT FAIR/Nantwich Civic Hall, Market Street, Nantwich, Cheshire**
Stancie Kutler Crafts

Nov 27   **THE BATH 3RD ANNUAL CHRISTMAS CRAFT FAIR/St Gregory's School, Bath**
West Country Craft Fairs   *See display advertisement*

Nov 27   **CRAFT & GIFT FAIR/Barnet Library, Stapylton Road, Barnet, Herts**
Marie Margaret Promotions

Nov 27-28   **CRAFT FAYRE/Blakemere Craft Centre, Chester Road, Sandiway, Northwich, Cheshire**
Blakemere Craft Centre   *See display advertisement*

Nov 27-28   **CRAFT FAIR/The Ingestre Suite, County Showground, Weston Road, Stafford, Staffs**
Central Promotions   *See display advertisement*

Nov 27-28   **CRAFT FAYRE/Quarry Bank Mill, Styal, Cheshire**
Cheshire Fayre   *See display advertisement*

Nov 27-28   **CRAFT FAIR/Brigade Hall, Bakewell, Derbys**
Cottage Creations Craft Fairs

Nov 27-28   **CRAFT, DESIGN & GIFT FAIR/Wyndley Garden Centre, Warwick Road, Knowle, Warks**
Cottage Industries Association   *See display advertisement*

Nov 27-28   **THE CHRISTMAS GIFTS FAIR/Capesthorne Hall, nr Macclesfield, Cheshire**
Countrywide Events

Nov 27-28   **CHRISTMAS CRAFT FAIR/RHS Rosemoor Garden, Torrington, Devon**
Creativity

Nov 27-28   **CHRISTMAS CRAFT FAIR/Woodville Halls, Gravesend, Kent**
East Kent Fairs   *See display advertisement*

Nov 27-28   **CHRISTMAS CRAFTS/Solihull College, Solihull, West Midlands**
Hobby Horse Design & Craft Fairs

| Nov 27-28 | **YORKSHIRE CHRISTMAS FESTIVAL OF CRAFTS & FINE FOODS/ Knavesmere Suite, York Race Course, North Yorks** |
| | Jean Welch Shows *See display advertisement* |

Nov 27-28   **YORKSHIRE CHRISTMAS FESTIVAL OF CRAFTS & FINE FOODS/ Knavesmere Suite, York Race Course, North Yorks**
Jean Welch Shows   *See display advertisement*

Nov 27-28   **NATIONAL CHRISTMAS LACEMAKER'S FAIR/National Exhibition Centre, Birmingham, West Midlands**
John & Jennifer Ford

Nov 27-28   **CHRISTMAS CRAFTS AT KNEBWORTH/Knebworth House & Gardens, Junction 7 A1M, Stevenage, Herts**
Living Heritage Craft Shows Ltd   *See display advertisement*

Nov 27-28   **MEDIEVAL CHRISTMAS IN LUDLOW/Ludlow Castle, Ludlow, Salop   (provisional title)**
Ludlow Castle Festival of Crafts

Nov 27-28   **CRAFT FAIR/Queens Hall, Corn Exchange, High Street, Rochester, Kent**
M B County Fairs

Nov 27-28   **YULETIDE CRAFT FESTIVAL/Ragley Hall, Alcester, Warks**
MGA Fairs   *See display advertisement*

Nov 27-28   **CRAFT FAIR/Newstead Abbey, Mansfield, Notts**
Oak Craft Fairs   *See display advertisement*

Nov 27-28   **CRAFT & GIFT FAYRE/Ferneham Hall, Fareham, Hants**
Something Special Craft & Gift Fayres

Nov 27-28   **VICTORIAN CHRISTMAS/Southend-on-Sea, Essex**
Special Events - Southend Borough Council

Nov 27-28   **JUST ARTS & CRAFTS/Chatham Historic Dockyard, Chatham, Kent**
Traditional Crafts Ltd   *See display advertisement*

Nov 27-Dec 23 **CARDIFF AT CHRISTMAS CRAFT FESTIVAL/St John's Square,Cardiff**
(provisional)   Craft*Folk

Nov 28   **CRAFT FAIR/Spelthorne Leisure Centre, Knowle Green, Staines, Middx**
Cottage Craft Fairs   *See display advertisement*

Nov 28   **CRAFT FAIR/Lacock Village Hall, Lacock, nr Chippenham, Wilts**
Countrycraft

Nov 28   **CRAFT FAIR/Lancaster University Conference Centre, Lancs**
Creative Crafts Association   *See display advertisement*

Nov 28   **ARTS & CRAFTS FAIR/British Wheelchair Sports Foundation, Stoke Mandeville, Bucks**
Falcon Fairs

Nov 28   **CHRISTMAS CRAFT FAIR/Leisure Centre, Bepton Road, Midhurst, West Sussex**
Grange Craft Fairs

Nov 28   **CRAFT FAIR/Courage Hall, Brentwood Boys School, Middleton Hall Lane, Brentwood, Essex**
Hallmark Fairs

Nov 28	**CRAFT FAIR/Dunkenhalgh Hotel, Clayton-le-Moors, nr Accrington, Lancs** Heritage Fairs
Nov 28	**ARTS & CRAFTS FAIR/Ripley Town Hall, Ripley, nr Harrogate, North Yorks** Jean Bryon
Nov 28	**CRAFT FAIR/North Devon College, Barnstaple, Devon** Kevin Murphy Craft Fairs
Nov 28	**CRAFT & GIFT FAIR/St George Swallow Hotel, Harrogate, North Yorks** Quality Craft & Gift Fairs *See display advertisement*
Nov 28	**CRAFT FAIR/The Manor Hall, Manor Road, Chigwell, Essex** Quality Craft Fairs
Nov 28	**CRAFT FAIR/Holiday Inn, Seaton Burn, nr Newcastle upon Tyne, Tyne & Wear** Quintet Promotions
Nov 28	**CRAFTS FOR CHRISTMAS AT ST DONAT'S CASTLE/St Donat's, nr Llantwit Major, South Glam** St Donats Arts Centre
Nov 28	**THE STRATFORD-UPON-AVON 3RD ANNUAL CHRISTMAS CRAFT FAIR/ Royal Shakespeare Theatre, Stratford-upon-Avon, Warks** West Country Craft Fairs *See display advertisement*
Nov 28	**CRAFT FAIR/Longfield Suite, Prestwich, Manchester** West Pennine Promotions
Dec 1-3	**VICTORIAN CHRISTMAS EVENINGS AT AVONCROFT MUSEUM/ Bromsgrove, Worcs** Hobby Horse Design & Craft Fairs
Dec 2	**LATE NIGHT CRAFT FAIR/Village Hall, Lewes Road, Ditchling, nr Hassocks, West Sussex** Craft Developments
Dec 2	**CRAFT GUILD CHRISTMAS SHOPPING EVENT/Martin Mere Wildfowl & Wetlands Trust Centre, Burscough, nr Ormskirk, Lancs** The Craft Guild of West Lancashire
Dec 3-4	**CRAFT FAIR/Kensington Town Hall, Hornton Street, London W8** Eden Crafts
Dec 3-5	**CHRISTMAS CRAFT & GIFT FAIR/Purbeck and Tregonwell Halls, Bourne- mouth International Centre, Dorset** BIC Exhibitions
Dec 3-5	**DICKENSIAN CHRISTMAS CRAFT FAYRE/Heritage Museum, Gaydon, Warks** Four Seasons (Events) Ltd
Dec 3-5	**CHRISTMAS SHOPPING FAYRE/Westpoint, Exeter, Devon** Grandstand Events Ltd
Dec 3-5	**CRAFT FAIR/St William's College, York, North Yorks** Keld Craft Fairs

Dec 3-5	**THE ALEXANDRA PALACE CHRISTMAS CRAFT FAIR/THE FESTIVE TABLE/ Alexandra Palace, North London**	
	Marathon Event Management Ltd	*See display advertisement*
Dec 3-5	**CRAFTS FOR CHRISTMAS - WEST COUNTRY/Bath & West Showground, Shepton Mallet, Somerset**	
	Rural Crafts Association	*See display advertisement*
Dec 3-5	**THE CRAFT MOVEMENT/Queen Charlotte Hall, Richmond, Surrey**	
	The Craft Movement	
Dec 3-5	**LIVE CRAFTS SHOW/Highclere Castle, nr Newbury, Berks**	
	The Exhibition Team Ltd	*See display advertisement*
Dec 3-5	**FORT PURBROOK CRAFT FAYRE/Portsdown Hill, Cosham, Portsmouth, Hants**	
	Woodland Crafts	*See display advertisement*
Dec 3-12	**SWANSEA CHRISTMAS STREET MARKET/Swansea, West Glam**	
	Wales Craft Council	
Dec 3-23 (provisional)	**CRAFT & GIFT MARKET/Old Market Square, Nottingham, Notts**	
	Nottingham City Council	
Dec 4	**CRAFT MARKET/Fisher Hall, Guildhall Place, Cambridge, Cambs**	
	Balthazar	
Dec 4	**CRAFT FAIR/Corn Exchange, Haddington, East Lothian**	
	Border Fairs	
Dec 4	**CRAFT FAIR/Community Centre, Pond Road, Shoreham-by-Sea, West Sussex**	
	Craft Developments	
Dec 4	**ARTS & CRAFTS FAYRE/Creech Castle, Bathpool, Taunton, Somerset**	
	Fountain Fayres & Exhibitions	
Dec 4	**CRAFT FAIR/Bridport Arts Centre, Bridport, Dorset**	
	J M Evans	
Dec 4	**CRAFT & GIFT FAIR/Barnet Library, Stapylton Road, Barnet, Herts**	
	Marie Margaret Promotions	
Dec 4	**CRAFT FAIR/The Castle Hall, Hertford, Herts**	
	Quality Craft Fairs	
Dec 4	**HADDENHAM FESTIVAL & CRAFT FAYRE/Haddenham Village Hall, Church Way, Haddenham, Bucks**	
	R J Heydon	
Dec 4	**ART & CRAFT FAIR/The Arts Centre, Biddick Lane, Fatfield, Washington, Tyne & Wear**	
	The Arts Centre	
Dec 4	**LYME REGIS CHRISTMAS CRAFT FAIR/Marine Theatre, Lyme Regis, Dorset**	
	West Country Craft Fairs	*See display advertisement*
Dec 4-5	**CRAFT FAYRE/Park Farm Garden Centre, Landford, Salisbury, Wilts**	
	Avocet Crafts	

Dec 4-5	**CRAFT FAYRE/Blakemere Craft Centre, Chester Road, Sandiway, Northwich, Cheshire**
	Blakemere Craft Centre *See display advertisement*

Dec 4-5	**GOODWOOD CHRISTMAS CRAFT & GIFT FAYRE/Goodwood, nr Chichester, West Sussex**
	Buckingham Publicity *See display advertisement*

Dec 4-5	**CRAFT FAYRE/Fenton Manor, Fenton, Stoke-on-Trent, Staffs**
	Cheshire Fayre *See display advertisement*

Dec 4-5	**CRAFT, DESIGN & GIFT FAIR/Jardinerie Garden Place, Kenilworth Road (A452), Hampton-in-Arden, West Midlands**
	Cottage Industries Association *See display advertisement*

Dec 4-5	**CRAFT FAIR/Haydock Park Racecourse Exhibition Centre, St Helens, Merseyside**
	Creative Crafts Association *See display advertisement*

Dec 4-5	**CHRISTMAS CRAFT FAIR/Town Hall, Dover, Kent**
	East Kent Fairs *See display advertisement*

Dec 4-5	**HARROGATE CHRISTMAS FESTIVAL OF CRAFTS & FINE FOODS/Crown Hotel, Harrogate, North Yorks**
	Jean Welch Shows *See display advertisement*

Dec 4-5	**CRAFT FAIR/Wyvern Hall, Swallows Leisure Centre, Central Avenue, Sittingbourne, Kent**
	M B County Fairs

Dec 4-5	**CRAFT FAIR/Lyndhurst Community Centre, Lyndhurst, Hants**
	Oakleaf Craft Fairs *See display advertisement*

Dec 4-5	**CRAFT FAIR/Sandringham Park, Norfolk**
	Rainbow Fair

Dec 4-5	**VICTORIAN CHRISTMAS CRAFT FAIR/The Argory, Derrycaw Road, Moy, Dungannon, Co Armagh**
	The National Trust, The Argory

Dec 4-5	**JUST ARTS & CRAFTS/Rosebery Suites, Epsom Racecourse, Epsom, Surrey**
	Traditional Crafts Ltd *See display advertisement*

Dec 4-5 (provisional)	**RICHMOND FELLOWSHIP CRAFT FAIR/8 Addison Road, London W14**
	Richmond Fellowship Craft Fair

Dec 4-12	**BRITISH CRAFTS SHOWCASE AT L'ARTIGIANATO MILAN EXHIBITION/ Fiera Milano, Milano, ITALY**
	Rural Crafts Association *See display advertisement*

Dec 5	**CRAFT FAIR/Northwood Stadium, Keelings Road, Northwood, nr Hanley, Stoke-on-Trent, Staffs**
	Archer Promotions

Dec 5	**CHRISTMAS CRAFT SHOW/The Belfry, Wishaw, Sutton Coldfield, West Midlands**
	CFL Craft Shows

Dec 5	**CRAFT FAIR/The Moat House Hotel, M54 Junction 5, Telford, Salop**
	Central Promotions *See display advertisement*

Dec 5   **CRAFT FAIR/The Moat House Hotel, M54 Junction 5, Telford, Salop**
Central Promotions *See display advertisement*

Dec 5   **CRAFT FAIR/Loddon Valley Leisure Centre, Chalfont Way, Lower Earley, nr Reading, Berks**
Cottage Craft Fairs *See display advertisement*

Dec 5   **CRAFT FAIR/Keresforth Hall, Barnsley, South Yorks**
Cottage Creations Craft Fairs

Dec 5   **CRAFT FAIR/Lacock Village Hall, Lacock, nr Chippenham, Wilts**
Countrycraft

Dec 5   **CHRISTMAS CRAFT FAIR/Kings of Wessex School, Cheddar, Somerset**
Creativity

Dec 5   **ARTS & CRAFTS FAIR/Bushey Hall School, Bushey, Herts**
Falcon Fairs

Dec 5   **CRAFT FAIR/Beaumanor Hall, Woodhouse Eaves, nr Loughborough, Leics**
Heathfield Craft Fairs

Dec 5   **CHRISTMAS CRAFT FAIR/Gargrave Village Hall, Gargrave, nr Skipton, North Yorks**
Heritage Fairs

Dec 5   **CRAFT FAIR/Beverley Leisure Centre, Flemingate (opposite Army Museum), Beverley, East Yorks**
Holland Fairs

Dec 5   **CRAFT FAIR/Leisure Centre, Chepstow, Gwent**
Kevin Murphy Craft Fairs

Dec 5   **CRAFT FAIR/Hinchingbrooke House, Huntingdon, Cambs**
Kingfisher Promotions

Dec 5   **CRAFT FAIR/Stone Manor Hotel, Stone, nr Kidderminster, Worcs**
Laurel Crafts

Dec 5   **CRAFT FAIR/The Bellhouse Hotel, Oxford Road (A40), Beaconsfield, Bucks**
Midas Fairs

Dec 5   **CRAFT FAIR/Royal Chace Hotel, The Ridgeway, Enfield, Middx**
Quality Craft Fairs

Dec 5   **CRAFT FAIR/Friendly Hotel, West Boldon, Tyne & Wear**
Quintet Promotions

Dec 5   **THE NEW FOREST 4TH ANNUAL CHRISTMAS CRAFT FAIR/Lyndhurst Park Hotel, Lyndhurst, Hants**
West Country Craft Fairs *See display advertisement*

Dec 6   **TIVERTON CRAFT FAIR/The Pannier Market, Tiverton, Devon**
Tiverton Craft Fair

Dec 6-8   **CRAFT MARKET/Fisher Hall, Guildhall Place, Cambridge, Cambs**
Balthazar

Dec 7   **RURAL CRAFTS ASSOCIATION AT THE ROYAL WELSH WINTER FAIR/**
Royal Welsh Showground, Llanelwedd, Builth Wells, Powys
Rural Crafts Association   *See display advertisement*

Dec 10-11   **DISS CHRISTMAS CRAFT FAIR/Corn Hall, Market Hill, Diss, Norfolk**
Four Seasons Fairs

Dec 10-12   **CRAFTS FOR CHRISTMAS/Blickling Hall, Blickling, nr Norwich, Norfolk**
Eastern Events Ltd   *See display advertisement*

Dec 11   **CRAFT & GIFT FAIR/The Harlington Centre, High Street, Fleet, Hants**
Aquarius Fairs

Dec 11   **CRAFT MARKET/Fisher Hall, Guildhall Place, Cambridge, Cambs**
Balthazar

Dec 11   **CRAFT FAYRE/The Town Hall, Torquay, Devon**
Cherrycraft Fayres & Festivals

Dec 11   **DULWICH CRAFT FAIR/St Barnabas Hall, Dulwich, London SE21**
Dulwich Craft Fairs

Dec 11   **CRAFT MARKET/Methodist Church Hall, Ashton Square, Dunstable, Beds**
Dunstable Craft Market

Dec 11   **CHRISTMAS CRAFT FAIR/Guildhall, Sandwich, Kent**
East Kent Fairs   *See display advertisement*

Dec 11   **ARTS & CRAFTS FAIR/Town Hall, Towcester, Northants**
Falcon Fairs

Dec 11   **ARTS & CRAFTS FAYRE/Somerset Hall, Portishead, nr Bristol**
Fountain Fayres & Exhibitions

Dec 11   **CRAFTS & COLLECTABLES FAIR/ Parish Hall, Culcheth, nr Warrington, Cheshire**
Gem Fairs

Dec 11   **CRAFT FAIR/Bridport Arts Centre, Bridport, Dorset**
J M Evans

Dec 11   **CRAFT FAIR/Exmouth Pavilion, Exmouth, Devon**
J M Evans

Dec 11   **MID SUSSEX CRAFT SHOW/Clair Hall, Sussex**
Jets Quality Craft Fairs

Dec 11   **CRAFT FAIR/Guildhall, Plymouth, Devon**
Kevin Murphy Craft Fairs

Dec 11   **CRAFT & GIFT FAIR/Barnet Library, Stapylton Road, Barnet, Herts**
Marie Margaret Promotions

Dec 11   **CRAFT FAIR/Market Hall, Abergavenny, Monmouthshire**
Monmouthshire County Council

Dec 11-12   **CRAFT FAYRE/ Craft Centre, Chester Road, Sandiway, Northwich, Cheshire**
Blakemere Craft Centre   *See display advertisement*

| Dec 11-12 | **CRAFT FAIR/Brigade Hall, Bakewell, Derbys** |
| | Cottage Creations Craft Fairs |

Dec 11-12   **CRAFT FAIR/Brigade Hall, Bakewell, Derbys**
Cottage Creations Craft Fairs

Dec 11-12   **CRAFT, DESIGN & GIFT FAIR/Dobbies Gardening World, A5, Penkridge, nr Cannock, Staffs**
Cottage Industries Association   *See display advertisement*

Dec 11-12   **CRAFT FAIR/St William's College, York, North Yorks**
Keld Craft Fairs

Dec 11-12   **CRAFT FAIR/Ely Maltings, Ely, Cambs**
Kingfisher Promotions

Dec 11-12   **CRAFT FAIR/Sevenoaks Community Centre, Otford Road, Sevenoaks, Kent**
M B County Fairs

Dec 11-12   **CRAFT FAIR/The Pavilion, Buxton, Derbys**
Town & Country Craft Fairs

Dec 12   **CRAFT FAIR/Leisure Centre, Thames Drive, Biddulph, Staffs**
Archer Promotions

Dec 12   **CRAFT FAIR/Community Centre, Kinver, nr Stourbridge, West Midlands**
Central Promotions   *See display advertisement*

Dec 12   **CRAFT FAIR/Kingfisher Hotel, Wall Heath, nr Kingswinford, West Midlands**
Central Promotions   *See display advertisement*

Dec 12   **CRAFT FAIR/Rivermead Complex, Richfield Avenue, Caversham, Reading, Berks**
Cottage Craft Fairs   *See display advertisement*

Dec 12   **CRAFT FAIR/Lacock Village Hall, Lacock, nr Chippenham, Wilts**
Countrycraft

Dec 12   **CRAFT FAIR/Altrincham Leisure Centre, Altrincham, Cheshire**
Creative Crafts Association   *See display advertisement*

Dec 12   **CRAFT FAIR/The Platform, Morecambe, Lancs**
Creative Crafts Association   *See display advertisement*

Dec 12   **CRAFT & GIFT FAIR/Barton Village Hall, nr Preston, Lancs**
Golden Age Fairs

Dec 12   **CRAFT FAIR/Elvaston Castle, Borrowash, Derbys**
Heathfield Craft Fairs

Dec 12   **CRAFT FAIR/Chase Hotel, Ross-on-Wye, Herefordshire**
Kevin Murphy Craft Fairs

Dec 12   **CRAFT FAIR/Victoria Hall, Bourton-on-the-Water, Glos**
M&B Crafts

Dec 12   **CRAFT FAIR/Market Hall, Abergavenny, Monmouthshire**
Monmouthshire County Council

Dec 12   **CRAFT & GIFT FAIR/Hilton National, Garforth, Leeds, West Yorks**
Quality Craft & Gift Fairs   *See display advertisement*

Dec 12 **CRAFT FAIR/Park Hotel, Seafront, Tynemouth, Tyne & Wear**
Quintet Promotions

Dec 13-15 **CRAFT MARKET/Fisher Hall, Guildhall Place, Cambridge, Cambs**
Balthazar

Dec 15 **CRAFT FAYRE/Craft Centre, Chester Road, Sandiway, Northwich, Cheshire**
Blakemere Craft Centre   *See display advertisement*

Dec 15 **CRAFT FAIR/Town Hall, Northallerton, North Yorks**
Keld Craft Fairs

Dec 16-24 **CRAFTS AT CROYDON CHRISTMAS FESTIVITIES/High Street, Croydon, Surrey**
Eden Crafts

Dec 18 **CRAFT MARKET/Fisher Hall, Guildhall Place, Cambridge, Cambs**
Balthazar

Dec 18 **CRAFT FAIR/Burgh Hall, Peebles**
Border Fairs

Dec 18 **ARTS & CRAFTS FAIR/Town Hall, Brackley, Northants**
Falcon Fairs

Dec 18 **ART & CRAFT FAIR/The Arts Centre, Biddick Lane, Fatfield, Washington,**
(provisional) **Tyne & Wear**
The Arts Centre

Dec 18-19 **CRAFT FAYRE/Craft Centre, Chester Road, Sandiway, Northwich, Cheshire**
Blakemere Craft Centre   *See display advertisement*

Dec 18-19 **CRAFT FAIR/Guildhall, Salisbury, Wilts**
Kevin Murphy Craft Fairs

Dec 19 **CRAFT FAIR/Whitchurch Leisure Centre, High Street, Whitchurch, Salop**
Archer Promotions

Dec 19 **CRAFT FAIR/The Pemberton Centre, Rushden, Northants**
Cambridge Craft Fairs

Dec 19 **CRAFT FAIR/The Town Hall, Crown Centre, Stourbridge, West Midlands**
Central Promotions   *See display advertisement*

Dec 19 **CRAFT FAIR/Olde House Trading Post, Chesterfield, Derbys**
Cottage Creations Craft Fairs

Dec 19 **ARTS & CRAFTS FAIR/Woburn Village Hall, Woburn, Beds**
Falcon Fairs

Dec 19 **ARTS & CRAFTS SHOW/Lauderdale House, Highgate Hill, London N6**
Lauderdale Arts & Crafts

Dec 19 **CRAFT & GIFT FAIR/Pudsey Civic Hall, nr Leeds, West Yorks**
Quality Craft & Gift Fairs   *See display advertisement*

Dec 20-24 **CRAFT MARKET/Fisher Hall, Guildhall Place, Cambridge, Cambs**
Balthazar

ALTERNATIVE CRAFT MARKETING OPTIONS

This section highlights a range of different craft marketing opportunities which do not lend themselves to inclusion in the main event calendar as detailed on the preceding pages. Contact telephone numbers are given here, but full details on the firms and organisations mentioned below can be found in the appropriate section, beginning on page XXX. All charges quoted here are net of VAT unless otherwise stated.

A&J FAIRS Tel: 01705 427373

A&J specialises in week-long craft fairs in shopping centres and already has firm dates for nearly 70 such events taking place right through 1999. The shopping centres chosen by A&J for 1999 are: Chequers, Maidstone, Kent; Belfry, Redhill, Surrey; Cascades, Portsmouth, Hants; Fareham Shopping Centre, Hants; Meridian, Havant, Hants; Port Solent Shopping Centre, Hants; and Royal Priors, Leamington Spa, Warks.

Chequers dominates this programme with 26 weeks, and then Port Solent (14), Belfry (7), Meridian (6), Fareham (6), Cascades (5) and Royal Priors (4). The Fareham programme, however, is subject to confirmation. Approximately 12 sites are available at each event at an average price of £185 per week. Exhibitors new to A&J need to send in photographs. Details from Alice or John O'Farrell.

ABERYSTWYTH ARTS CENTRE Tel: 01970 622895/622887

Exhibitions of contemporary art and craft are held throughout the year, in addition to which there is a theatre, craft shop, bookshop and cafe. The centre also holds concerts, courses and activities. The main gallery, craft shop, foyer, cafe and special Ceramic Series exhibitions are open Monday to Saturday from 10am-5pm.

The centre traditionally stages a Christmas Craft Fair, held in the foyer gallery, which runs from the second week in November right through until the last open day before christmas. There are usually around 80 craftspeople with work for sale.

AMBERLEY MUSEUM Tel: 01798 831370

Based mid-way between Arundel and Storrington in West Sussex, this working museum has a resident team of craftspeople who can be seen exercising time-honoured skills on every day of its season. Using traditional materials and tools, they produce a range of fine wares, while the museum offers a base from which they earn their living and keep their trades alive.

In addition to its regular activities, the museum runs a programme of special events and in 1998 this included a woodworking show in the autumn. Crafts are on sale throughout the season. More information from Shirley Fagg.

ANGEL ROW GALLERY Tel: 0115 947 6334

Sited in the Central Library Building in Nottingham, Angel Row Gallery sells a variety of contemporary craft throughout the year. All exhibitors are chosen by the Crafts and Exhibitions Officers. At Christmas they usually have a bigger selling show; again, all work is chosen by the officers. Makers and designers who wish to have their work considered for display/sale in the gallery should send slides, CV and personal statement. More details from Stephanie Potts.

ARCHER PROMOTIONS Fax: 01782 827718

In addition to the craft fairs held in the Stoke-on-Trent area and in Congleton (detailed in the previous section), Archer Promotions also holds a Craft and Collectors market in the Market Square, Leek, Staffs each and every Saturday throughout the year. Bookings taken each week. Speak to Kevin Harper.

BLACKTHORPE BARN CRAFTS MARKETS Tel: 01359 271203

These are held in Rougham, nr Bury St Edmunds, Suffolk at a cost of around £35 per day. Around 50 sites are available at each event, which feature quality crafts only. Exhibitors new to Blackthorpe need to send in photographs. No other details for 1999 were to hand at the time of going to press. Up-to-date information can be obtained from Katie Millard.

BOTANY BAY VILLAGES Tel: 01257 261220

A sympathetically restored 150,000 square foot mill adjacent to Junction 8 of the M61 in Chorley, Lancs, this complex is described as a unique and unusual shopping and leisure experience, spread over five themed floors. Botany Bay offers individual retail units and professional sales staff to sell on makers' behalf.

There is free TV, radio and press advertising, 24-hour CCTV and car parking. There are five million adults within one hour's drive and there are regular coach parties, on-site restaurants and a children's play centre. Craft units are available from £21 per week, fully inclusive of business rates and service charge. Details available from Tom Morgan.

BROAD STREET MALL Tel: 0118 957 6633

Broad Street Mall in Reading, Berks has two craft barrows available on a weekly basis throughout the year. Approximate cost is £35 per day, with extra charged for the barrow itself and provision of electricity, if required. Exhibitors new to Broad Street Mall need to send in photographs. Details from Carole Kirk.

CAMDEN LOCK MARKET Tel: 0171 284 2084

The original art and craft market at Camden, set in picturesque canal-side surroundings. World famous for funky fashion, arts and crafts.

The market is open seven days a week and stall rents are charged at £8 Monday-Wednesday for stalls inside and £7 for outside; £9 inside and £8 outside Thursday and Friday; £31 inside and £27 outside on Saturday; and £45 inside and £38 outside on Sunday. For turn-up, trading times and other details, contact Allan, Barney or Eamon.

COCKPIT ARTS Tel: 0171 419 1959

This centre of excellence in Holborn, within 15 minutes walk of Covent Garden, the City and Hatton Garden, provides studios and a supportive environment for some of this country's top contemporary craftspeople. Each year, approximately 115 people, mostly working in shared studios, open their doors to over 3,000 public and trade buyers during the last weekend in June (Summer Festival) and November (Winter Festival).

For the Winter Festival, craftspeople from outside Cockpit Arts are invited to exhibit. However, acceptance is subject to work being of the very highest quality, rarity and to space availability.

Cockpit Arts has an education and training programme, regularly running courses in a variety of crafts and offering in-house training to craftspeople who require it. Open craft workshops and demonstrations usually take place during the Summer Festival.

CROESOSWALLT CRAFTS Tel: 01691 652423

Croesoswallt Crafts runs a market stall in Powis Hall Market, Oswestry, Salop on Wednesdays and Saturdays, plus occasional extra days at Christmas and on Public Holidays. They sell work by artists and craftspeople from the Oswestry and Welsh Borderland area, with the stall being run by members of the Oswestry & Welsh Border Craft Circle.

The hours of the market are approximately 9am-4pm. Work must be designed or made in the area and not made up from kits. They are also governed by overall market rules, so cannot sell items already being sold by any other indoor stall. Croesoswallt specialises in locally made crafts and are the only retail outlet for some items. Feel free to visit the stall on market days to discuss sales, or telephone Sue Franklin.

EDEN CRAFTS Tel: 0181 788 4434

In addition to its craft fairs in Wimbledon, New Malden, Guildford, Croydon, Chelsea and Kensington (detailed in previous section), Eden Crafts will organise six craft fairs for 1999 in the Arndale Shopping Centre, Wandsworth, London. These are scheduled to run March 22-27, April 5-10, May 24-29, August 30-September 4, October 25-30 and November 8-27. Details from Dina Samara.

FAIRKYTES ARTS CENTRE Tel: 01708 456308

Based in Billet Lane, Hornchurch, Essex, the Fairkytes Arts Centre provides a venue which is bookable by craft groups. Speak to John Shadwell.

FORESIGHT Tel: 01634 263886

The Anglesey Shopping Centre, New Road, Gravesend, Kent is the venue for Foresight's programme of six craft events. The dates are subject to confirmation, but provisionally will be the trading weeks commencing March 22, May 3, June 21, August 30, October 4 and November 1.

There are 12 sites available for each event at costs averaging out at £22 per day. Exhibitors new to Foresight need to send in photographs. Details from Linda Collins-Stevenson.

FORUM GROUP Tel: 01782 595805

Forum Group organises the twice-weekly markets at The Stones, High Street Market, Newcastle-under-Lyme, Staffs. The Tuesday market tends towards antiques and collectors, but the Thursday market, which runs from 8am-3pm, does have arts and crafts stalls. Details from Geoffrey Baskin.

GRANARY WHARF FESTIVAL MARKET Tel: 0113 244 2020

Granary Wharf will be holding its craft market at its site at The Canal Basin, Leeds, West Yorks every weekend in 1999. There are between 60 and 80 stands available at a cost working out at between £10 and £20 per day. A high standard of craft is sought.
Entertainment is staged on each market day: first Sunday of the month, children's entertainment; third Sunday of the month, Brass Band Day. There are also regular events throughout the year. There is generally a good chance of late booking, although early booking is advised for the Christmas period. Details from Suzanne Farmer.

GRANGE CRAFT FAIRS Tel: 01730 816841

In addition to its Christmas Craft Fair (detailed in previous section), the Grange Leisure Centre, Bepton Road, Midhurst, West Sussex holds a monthly market on the third Saturday of each month, plus one extra date on December 4. These are general markets, open 9.30am-3pm.
Specialist events next year will include nine book fairs, seven table top sales and a Modellers Exhibition on March 7. Details from Pat Bryant.

GREEN CLOSE STUDIOS LTD   Tel: 01524 221233

Commitment to studio rental for an ongoing period is a prerequisite for participation in sales through this venue, which is at Green Close Barn, Melling, Carnforth, Lancs. Costs are quoted at around £6 per day, but makers must make further enquiries to see what this entails as full details were not to hand at the time of going to press. Green Close seeks the very highest standard of craft work and needs to actually see original work first. Speak to Susan Flowers.

GREENWICH MARKET Tel: 0171 247 6590

A vibrant, well established market set in the very heart of London's historic village on the Thames.   Antiques and collectables pre-1960 on Thursdays; arts and crafts on Fridays, Saturdays and Sundays.
Good booking opportunities, but photographs needed from new applicants and a high quality of crafts sought. For further details and 1999 prices, contact Mark Freeman.

KIRKLEES METROPOLITAN COUNCIL Tel: 01484 223733

The council organises the Holmfirth Craft Market which is held weekly at Holmfirth Market, Huddersfield Road/Hollowgate, nr Huddersfield, West Yorks. There are 40 stands available at a cost of £10 per day.
The council also organises the bi-annual Huddersfield Craft Market at Huddersfield Open Market, Broom Street, Huddersfield, West Yorks. There are 120 stalls available for these two events at a cost of £20 per day. Dates were not to hand at the time of going to press. Speak to Mr T Woodfine about Holmfirth, but for Huddersfield telephone Mrs J Edgar on 01484 223730.

L.A.C.E. Tel: 01282 452637

Lee's Arts & Crafts Exhibitions will stage eight week-long craft exhibitions in shopping centres in 1999, four in Oldham and four in Sheffield.   Provisional dates for Oldham are trading weeks commencing March 1, May 10, August 23 and November 1 - while for Sheffield they are March 8, April 26, September 13 and November 22. Five to six sites are available at each event at a cost of £25 per day. Exhibitors need to provide their own tables. Details from Jim Whittaker.

LANCASTRIAN FAIRS Tel: 01282 430670

In addition to its wide programme of fairs held in York, Hebden Bridge, Gargrave and Settle (detailed in previous section), Lancastrian Fairs also stages an Antique & Craft Fair every Monday and Wednesday in the Town Hall, Skipton, North Yorks. Typical costs of Lancastrian Fairs' events are in the order of £15 per day. Details from Kevin Townson.

MAURTRAID CRAFT SHOWS Tel: 01908 271833

In addition to its craft shows in Slough (detailed in the previous section), Maurtraid has scheduled two week-long and two four-day events to be held at the Central Milton Keynes

Shopping Centre, Bucks. These will be held March 9-14, June 17-20, September 16-19 and October 26-31.

Maurtraid is also hoping to stage a craft show at the Trafford Shopping Centre in Manchester, but the dates are not yet confirmed. A high standard of crafts is sought in all cases and exhibitors new to Maurtraid need to send in photographs. Details from Sue Preedy.

MONMOUTHSHIRE COUNTY COUNCIL Tel: 01873 735811

The council organises the Abergavenny craft fairs (listed in previous section) but also several others. Every Tuesday, Friday and Saturday in the Market Hall and adjoining car parks in Abergavenny, there is a general retail market; this highlights crafts and gifts on Bank Holidays. Opening times are 8am-5pm and it is one of the largest in Wales.

Craft fairs are also held monthly from April to December in The Shire Hall, Monmouth where, on the forecourt, there is also the Monmouth Retail Market every Friday and Saturday from 8am-5pm. A retail market also takes place on the pedestrianised shopping area in Caldicot every Tuesday, opening 8am-5pm. The craft events, like the others, feature free admission to the buying public. The council's contact is Mr G Harris.

NEWCASTLE ARMSTRONG BRIDGE CRAFT MARKET Tel: 0191 232 8520 Extn: 6112

The city's Public Health & Environmental Protection Department administers this open air craft market which is held each Sunday throughout the year at Armstrong Bridge, Heaton, Newcastle upon Tyne, Tyne & Wear. Annual permits are granted to stallholders who produce their own craft items. The permit prescribes the goods that may be sold and currently it costs £114. Approximately 70 permits are issued each year. It is an offence to trade without a permit. Details from Mr P Sweet.

OLD SPITALFIELDS MARKET Tel: 0171 247 6590

A unique cosmopolitan arts and cultural centre in the heart of the City of London. Home to one of Britain's largest organic markets, sports facilities, foods, craft stalls, fashion and gifts. Open Sunday to Friday with 200 pitches available. Pitches charged at £5 for the weekdays and £30 for a Sunday. No bookings required. Details from Eric Graham.

STAMFORD ARTS CENTRE (CRAFT SHOWCASES) Tel: 01780 763203

Based in St Mary's Street in the fine Georgian conservation town of Stamford, Lincs, this multi-purpose arts centre houses two prominent craft showcases, with a changing programme of exhibitions throughout the year. Selected work features the best in local contemporary craft design from the East Midlands and East Anglia, as well as exhibitions by national makers. Work is selected for quality and design across a wide range of media and submissions are sought throughout the year. Speak to Carol Palmer.

STAPEHILL ABBEY, CRAFTS & GARDENS Tel: 01202 861686

Stapehill holds Spring and Autumn craft fairs, as listed in the previous section. However, within the Abbey Buildings at 276 Wimborne Road West, Stapehill, nr Wimborne, Dorset there are also craft units sometimes available to rent. Details on availability and prices from Sheena Tinsdale.

THE CRAFTER'S MARKETPLACE Tel: 01332 267750

A new concept in craft retailing, this city centre store in Derby, which opened in July 1997, is dedicated to selling hand-crafted products direct to the public. With no entry charge and situated on the inner ring road just 200 yards from Derby's pedestrian precinct, the store brings quality crafts to the general public 361 days a year. Trained staff look after the booths and sell stock, also taking special orders on makers' behalf. Booths are available in a variety of sizes from £40 a month with a 12.5% sales commission (inclusive of VAT). Details from Cliff Bloomfield.

WALFORD MILL CRAFT CENTRE Tel: 01202 841400

A converted mill about a quarter of a mile north of Wimborne, Dorset in a quiet riverside setting. The shop and exhibition gallery was selected by the Crafts Council for quality and is therefore on the new regional list. The shop has a wide range of contemporary craftwork, much of it from local craftspeople, while the gallery has about eight different exhibitions each year.

Debbie Kirby dyes and weaves fine silk in her workshop and has a range of items for sale, including ties, scarves and wall hangings. Kate Arbon has her workshop by the river where she makes a unique selection of jewellery using precious metals and stones. The top floor of the mill houses a craft school which runs courses in many skills for children and adults and, across the courtyard, is a licensed restaurant offering lunches and teas. Open every day 10am-5pm, but closed on Mondays from January to March. Details from Philip Goulden.

WEST COUNTRY CRAFT FAIRS Tel: 01749 677049

Besides its extensive programme of craft fairs, shows and festivals (detailed in previous section), West Country Markets will stage the Lyme Regis Indoor Craft Market at the Marine Theatre, Lyme Regis, Dorset every Thursday in 1999 from July 8 until September 2. Opening times will be 10am-5pm. Details from Fred Wilcox.

WOODLAND CRAFTS Tel: 01243 641306

Fairs taking place in Cosham, Fareham, Lancing, Southsea and Shoreham-by-Sea are all detailed in the previous section, but Woodland also runs six-day events in two shopping centres, the County Mall in Crawley, West Sussex and Fareham Shopping Mall in Hants.

Four confirmed dates for Crawley are: March 9-14, June 8-13, August 10-15 and October 12-17. Three confirmed for Fareham are: March 16-21, April 20-25 and June 15-20. More dates are yet to follow. Details from Paul Bishopp.

WYESIDE ARTS CENTRE Tel: 01982 552555

'Crafts Wyeside' is situated in the foyer area of the centre, a sympathetically remodelled Victorian market hall building on the banks of the River Wye in the small market town of Builth Wells. Beautifully designed craftcases offer a wide range of the very best craftwork from Mid-Wales and the Borders. An innovative computer graphic display details current work. A growing portfolio of information helps customers find their way to the wide variety of craftspeople's studios and other outlets in the region. Wyeside Gallery offers exhibitions throughout the year, encompassing all forms of contemporary arts and crafts by both established and up-and-coming figures.

Craft fairs are organised throughout the year, held in the unique setting of the original arcaded Victorian market hall. More information from Natalie Bass.

EVENT ORGANISERS AND OTHER KEY CONTACTS

In preparing the following section we have questionnaired British organisers of craft events and other organisations providing craft marketing opportunities. The initial contact details are self-explanatory and now include email and website addresses where we have been advised of them.

The remaining part of each entry comprises answers to the eight key questions that we have posed. We asked for details on the following:

Number of events organised each year

Number of stands available at these events

Average admission charge to the general public

Average daily stand/space charge for exhibitors

Details of extra charges (e.g. electricity)

Late booking opportunities

Whether photographs are required from new exhibitors

Selection policy

You should find analysis of the answers straightforward, with the exception of selection policy which requires some further explanation. Organisers have been asked to label their policy A, B, C or D, signifying the following:

A = Very Strict (probably only the highest quality of design, display and skill allowed, in many cases from graduate designers/artists/craftworkers).
B = Highly Considered (all craft, makers only permitted and only highly skilled workers allowed after full examination of work and/or photographs).
C = Liberal (mostly craft, favouring maker exhibitors, but only gentle or no sanction exercised as to design ability or skill level).
D = High Flexible (bought-in and/or non-craft goods permitted; no sanction as to quality exercised).

Except where otherwise noted, the stand/space costs quoted in each entry are the average daily exhibiting cost, net of VAT. Sometimes you will find a range of costs noted, particularly where organisers operate in a variety of venues.

This has inevitably been a process of self-certification by event organisers and therefore there is still no substitute for our usual advice to craftworkers to visit the events of organisers you may wish to book up with to make sure they suit your work, your style and your pocket. If, in undertaking this exercise, you feel the information we've carried has changed, then we'd like to hear from you so that we can take up any such discrepancies with organisers and, where merited, correct entries.

You will in a limited number of cases find certain information omitted from the entries. This is either because it was not provided by the time we went to press or is not relevant in a particular case.

We must emphasise that while every effort has been made to ensure the provision of accurate information, both here and throughout the book, details have been provided by others and we have accepted and printed them in good faith. We cannot under any circumstances accept liability, financial or otherwise, for any error or omission.

The entries constitute a guide to each organiser's policy but all the elements of this need to be double-checked before undertaking any financial commitment. We have neither sought nor accepted payment for any standard entry. However, some organisations have chosen to take paid advertising and they are represented in bold type. In some cases, these adverts contain additional useful information and they can be located by checking the index of advertisers on page 216

LIVE Crafts

Live Crafts Shows give the visitor a chance to meet the makers, see them at work and purchase some of the finest examples of purely handmade British Art, Craft, Fashion & Design.

13,14 FEBRUARY	**ASCOT EXHIBITION CENTRE**, Ascot Racecouse, Berkshire
27,28 FEBRUARY	**BROOKLANDS**, Weybridge, Surrey
20,21 MARCH	**BLETCHLEY PARK**, Bletchley, Buckinghamshire
2,3,4,5 APRIL	**MARLBOROUGH COLLEGE**, Marlborough, Wiltshire
17,18 APRIL	**BOUGHTON MONCHELSEA PLACE**, Nr Maidstone, Kent
24,25 APRIL	**BATH RACECOURSE**, Bath, Somerset
1,2,3 MAY	**CHILTERN OPEN AIR MUSEUM**, Chalfont St Giles, Buckinghamshire
14,15,16 MAY	**MAPLEDURHAM HOUSE**, Nr Reading, Oxfordshire
29,30,31 MAY	**BREAMORE HOUSE**, Fordingbridge, Hampshire
4,5,6 JUNE	**LOSELEY HOUSE**, Compton, Nr Guildford, Surrey
25,26,27 JUNE	**GREAT MISSENDEN**, Buckinghamshire
9,10,11 JULY	**FIRLE PLACE**, Lewes, East Sussex
23,24,25 JULY	**BERKELEY CASTLE**, Nr Gloucester, Gloucestershire
30,31 JUL & 1 AUG	**BASILDON PARK**, Lower Basildon, Reading, Berkshire
20,21,22 AUGUST	**PARHAM PARK**, Pulborough, West Sussex
28,29,30 AUGUST	**HIGHCLERE CASTLE**, Nr Newbury, Berkshire
3,4,5 SEPTEMBER	**BOUGHTON MONCHELSEA PLACE**, Nr Maidstone, Kent
17,18,19 SEPTEMBER	**OSTERLEY PARK**, Isleworth, Middlesex
25,26 SEPTEMBER	**OAKLANDS COLLEGE**, St Albans, Hertfordshire
2,3 OCTOBER	**HOGHTON TOWER**, Nr Preston, Lancashire
9,10 OCTOBER	**BLETCHLEY PARK**, Bletchley, Buckinghamshire
16,17 OCTOBER	**ASCOT EXHIBITION CENTRE**, Ascot Racecourse, Berkshire
23,24 OCTOBER	**TO BE CONFIRMED** (replaces Charterhouse), Surrey
6,7 NOVEMBER	**BATH RACECOURSE**, Bath, Somerset
13,14 NOVEMBER	**BUCKS COLLEGE**, Newlands Park Campus,
& 20,21 NOVEMBER	Chalfont St Giles, Buckinghamshire
25,26,27,28 NOV	**LOSELEY HOUSE**, Compton, Nr Guildford, Surrey
3,4,5 DECEMBER	**HIGHCLERE CASTLE**, Nr Newbury, Berkshire

As well as Live Crafts, The Exhibition Team Ltd are also organising:
CRAFT IN ACTION 1999
Held at the **LINCOLNSHIRE SHOWGROUND**, Lincoln
19,20,21 FEBRUARY & 19,20,21 NOVEMBER

For more information on any of the above events please contact:
THE EXHIBITION TEAM LTD
Events House, Wycombe Air Park, Marlow, Buckinghamshire SL7 3DP
Tel: 01494 450504 - Fax: 01494 450245

3D/2D CRAFT & DESIGN FAIRS
Unit 3, Albion Business Centre
78 Albion Road
Edinburgh EH7 5QZ
Tel: 0131 661 6600
Fax: 0131 661 0012
Contact: Kathy Mills
Number of Events: 50
Number of Stands: 70
Public Admission Price: 80p (halls); £2 (marquees).
Stand/Space Costs: £35/day (halls); £55/day (marquees), no extras.
Late Booking Opportunities: Not many
Photographs: Yes
Selection Policy: A

A&J FAIRS
12 Landport Terrace
Portsmouth
Hants PO1 2RG
Tel: 01705 427373
Fax: 01705 427374
Contact: Alice or John O'Farrell
Number of Events: 68
Number of Stands: Approx 12
Public Admission Price: Nil
Stand/Space Costs: £185 per week.
Late Booking Opportunities: Some
Photographs: Yes
Selection Policy: C
Week-long fairs in shopping centres, all but one in the south of England; see section on Alternative Craft Marketing Options.

ABERYSTWYTH ARTS CENTRE
Penglais Hill
Aberystwyth
Dyfed
SY23 3DE
Tel: 01970 622887/01970 621903
Fax: 01970 622883
Contact: Eve Ropek or Sally Smith
A broad range of activities; see section on Alternative Craft Marketing Options for full details.

ALWINTON BORDER SHEPHERDS SHOW
c/o Biddlestone
Townfoot, Rothbury
Morpeth
Northumberland
NE65 7DX
Tel: 01669 630246
Contact: Mrs E Dixon
Number of Events: 1

Number of Stands: 40
Public Admission Price: £3
Stand/Space Costs: £20/day, no extras.
Late Booking Opportunities: Rare
Photographs: No
Selection Policy: C

AMBERLEY MUSEUM
Amberley
Arundel
West Sussex
BN18 9LT
Tel: 01798 831370
Fax: 01798 831831
Website: www.fastnet.co.uk/amberley.museum/
Contact: Shirley Fagg
Public Admission Price: £5.20 (to museum).
Crafts on sale throughout the season; see section on Alternative Craft Marketing Options.
Late Booking Opportunities: Some
Photographs: They prefer to see the actual work
Selection Policy: B

AMBLESIDE HORTICULTURAL & CRAFT SOCIETY
8 Loughrigg Park
Ambleside
Cumbria LA22 0DY
Tel: 01539 432904
Number of Events: 1
Number of Stands: 35
Public Admission Price: £3
Stand/Space Costs: £70 for three days.
Electricity charged at £10 extra.
Late Booking Opportunities: Some
Photographs: No
Selection Policy: B

ANGEL ROW GALLERY
Central Library Building
3 Angel Row
Nottingham
Notts NG1 6HP
Tel: 0115 947 6334
Fax: 0115 947 6335
Contact: Stephanie Potts
Public Admission Price: Nil
A variety of contemporary crafts are sold throughout the year; see section on Alternative Craft Marketing Options.
Photographs: Yes
Selection Policy: A

APHRODITE
50 Westminster Road
Morecambe
Lancs LA4 4JD
Tel: 01524 426875
Contact: Amanda Barker
Number of Events: 110
Number of Stands: 6-40
Public Admission Price: Nil
Stand/Space Costs: £10-£25/day, no
extras.
Late Booking Opportunities: Some
Photographs: No
Selection Policy: C

AQUARIUS FAIRS
Eastside, Frog Lane
Mapledurwell, nr Basingstoke
Hants
RG25 2LP
Tel: 01256 363311
Fax: 01256 465559
Contact: Elaine Cashmore
Number of Events: 12-15
Number of Stands: 35
Public Admission Price: 20p-£1
Stand/Space Costs: £20-£30/day, no
extras.
Late Booking Opportunities: Some
Photographs: Yes, and sometimes they
personally vet work.
Selection Policy: B for pure craft; C for
gift/craft events.

ARCHER FAIRS
1 Merlin Close
Wedgwood Farm Estate
Oxford, Stoke-on-Trent
Staffs ST6 6UW
Fax: 01782 827718
Contact: Kevin Harper
Number of Events: 30
Number of Stands: 30+
Public Admission Price: 50p
Stand/Space Costs: £16/day, no extras.
Late Booking Opportunities: Some
Photographs: No
Selection Policy: C

ARIGINAL FAYRES
The Retreat
79 Hickton Road
Swanwick
Derbys
DE55 1AG
Tel: 01773 603187
Fax: 01773 603187

Contact: Val Bacon
Number of Events: 40
Number of Stands: 20-100
Public Admission Price: Nil
Stand/Space Costs: £25-£135/day, no
extras.
Late Booking Opportunities: Some
Photographs: No
Selection Policy: B
Specialises in Wedding Fayres, some with
Fashion Shows.

ARROW MANAGEMENT & MARKETING LTD
119 Thorpe Road
Peterborough
Cambs PE3 6JU
Tel: 01733 894440
Fax: 01733 894440
Contact: Phil Wing
Number of Events: 3-5
Number of Stands: 25
Public Admission Price: Adults £4
Stand/Space Costs: £6-£25/day, inclusive
of electricity.
Tables charged extra at £2.50.
Late Booking Opportunities: Some
Photographs: No
Selection Policy: C

ART IN ACTION
96 Sedlescombe Road
Fulham
London SW6 1RB
Tel: 0171 381 3192
Fax: 0171 381 0605
Contact: Bernard Saunders - Organiser
Number of Events: 1
Number of Stands: 80
Public Admission Price: £5-£9 (1998)
depending on status.
Stand/Space Costs: £45 per ft (between 6ft
and 12ft) for 4 days.
Extras: Table £10 + VAT; Electricity £40 +
VAT.
Late Booking Opportunities: Some
Photographs: Yes
Selection Policy: B

ARTISAN
Edinburgh Contemporary Craft
Festival Ltd
6 Darnaway Street
Edinburgh
EH3 6BG
Tel: 0131 225 2059
Fax: 0131 225 2770

Email: artisan2uk@aol.com
Website: www.dunbrowsin.demon.co.uk
Contact: Sherril Fraser
Number of Events: 1
Number of Stands: 150
Public Admission Price: £5
Stand/Space Costs: Approx £100/day, no extras.
Late Booking Opportunities: None
Photographs: Transparencies required.
Selection Policy: A

AVOCET CRAFTS
4 West Lane
North Baddesley
Southampton
Hants SO52 9GB
Tel: 01703 730321
Contact: Gail Ingram
Number of Events: 10
Number of Stands: 40
Public Admission Price: 50p
Stand/Space Costs: £35/day, no extras.
Late Booking Opportunities: Rare
Photographs: Yes
Selection Policy: B

BALTHAZAR
PO Box 82
Cambridge
Cambs CB2 2XQ
Tel: 01223 247370
Contact: Roz Myers
Number of Events: 60 one-day craft markets.
Number of Stands: 30
Public Admission Price: Nil
Stand/Space Costs: £20 for stall of 6ft frontage by 2ft 6in depth.
Tables charged extra at £1 if needed.
Late Booking Opportunities: Some
Photographs: Yes
Selection Policy: B/C

BEAD SOCIETY OF GREAT BRITAIN
1 Casburn Lane
Burwell
Cambs
CB5 0ED
Contact: Carole Morris
Number of Events: 1
Number of Stands: 60-70
Public Admission Price: £1
Stand/Space Costs: £30 per 6ft table.
Electricity charged extra at £2.50.
Stalls available only to Society members.
SAE for details.

BERNARD DIMMELOW
8 Chesterfield Close
Eythrope
Stone
Bucks HP17 8PY
Tel: 01296 747544
Email: 101563.437@compuserve.com
Contact: Bernard Dimmelow
Number of Events: 2
Number of Stands: 45
Public Admission Price: Visitors pay on gate for whole of show.
Stand/Space Costs: £35/day in craft marquee at The Wycombe Show and £55/day in craft marquee at The Thame Show; no extras.
Late Booking Opportunities: Some
Photographs: No
Selection Policy: C

BIC EXHIBITIONS
Bournemouth International Centre
Exeter Road
Bournemouth
Dorset BH2 5BH
Tel: 01202 456501
Fax: 01202 456500
Email:louise.burridge.bic@bournemouth.gov.uk
Website: www.bournemouth.gov.uk
Contact: Louise Burridge
Number of Events: 2
Number of Stands: 100
Public Admission Price: £1.50
Stand/Space Costs: £40/day.
Electricity charged extra at £17.50 + VAT.
Late Booking Opportunities: Some
Photographs: No
Selection Policy: C

BLACK ISLE SHOW
Black Isle Farmers' Society
Drumournie
5 Dochfour Drive
Inverness IV3 5EB
Tel: 01463 233957
Fax: 01463 243777
Email: BIFS1836@aol.com
Contact: Bruce Graham
Number of Events: 1
Number of Stands: 300
Public Admission Price: £2-£5, depending on status (1998).
Stand/Space Costs: £75 for craft exhibitors, no extras.
Late Booking Opportunities: Rare
Photographs: Yes
Selection Policy: B

BLACKTHORPE BARN CRAFTS MARKETS
Estate Office
Rougham
Bury St Edmunds
Suffolk IP30 9LZ
Tel: 01359 271203
Fax: 01359 271555
Email: barn@rougham.force9.co.uk
Contact: Katie Millard
Number of Events: 5
Number of Stands: 50
Public Admission Price: £1 (£4 season ticket).
Stand/Space Costs: £35/day, no extras.
Late Booking Opportunities: Some
Photographs: Yes
Selection Policy: B

BLAKEMERE CRAFT CENTRE
Chester Road
Sandiway
Northwich
Cheshire CW8 2EB
Tel: 01606 883261
Fax: 01606 301495
Contact: Lorraine Nevett
Number of Events: 60
Number of Stands: 20
Public Admission Price: Nil
Stand/Space Costs: £17.50/day.
Electricity used over 250W charged extra.
Late Booking Opportunities: Some
Photographs: Yes
Selection Policy: B

BOLTON METROPOLITAN BOROUGH
Leisure Services Department
The Wellsprings
Civic Centre, Bolton
Lancs
BL1 1US
Tel: 01204 522311 Extn: 4070
Fax: 01204 365034
Contact: Mike Coleman
Number of Events: 1
Public Admission Price: Nil
Stand/Space Costs: On application
Craft marquee at the Bolton Show.

BORDER FAIRS
Glenormiston Lodge
Innerleithen
Peeblesshire
EH44 6RD
Tel: 01896 831306
Contact: Paul MacNaughton
Number of Events: 40

Number of Stands: 30
Public Admission Price: 60p
Stand/Space Costs: £17/day, no extras.
Late Booking Opportunities: Some
Photographs: No
Selection Policy: C

BOROUGH OF PENDLE E.D.U.
Pendle Business Centre
Trafalgar Court, Commercial Road
Nelson
Lancs BB9 9BT
Tel: 01282 661682
Fax: 01282 661680
Email: j.johnson@unix1.pendle.gov.uk
Contact: Joanne Johnson
Number of Events: 1
Number of Stands: 30-40
Public Admission Price: Nil
Stand/Space Costs: On application.
Late Booking Opportunities: Some
Photographs: No
Selection Policy: C

BOTANY BAY VILLAGES
Canal Mill
Botany Brow, Chorley
Lancs PR6 9AF
Tel: 01257 261220
Fax: 01257 230888
Contact: Tom Morgan
Number of Stands: 120 sites on permanent
craft floor plus craft
marquees in the summer.
Public Admission Price: £2-£2.50
Late Booking Opportunities: Some
Photographs: No
Selection Policy: B
See section on Alternative Craft Marketing
Options for full details.

BOURNEMOUTH & POOLE DOLLS HOUSE & MINIATURE FAIR
422 Ashley Road
Parkstone, Poole
Dorset
BH14 0AA
Tel: 01202 745418
Contact: Mr or Mrs Earl
Number of Events: 1
Number of Stands: 50+
Public Admission Price: £2.50
Stand/Space Costs: £39.50/day.
Electricity charged extra at £7.
Late Booking Opportunities: Some
Photographs: Yes
Selection Policy: B

BRANCEPETH CASTLE CRAFT FAIRS
Brancepeth Castle
Durham
Co Durham DH7 8DF
Tel: 0191 378 0628/01223 355336
Contact: Mrs F M Dobson/Mrs A C Hobbs
Number of Events: 2
Number of Stands: 80
Public Admission Price: £1-£1.50
Stand/Space Costs: £79.50 for six ft (min.)
for all three days.
Tables, if required, charged at £2 per ft per
three-day fair.
Late Booking Opportunities: Some
Photographs: Yes
Selection Policy: B

BRECKNOCKSHIRE AGRICULTURAL SOCIETY
Show Office
13 The Bulwark, Brecon
Powys LD3 7AD
Tel: 01568 708760
Fax: 01568 708760
Contact: Janet Vaughan
Number of Events: 1
Number of Stands: 30
Public Admission Price: Not confirmed.
Stand/Space Costs: Not confirmed.
Late Booking Opportunities: Some
Photographs: No
Selection Policy: C

BRENTWOOD FAIRS
16 Eaton Drive
Alderley Edge
Cheshire SK9 7RA
Tel: 01625 590602
Fax: 01625 590602
Contact: Sylvia Wood
Number of Events: 20
Number of Stands: 50
Public Admission Price: £2.50
Stand/Space Costs: £50/day, no extras.
Late Booking Opportunities: Some
Photographs: Yes
Selection Policy: B

BRIDLINGTON MODEL BOAT SOCIETY
c/o 46 Manorfield Avenue
Driffield
East Yorks YO25 5HP
Tel: 01377 252550
Fax: 01377 252550
Email: fozzie46@aol.com
Website: www.members.wbs.net/
homepages/6/m/b/bmbs4u/index.html

Contact: John Foster
Number of Events: 1
Number of Stands: 90
Public Admission Price: £1.50
Stand/Space Costs: £15/day, no extras.
Late Booking Opportunities: Some
Photographs: No
Selection Policy: C

BRITISH LAPIDARY & MINERAL DEALERS ASSOCIATION
c/o 264 Wharf Road, Ealand
North Lincs DN17 4JN
Tel: 01724 710361 (up to 21.00h)
Fax: 01724 710361
Contact: David Precious
Number of Events: 4
Number of Stands: 90
Public Admission Price: £2 (accompanied
under-14s free).
Stand/Space Costs: £50/day, no extras.
Late Booking Opportunities: Some
Photographs: No
Selection Policy: D

BRITISH TOYMAKERS GUILD
124 Walcot Street
Bath BA1 5BG
Tel: 01225 442440
Contact: Robert Nathan
Number of Events: 1
Number of Stands: 60
Public Admission Price: £2.50
Stand/Space Costs: On application.
Late Booking Opportunities: Nearly always
Photographs: The Guild insists on actually
seeing the work.
Selection Policy: B/C and only members of
the Guild.

BROAD STREET MALL
203 Broad Street Mall
Reading
Berks RG1 7QE
Tel: 0118 957 6633
Fax: 0118 956 9319
Contact: Carole Kirk
Number of Events: Craft pitches available
throughout the year.
Number of Stands: 2 at any one time
Public Admission Price: Nil
Stand/Space Costs: £35/day.
Electricity and Craft Barrows charged extra.
Late Booking Opportunities: Some
Photographs: Yes
Selection Policy: D, but still subject to
some sanction of quality.

BROOME PARK COUNTRY & CRAFT FAIR
Show Office, c/o Relyon Group
Poulton Close
Dover
Kent CT17 0HL
Tel: 01304 242711
Fax: 01304 241058
Contact: Jean Philpott or George Saunders
Number of Events: 1
Number of Stands: 60
Public Admission Price: £4
Stand/Space Costs: £25/day, no extras.
Late Booking Opportunities: Some
Photographs: No
Selection Policy: C

BUCKINGHAM PUBLICITY
11 High Street
Old Portsmouth
Hants PO1 2LP
Tel: 01705 677200
Fax: 01705 677900
Contact: Jon Harris
Number of Events: 20
Number of Stands: 70-100
Public Admission Price: £4 (adults)
Stand/Space Costs: Varies greatly.
Electricity and Lights charged extra.
Late Booking Opportunities: Rare
Photographs: No
Selection Policy: A

CADEBY STEAM & COUNTRY FAIR
252 Higham Lane
Nuneaton
Warks CV11 6AR
Tel: 01203 382263
Contact: Brenda Vernon
Number of Events: 1
Number of Stands: 30
Public Admission Price: £2.50
Stand/Space Costs: £25 for the two days;
no extras.
Late Booking Opportunities: Nearly
always
Photographs: No
Selection Policy: C

CAILE CRAFT FAIRS
8 Arundel Way
Meadow Green
Meadowfield
Co Durham DH7 8UT
Tel: 0191 378 1923 (day + evening)
Fax: 0191 378 1923
Contact: Margaret Hodge

Number of Events: 12
Number of Stands: 20-36
Stand/Space Costs: On application.
Late Booking Opportunities: Some
Photographs: Yes
Selection Policy: B

CAMBRAY FAIRS
6 Hudson Close
Harthill
Sheffield S26 7WB
Tel: 01909 770531
Fax: 01909 774265
Contact: Judith Dawson
Number of Events: 10
Number of Stands: 20-40
Public Admission Price: 50p
Stand/Space Costs: £20/day, no extras.
Late Booking Opportunities: Some
Photographs: Yes
Selection Policy: B/C

CAMBRIDGE CRAFT FAIRS
PO Box 56
Wellingborough
Northants NN8 1SF
Tel: 01933 225674
Contact: Gillian McNern or David Smith
Number of Events: 8
Number of Stands: 150
Public Admission Price: £1 (children free).
Stand/Space Costs: £30/day, no extras.
Late Booking Opportunities: Some
Photographs: No
Selection Policy: B/C

CAMDEN LOCK MARKET
See Urban Space Management

CASTLE BROMWICH HALL GARDENS TRUST
Chester Road
Castle Bromwich
Birmingham
West Midlands
B36 9BT
Tel: 0121 749 4100
Fax: 0121 749 4100
Number of Events: 2
Number of Stands: 40
Public Admission Price: £2.50 (children
free).
Stand/Space Costs: £15/day.
Tables charged extra at £3.50.
Late Booking Opportunities: Some
Photographs: No
Selection Policy: C

CASTLE POINT BOROUGH COUNCIL
Council Offices
Kiln Road, Benfleet
Essex SS7 1TF
Tel: 01268 882200
Fax: 01268 882464
Contact: Sharon Whitty
Number of Events: 2
Number of Stands: 10-50
Public Admission Price: Nil
Stand/Space Costs: £10-£25/day.
Tables charged extra at £3.
Late Booking Opportunities: Nearly
always
Photographs: No
Selection Policy: C

CENTRAL PROMOTIONS
5 Forsythia Close
Telford
Salop TF2 9TA
Tel: 01952 200992
Contact: David Bushill
Number of Events: 35
Number of Stands: 50
Public Admission Price: 60p
Stand/Space Costs: £25/day, no extras.
Late Booking Opportunities: Some
Photographs: Yes
Selection Policy: C

CFL CRAFT SHOWS
Stainsby Bungalow, Main Road
Smalley
Derbys DE7 6DS
Tel: 01332 883479 (day + evenings)
Fax: 01332 882639
Email: CFL@Israel.globalnet.co.uk
Website: www.user.globalnet.co.uk/
~israel
Contact: Lee or Eleanor Israel
Number of Events: 20
Number of Stands: 20-150
Public Admission Price: £1.25-£3.25
Stand/Space Costs: £35/day, no extras.
Late Booking Opportunities: Rare
Photographs: Yes
Selection Policy: B

CHERRYCRAFT FAYRES & FESTIVALS
155 Lymington Road
Torquay
Devon TQ1 4BE
Tel: 01803 327822
Fax: 01803 322634
Contact: Walt Comber
Number of Events: 20

Number of Stands: 20-60
Public Admission Price: Nil
Stand/Space Costs: £21/day, no extras.
Late Booking Opportunities: Nearly always
Photographs: Yes
Selection Policy: B

CHERTSEY AGRICULTURAL ASSOCIATION
c/o 24 Oakway Drive
Frimley
Surrey GU16 5LF
Tel: 01276 26797
Contact: Mrs E Rooks
Number of Events: 1
Number of Stands: 50
Public Admission Price: £4
Stand/Space Costs: £30 for one day; £55
for the two days.
Extras (for two days): Tables £5; Electricity £5.
Late Booking Opportunities: Some
Photographs: No
Selection Policy: C/D

CHESHIRE FAYRE
PO Box 51
Macclesfield
Cheshire SK10 4EL
Tel: 01625 430519
Fax: 01625 430519
Email: langley@chesfayr.u-net.com
Contact: Colin or Doreen Langley
Number of Events: 17
Number of Stands: 75
Public Admission Price: £1.50
Stand/Space Costs: £46/day; no extras.
Late Booking Opportunities: Rare
Photographs: Yes
Selection Policy: B

COCKPIT ARTS
Cockpit Yard
Northington Street
London WC1N 2NP
Tel: 0171 419 1959
Fax: 0171 916 2455
Email: cockpit@easynet.co.uk
Contact: Katie Tyssen
Number of Events: 2
Number of Stands: 10
Public Admission Price: £2.50
Stand/Space Costs: £50/day, no extras.
Late Booking Opportunities: Rare
Photographs: Yes
Selection Policy: A
See also section on Alternative Craft
Marketing Options for details on work-
shops, courses and contemporary crafts.

COTSWOLD CRAFTSMEN
Whalley Cottage
Whittington
Cheltenham
Glos GL54 4HB
Tel: 01993 823678
Fax: 01242 821036
Contact: Jane Ann Rowe
Number of Events: 3
Number of Stands: 20
Public Admission Price: £1
Photographs: Yes
Selection Policy: B
Shows and exhibitions/sales are only for the 30 or so members of the guild, drawn from the Cotswolds area.

COTTAGE CRAFT FAIRS
122 Sevenoaks Road
Orpington
Kent BR6 9JZ
Tel: 01689 852121
Fax: 01689 856561
Contact: Bob Jack
Number of Events: 20
Number of Stands: 50+
Public Admission Price: £1
Stand/Space Costs: £30-£35/day, no extras.
Late Booking Opportunities: Some
Photographs: Yes
Selection Policy: B/C

COTTAGE CREATIONS CRAFT FAIRS
Holly Cottage
56 Salisbury Road
Dronfield
Derbys
S18 6UG
Tel: 01246 412620
Contact: Maurice Green
Number of Events: 60
Number of Stands: 35
Public Admission Price: 50p
Stand/Space Costs: £25/day, no extras.
Late Booking Opportunities: Some
Photographs: No
Selection Policy: C

COTTAGE INDUSTRIES ASSOCIATION
25 Hughes Avenue
Wolverhampton
West Midlands
WV3 7AU
Tel: 01902 332901
Fax: 01902 332901
Contact: John Jeater

Number of Events: 50
Number of Stands: 50
Public Admission Price: Nil
Stand/Space Costs: £30/day.
Extras: Electricity £5/two days; Extra Tables £5/two days.
Late Booking Opportunities: Nearly always
Photographs: No
Selection Policy: C, except for Bristol Balloon Fiesta which is 'A' (British Crafts only).

COTTAGE INDUSTRY SHOWS
Great Oaks Granary
Kennel Lane
Windlesham
Surrey GU20 6AA
Fax: 01276 479255
Contact: Brenda Gosling
Number of Events: 2-4
Number of Stands: 50-80
Public Admission Price: £2
Stand/Space Costs: £70-£80/day, no extras.
Late Booking Opportunities: Some
Photographs: Yes
Selection Policy: A/B

COUNTRY COTTAGE CRAFTS
Trunch Hill
Denton
Harleston
Norfolk IP20 0AE
Tel: 01986 788757
Contact: David Hicks
Number of Events: 5
Number of Stands: 100
Public Admission Price: £1.50-£3, depending on status.
Stand/Space Costs: £30-£50/day.
Extras: Tables £5; Chairs £2.50.
Late Booking Opportunities: Some
Photographs: Yes
Selection Policy: B

COUNTRYCRAFT
5 Boucher Place
St Werburghs
Bristol BS2 9YY
Tel: 0117 955 7936
Contact: Sandra Atkins
Number of Events: 42
Number of Stands: 20
Public Admission Price: Nil
Stand/Space Costs: £16/day, no extras.
Late Booking Opportunities: Rare
Photographs: Yes
Selection Policy: B

COUNTRYWIDE EVENTS

10 Naseby Drive
Loughborough
Leics LE11 4NU
Contact: Clive Gregory
Number of Events: 14
Number of Stands: 55
Public Admission Price: £2
Stand/Space Costs: £80/day, no extras.
Late Booking Opportunities: Some
Photographs: Yes
Selection Policy: B

COUNTY CRAFTS

PO Box 2
Ratby
Leics
LE6 0XT
Tel: 0116 239 4366
Mobile: 0850 394366
Contact: Marcus Pateman

COWPIE COUNTRY SHOW

7 Old School Lane
Brockham Green
Betchworth
Surrey RH3 7JP
Tel: 01737 842042 (day/evening)
Contact: Hilary Budd
Number of Events: 1
Number of Stands: 100
Public Admission Price: £5
Stand/Space Costs: Inside, £6 per ft/day;
Outside, £3 per ft/day.
Extras: Electricity £10; Tables (6ft) £5.
Late Booking Opportunities: Some
Photographs: Not compulsory, but
appreciated.
Selection Policy: C

CRAFT CARNIVAL

Hill Butts House
Kingston Lacy
Wimborne
Dorset
BH21 4DS
Tel: 01202 842407
Fax: 01202 842407
Contact: Kati Zombory-Moldovan
Number of Events: 6
Number of Stands: 100-150
Public Admission Price: £2
Stand/Space Costs: £30/day.
Electricity charged extra at £15
Late Booking Opportunities: Some
Photographs: Yes
Selection Policy: C

CRAFT DEVELOPMENTS

14 Portway
Steyning
West Sussex BN44 3QF
Tel: 01903 813657
Contact: Mrs Jackie Martin
Number of Events: 20
Number of Stands: 20-30
Public Admission Price: Nil
Stand/Space Costs: £23/day, no extras.
Late Booking Opportunities: Rare
Photographs: Yes
Selection Policy: C

CRAFT*FOLK

PO Box 26
Dinas Powys
South Glam CF64 4YR
Tel: 01222 514732
Fax: 01222 514732
Email: craft*folk@potterco.demon.co.uk
Contact: Angie Coutts or Maxine Hird
Number of Events: 10
Number of Stands: 30-50
Public Admission Price: Nil
Stand/Space Costs: £20-£50/day.
Tables, Chairs and Frontsheets charged
extra.
Late Booking Opportunities: Some
Photographs: Yes
Selection Policy: B

CRAFT IN ACTION

Arcus Veni
21 Upton Gardens
Upton upon Severn
Worcs WR8 0NU
Tel: 01684 592709
Number of Events: 35
Number of Stands: 20
Public Admission Price: Nil
Stand/Space Costs: £20/day.
Sometimes extra charges for electricity
and/or tables at the marquee events.
Late Booking Opportunities: None, as
vetting takes some time.
Photographs: Yes
Selection Policy: A

CRAFTS COUNCIL

44a Pentonville Road
Islington
London N1 9BY
Tel: 0171 278 7700
Fax: 0171 837 6891
Number of Events: 1
Number of Stands: 200+

Stand/Space Costs: Potential exhibitors must make a postal applications for forms. The Chelsea Crafts Fair is held over two weeks, with different displays in each week.
Photographs: Transparencies
Selection Policy: Juried event - Makers must supply a description of their activity, their exhibit proposal and four 35mm slides of current work.

CRAFTS IN ACTION
The All England Jumping Course
London Road
Hickstead
West Sussex
RH17 5NX
Tel: 01273 833884
Fax: 01273 835556
Email: marathon@btinternet.com
Contact: Dee Leek
Number of Events: 7
Number of Stands: 25
Public Admission Price: Show Gate price (not known).
Stand/Space Costs: £75/day, with some variation.
Electricity and Tables charged extra.
Late Booking Opportunities: Rare
Photographs: Yes
Selection Policy: A

CREATIVE CRAFTS ASSOCIATION
Primrose Cottage
Howards Lane
Eccleston, St Helens
Merseyside
WA10 5QD
Tel: 01744 750606
Contact: Sandra
Number of Events: 40
Number of Stands: 50+
Public Admission Price: £1
Stand/Space Costs: £25/day, no extras.
Late Booking Opportunities: Rare
Photographs: Yes
Selection Policy: B

CREATIVITY
33 Beechmount Drive
Weston-super-Mare
North Somerset BS24 9EY
Tel: 01934 813407
Fax: 01934 813407
Contact: Sally Packer
Number of Events: 6
Number of Stands: 30-50

Public Admission Price: Nil
Stand/Space Costs: £30/day.
Tables, Chairs and Electricity all charged extra at prevailing hire rates.
Late Booking Opportunities: Some
Photographs: Yes
Selection Policy: B

CREWE & NANTWICH CARNIVAL
Crewe & Nantwich Borough Council
Municipal Buildings, Earle Street
Crewe
Cheshire CW1 2BJ
Tel: 01270 537239
Fax: 01270 537322
Contact: Elaine Dodd
Number of Events: 1
Number of Stands: 100
Public Admission Price: Nil
Stand/Space Costs: £40/day.
Electricity charged extra.
Late Booking Opportunities: Some
Photographs: No
Selection Policy: D

CROESOSWALLT CRAFTS
c/o Powis Hall Market, Oswestry
Salop SY11 1PZ
Tel: 01691 652423
Contact: Sue Franklin
Number of Events: 1
Number of Stands: 20-30
Public Admission Price: Nil
Stand/Space Costs: £40/day, no extras.
Late Booking Opportunities: Some
Photographs: Yes
Selection Policy: B
See also section on Alternative Craft Marketing Options for details on twice-weekly market stalls.

CUMBRIA CRAFT GUILD
c/o Hollin Howe
Lonsties, Keswick
Cumbria CA12 4TD
Tel: 01768 771458
Contact: Val Blenkiron (Secretary)
Number of Events: 1
Number of Stands: N/A; this is the Guild's Exhibition.
Public Admission Price: £1
Stand/Space Costs: N/A; they have an entry/hanging fee only.
Late Booking Opportunities: N/A
Photographs: No, work is selected by examination of product.
Selection Policy: A

DALESWAY FESTIVALS LTD
The All England Jumping Course
London Road
Hickstead
West Sussex
RH17 5NX
Tel: 01273 833884
Fax: 01273 835556
Email: marathon@btinternet.com
Contact: Gary Bates
Number of Events: 8
Number of Stands: 120
Public Admission Price: £2
Stand/Space Costs: £50/day.
Electricity and Tables charged extra.
Late Booking Opportunities: Some
Photographs: Yes
Selection Policy: A

DEAN MANAGEMENT
PO Box 12
Chichester
West Sussex
PO20 7PH
Fax: 01243 641284
Website: www.deanmanagement.co.uk
Number of Events: 1
Public Admission Price: £2.50-£5.20,
depending on status.
Stand/Space Costs: £20/day.
Extras: Electricity £25; Tables £5.
Late Booking Opportunities: None
Photographs: On enquiry
Selection Policy: B

DOLLY DOMAIN FAIRS
45 Henderson Road
South Shields
Tyne & Wear
NE34 9QW
Tel: 0191 424 0400
Fax: 0191 424 0400
Contact: Liz or David Bonner
Number of Events: 6
Number of Stands: 65-92
Public Admission Price: £2.50
Stand/Space Costs: £48/day, no extras.
Late Booking Opportunities: Rare
Photographs: Yes
Selection Policy: B

DULWICH CRAFT FAIRS
25 Tewkesbury Avenue
Forest Hill
London
SE23 3DG
Contact: Nicholas Keogh

Number of Events: 3
Number of Stands: 45
Public Admission Price: £2
Stand/Space Costs: £60-£75/day, no
extras.
Late Booking Opportunities: Rare
Photographs: Yes
Selection Policy: A

DUNSTABLE CRAFT MARKET
c/o 5 Huckleberry Close
Luton
Beds
LU3 4AN
Tel: 01582 598442
Contact: Mike Kelly
Number of Events: 12
Number of Stands: 15-20
Public Admission Price: Nil
Stand/Space Costs: £15/day, no extras.
Late Booking Opportunities: Some
Photographs: Yes
Selection Policy: B

EAST KENT FAIRS
134/135 London Road
Dover
Kent
CT17 0TG
Tel: 01304 201644
Fax: 01304 201644 (ring first)
Contact: John Payne
Number of Events: 20
Number of Stands: 50-100
Public Admission Price: 50p
Stand/Space Costs: £25/day, no extras.
Late Booking Opportunities: Nearly
always
Photographs: No
Selection Policy: C

EAST MIDLANDS DOLL FAIRS
1 The Hallards
Eaton Socon
St Neots
Cambs
PE19 3QW
Tel: 01480 216372
Contact: Bruce King
Number of Events: 20
Number of Stands: 50-100
Public Admission Price: £2.50
Stand/Space Costs: £40/day, no extras.
Late Booking Opportunities: Some
Photographs: No
Selection Policy: C

EASTERN EVENTS LTD
Diggens Farm House
Buxton Road
Aylsham
Norfolk
NR11 6UB
Tel: 01263 734711
Fax: 01263 735134
Email: eastern.events@paston.co.uk
Website: www.paston.co.uk/
easternevents
Contact: John Wootten
Number of Events: 10
Number of Stands: 50-100
Public Admission Price: £2.50
Stand/Space Costs: £50/day.
Late Booking Opportunities: Some
Photographs: Yes
Selection Policy: B

EDEN CRAFTS
39 Ross Court
Putney Hill
Putney
London SW15 3NZ
Tel: 0181 788 4434
Fax: 0181 780 0993
Contact: Dina Samara
Number of Events: 20
Number of Stands: 30-140
Public Admission Price: Varies
Stand/Space Costs: £10-£30/per day.
Late Booking Opportunities: Some
Photographs: Yes
Selection Policy: A/B/C
See also section on Alternative Craft
Marketing Options.

ESSEX STEAM RALLY & COUNTRY SHOW
Barleylands Farm
Barleylands Road
Billericay
Essex
CM11 2UD
Fax: 01268 532032
Email: barleyfarm@aol.com
Contact: Jane Cowell
Number of Events: 2
Number of Stands: 20-150
Public Admission Price: £3-£5
Stand/Space Costs: £10/day.
Electricity charged extra.
Late Booking Opportunities: Some
Photographs: No
Selection Policy: C

EUSTON PARK RURAL PASTIMES
The Rectory
Honington
Bury St Edmunds
Suffolk
IP31 1RG
Tel: 01359 269265
Fax: 01359 269265
Contact: Tim Fogden
Number of Events: 1
Number of Stands: 30
Public Admission Price: £4
Stand/Space Costs: £25/day, no extras.
Late Booking Opportunities: Some
Photographs: No
Selection Policy: C

FAIR HAVENS & LITTLE HAVEN HOSPICES
Stuart House
47 Second Avenue
Westcliff-on-Sea
Essex
SS0 8HX
Fax: 01702 220351
Contact: Louise Gloyne
Number of Events: 2
Number of Stands: 30
Public Admission Price: Nil
Stand/Space Costs: £40/day, no extras.
Late Booking Opportunities: Some
Photographs: No
Selection Policy: D

FAIRKYTES ARTS CENTRE
51 Billet Lane
Hornchurch
Essex RM11 1AX
Tel: 01708 456308
Fax: 01708 475286
Contact: John Shadwell
Number of Events: 2
Number of Stands: 50
Public Admission Price: Nil
See also section on Alternative Craft
Marketing Options.

FALCON FAIRS
The Old Chequers
High Street
Wappenham
Northants
NN12 8SN
Tel: 01327 860578
Fax: 01327 860232
Contact: David Willis
Number of Events: 40

Number of Stands: 30
Public Admission Price: 50p
Stand/Space Costs: £25/day, no extras.
Late Booking Opportunities: Some
Photographs: No
Selection Policy: C

FIFE CRAFT ASSOCIATION
12 Valley Grove, Leslie
Glenrothes
Fife KY6 3BZ
Tel: 01592 743539 (day + evenings)
Contact: Peter Leigh
Number of Events: 18
Number of Stands: 25+
Public Admission Price: Nil
Stand/Space Costs: £15-£20/day, no extras.
Late Booking Opportunities: Some
Photographs: Yes
Selection Policy: B

FINCHCOCKS
Riseden
Goudhurst
Kent
TN17 1HH
Tel: 01580 211702
Fax: 01580 211007
Email: finchcocks@argonet.co.uk
Contact: Mrs Katrina Burnett
Number of Events: 2
Number of Stands: 80
Public Admission Price: £3.80
Stand/Space Costs: £35/day.
Tables charged extra.
Late Booking Opportunities: Some
Photographs: Yes
Selection Policy: C

FLOWERFIELDS ARTS CENTRE
(Coleraine Borough Council)
185 Coleraine Road
Portstewart
Co Londonderry
BT55 7HU
Tel: 01265 833959
Fax: 01265 835042
Email: flowerfield@dnet.co.uk
Contact: S Hunter
Number of Events: 1
Number of Stands: 28
Public Admission Price: 50p
Stand/Space Costs: £25/day, no extras.
Late Booking Opportunities: Rare
Photographs: Yes
Selection Policy: C

FOCAL POINT
76 Main Road
Long Bennington
nr Newark
Notts NG23 5DJ
Tel: 01400 281937
Fax: 01400 282051
Email: 100535.3116@compuserve.com
Website: www.focalpointuk.com
Contact: Robert Jordan
Number of Events: 2
Number of Stands: 150
Public Admission Price: N/A (Trade events).
Stand/Space Costs: On application.
Late Booking Opportunities: Rare
Photographs: Yes, and samples of work.
Selection Policy: A
These are craft sections at Trade Only exhibitions held at the
National Exhibition Centre.

FORESIGHT
5 Thames Avenue
Rainham
Kent ME8 9BN
Tel: 01634 263886
Fax: 01634 231394
Contact: Linda Collins-Stevenson
Number of Events: 6
Number of Stands: 12
Public Admission Price: N/A
Stand/Space Costs: £22/day.
Late Booking Opportunities: Some
Photographs: Yes
Selection Policy: C
See section on Alternative Craft Marketing Options for details on these shopping centre events.

FORUM GROUP
PO Box 465
Longton
Stoke-on-Trent
Staffs ST3 7SE
Tel: 01782 595805
Fax: 01782 596133
Contact: Geoffrey Baskin
Number of Events: 50
Number of Stands: 70
Public Admission Price: Nil
Stand/Space Costs: £12/day, no extras.
Late Booking Opportunities: Nearly always
Photographs: No
Selection Policy: D
See section on Alternative Craft Marketing Options.

FOUNTAIN FAYRES & EXHIBITIONS
40 Trewartha Park
Weston-super-Mare
North Somerset BS23 2RT
Tel: 01934 418437
Contact: Philip Barwell
Number of Events: 15
Number of Stands: 35-115
Public Admission Price: 35p-70p
Stand/Space Costs: £25-£30/day, no
extras.
Late Booking Opportunities: Some
Photographs: Yes
Selection Policy: B

FOUR SEASONS (EVENTS) LTD
1 Kineton Road
Southam
nr Leamington Spa
Warks CV33 0HZ
Tel: 01926 813374
Fax: 01926 813374
Contact: Ann Turner
Number of Events: 22
Number of Stands: 150
Public Admission Price: £3
Stand/Space Costs: £70/day, no extras.
Late Booking Opportunities: Rare
Photographs: Yes
Selection Policy: A/B

FOUR SEASONS FAIRS
6 Post Office Lane
Glemsford
Sudbury
Suffolk CO10 7RA
Fax: 01787 281855
Contact: Lorna Quick
Number of Events: 46
Number of Stands: 35-70
Public Admission Price: Nil
Stand/Space Costs: £30/day, no extras.
Late Booking Opportunities: Some
Photographs: Yes
Selection Policy: B

FRAMLINGHAM SPORTS CLUB
c/o Grove Farm Barns
Easton Road
Framlingham
Suffolk IP13 9LW
Tel: 01728 723320
Fax: 01728 723398
Contact: Richard Bull
Number of Events: 1
Number of Stands: 35-40
Public Admission Price: Nil

Stand/Space Costs: £15 for one day; £25
for both days, no extras.
Late Booking Opportunities: Some
Photographs: No
Selection Policy: C

FUTURE PUBLISHING LTD
30 Monmouth Street
Bath BA1 2BW
Tel: 01225 442244
Fax: 01225 732398
Email: agunning@futurenet.co.uk
Contact: Amanda Gunning
Number of Events: 2
Number of Stands: 150
Public Admission Price: £5-£6
Stand/Space Costs: On application.
Late Booking Opportunities: Rare
Photographs: Yes
Selection Policy: Needlecraft related
products only.

GATESHEAD FAIRS
"Longridge"
Longridge Road
Blaydon-on-Tyne
Tyne & Wear NE21 6JW
Contact: Ms Mary Edwards
Number of Events: 2
Number of Stands: 20
Public Admission Price: 50p
Stand/Space Costs: £25/day, no extras.
Late Booking Opportunities: Some
Photographs: Yes Selection Policy: B

GEM FAIRS
46 Greenmount Drive
Greenmount, Bury
Lancs BL8 4HA
Tel: 01204 883635
Contact: Mrs A R Lambert
Number of Events: 7+

GLASGOW CITY COUNCIL
Cultural & Leisure Services Dept
37 High Street
Glasgow G1 1LX
Tel: 0141 287 5190
Fax: 0141 287 3521
Contact: John Sackett
Number of Events: 1
Number of Stands: 50
Public Admission Price: £4
Stand/Space Costs: On application.
Late Booking Opportunities: Some
Photographs: No, not always
Selection Policy: D

GOLDEN AGE FAIRS
31 Hillcrest Avenue
Ingol, Preston
Lancs PR2 3UP
Tel: 01772 732877
Contact: Pauline or Alan
Number of Events: 20
Number of Stands: 40
Public Admission Price: 20p or free
Stand/Space Costs: £10-£25/day, no extras.
Late Booking Opportunities: Some
Photographs: No
Selection Policy: C

GOLDFINCH CRAFTS
4 Festival Avenue
Longfield
Kent DA3 7HR
Tel: 01474 703359 (day + evening)
Fax: 01474 703359
Email: john.goldfinch@virgin.net
Number of Events: 10
Number of Stands: 40-100
Public Admission Price: £1-£1.50
Stand/Space Costs: £40/day, no extras.
Photographs: No
Selection Policy: B/C

GOOD IDEAS CRAFT FAYRES
Narnia, 3 Dryad Way
Felpham
nr Bognor Regis
West Sussex PO22 7RQ
Tel: 01243 586220
Contact: Debby Addicott
Number of Events: 7
Number of Stands: Approx 20
Public Admission Price: Nil
Stand/Space Costs: £7.50/day, no extras.
Late Booking Opportunities: Some
Photographs: Yes, or visit arranged if local.
Selection Policy: B

GORING CHRISTMAS CRAFT FAIR
c/o Sweet Briar Cottage
High Street
Goring-on-Thames
Oxon RG8 9BB
Tel: 01491 874293
Contact: Mr J Munden
Number of Events: 1
Number of Stands: 33
Public Admission Price: 50p
Stand/Space Costs: £30/day, no extras.
Late Booking Opportunities: Rare
Photographs: Yes
Selection Policy: A

GRANARY WHARF
The Canal Basin
Leeds
West Yorks LS1 4BR
Tel: 0113 244 6570
Fax: 0113 245 0153
Email: enquiry@granary-wharf.co.uk
Website: www.granary-wharf.co.uk
Contact: Suzanne Farmer
Number of Events: 104
Number of Stands: 60-80
Public Admission Price: Nil
Stand/Space Costs: £10-£20/day, no
extras.
Late Booking Opportunities: Nearly
always
Photographs: Yes
Selection Policy: C
See section on Alternative Craft Marketing
Options.

GRANDSTAND EVENTS LTD
The Old Coach House
Boutport Street
Barnstaple
Devon EX31 1RW
Tel: 01271 378000
Fax: 01271 329133
Contact: Grahame Davidson
Number of Events: 3
Number of Stands: 250+
Public Admission Price: £1
Stand/Space Costs: £60/day.
Extras: Strip Lights £20; Double Sockets
£25; Tables £5.
Late Booking Opportunities: Some
Photographs: No
Selection Policy: C

GRANGE CRAFT FAIRS
The Grange Centre
Bepton Road
Midhurst
West Sussex GU29 9HD
Tel: 01730 816841
Fax: 01730 813757
Contact: Pat Bryant
Number of Events: 1
Number of Stands: 70
Public Admission Price: 60p-80p
Stand/Space Costs: £30/day, no extras.
Late Booking Opportunities: Some
Photographs: Yes
Selection Policy: C
Also general monthly market; see section
on Alternative Craft
Marketing Options.

GREEN CLOSE STUDIOS LTD
Green Close Barn
Melling
Carnforth
Lancs LA6 2RB
Tel: 01524 221233
Contact: Susan Flowers
Number of Events: 2
Number of Stands: 4
Public Admission Price: Nil
Stand/Space Costs: £6/day as part of a
commitment to studio rental for an
ongoing period.
Late Booking Opportunities: Rare
Photographs: No, they prefer to the actual
work in person.
Selection Policy: A
See section on Alternative Craft Marketing
Options.

GREENWICH MARKET
See Urban Space Management

HALLMARK FAIRS
8 Plymtree
Thorpe Bay
Southend-on-Sea
Essex
SS1 3RA
Tel: 01702 586262
Contact: Dennis or Pearl Baker
Number of Events: 8
Number of Stands: 100-120
Public Admission Price: £2
Stand/Space Costs: £38/day, no extras.
Late Booking Opportunities: Some
Photographs: Yes
Selection Policy: B

HARMONY HILL ARTS CENTRE
54 Harmony Hill
Lisburn
Co Antrim
BT27 4ES
Tel: 01846 678219
Fax: 01846 662679
Contact: Christina Hurson
Number of Events: 1
Number of Stands: 30
Public Admission Price: £1
Stand/Space Costs: £30/day, no extras.
Late Booking Opportunities: Rare
Photographs: Yes
Selection Policy: B
Also a continuing programme of exhibi-
tions and workshops throughout the year.

HEART OF ENGLAND CRAFTWORKERS
105 St George's Lane
Worcester
Worcs
WR1 1QS
Tel: 01905 21702
Fax: 01905 29285
Contact: Eddie or Chris Carless
Number of Events: 22
Number of Stands: 40
Public Admission Price: Nil
Stand/Space Costs: Varies.
Late Booking Opportunities: Some
Photographs: Yes
Selection Policy: A/B

HEATHFIELD CRAFT FAIRS
48 Little Lane
Kimberley
Notts
NG16 2PE
Tel: 0115 945 9321
Fax: 0115 945 9253
Contact: Shirley Keeling
Number of Events: 12
Number of Stands: 35-40
Public Admission Price: £1-£1.50
Stand/Space Costs: £35/day, no extras.
Late Booking Opportunities: Some
Photographs: Yes
Selection Policy: B

HENLEY & DISTRICT AGRICULTURAL ASSOCIATION LTD
Greenlands Farm, Dairy Lane
Hambleden
Oxon
RG9 3AS
Tel: 01491 410948/571301
Contact: J D Bird
Number of Events: 1
Number of Stands: 64
Public Admission Price: £6
Stand/Space Costs: £25/day.
Extras: Tables £8; Electricity £15.
Late Booking Opportunities: Rare
Photographs: No
Selection Policy: C

HEREFORDSHIRE COUNCIL
Cultural Services
PO Box 44
Leominster
Herefordshire HR6 8ZD
Tel: 01432 260614
Fax: 01568 611046
Email: mbateman@herefordshire.gov.uk

Contact: Melanie Bateman
Number of Events: 1
Number of Stands: 45
Public Admission Price: £1
Stand/Space Costs: £45/day, no extras.
Late Booking Opportunities: Some
Photographs: Yes
Selection Policy: B

HERITAGE FAIRS
'Farcroft'
Colne Road
Kelbrook
Lancs BB18 6TF
Tel: 01282 844037
Fax: 01282 844037
Contact: Carl Dart
Number of Events: 15
Number of Stands: 25-60
Public Admission Price: 50p-60p
Stand/Space Costs: £29-£49/day, no extras.
Late Booking Opportunities: Some
Photographs: Yes
Selection Policy: B/C

HOBBY HORSE DESIGN & CRAFT FAIRS
PO Box 3751
Solihull
West Midlands B91 3QF
Tel: 0121 711 4728
Fax: 0121 709 1012
Contact: Geoff Farnham
Number of Events: 14
Number of Stands: 60
Public Admission Price: £2.50
Stand/Space Costs: £40/day.
Electricity and Tables charged extra.
Late Booking Opportunities: Some
Photographs: Yes
Selection Policy: B

HOLLAND FAIRS
PO Box 46
Westella
nr Hull
East Yorks HU10 7YR
Tel: 0402 163060
Fax: 01482 654242
Contact: Cheryl
Number of Events: 10
Number of Stands: 50
Public Admission Price: £1
Stand/Space Costs: £15/day, no extras.
Late Booking Opportunities: Some
Photographs: No
Selection Policy: C

HOLMFIRTH ROUND TABLE
Tel: 01484 687413 (evenings only)
Contact: S Benison
Number of Events: 1

HOOK NORTON RURAL FAYRE
Highgrove Cottage
The Green
Hook Norton
Oxon OX15 5LE
Tel: 01608 737311
Contact: Diana Henderson
Number of Events: 1
Number of Stands: 36
Public Admission Price: £3
Stand/Space Costs: £25/day.
Electricity charged extra at £5.
Late Booking Opportunities: Some
Photographs: Yes
Selection Policy: C

HOVENDEN GALA & CRAFT FAIR
Redgate Villa
Foul Anchor
Tydd, Wisbech
Cambs PE13 5RF
Tel: 01945 585237
Contact: Mrs Joanna Kay
Number of Events: 1
Number of Stands: 20
Public Admission Price: £1
Stand/Space Costs: £20 for the one day, no extras.
Late Booking Opportunities: Nearly always
Photographs: No
Selection Policy: C
Craft fair held in conjunction with the annual gala at Hovenden House, a Leonard Cheshire home in Fleet, nr Spalding, Lincs.

ICHF LTD
Dominic House
Seaton Road, Highcliffe
Dorset BH23 5HW
Tel: 01425 272711
Fax: 01425 279369
Email: info@ichf.co.uk
Website: www.ichf.co.uk
Contact: Ray Dowdney
Number of Events: 20
Number of Stands: 250
Public Admission Price: £4.50
Stand/Space Costs: £300 for three days.
Electricity and Furniture charged extra.
Late Booking Opportunities: Rare
Photographs: Yes
Selection Policy: B

ISABEL HOSPICE CRAFT FAIRS
c/o 12 Blacksmith Close
Bishop's Stortford
Herts CM23 4GB
Contact: Joan Williams
Number of Events: 3
Number of Stands: 28
Public Admission Price: 50p
Stand/Space Costs: £20/day.
Additional Floor Space for Carousels etc.
available for extra £2.
Late Booking Opportunities: Some
Photographs: No
Selection Policy: C

J M EVANS
7 Tower Hill Road
Crewkerne
Somerset TA18 8BJ
Tel: 01460 78031
Contact: Ron or Joyce Evans
Number of Events: 30
Number of Stands: 30
Public Admission Price: Nil
Stand/Space Costs: £17/day, no extras.
Late Booking Opportunities: Some
Photographs: No
Selection Policy: B

JEAN BRYON
Wood View, 5 Ghyll Close
Steeton, nr Keighley
West Yorks BD20 6PW
Tel: 01535 653269
Contact: Jean Bryon
Number of Events: 10
Number of Stands: 25
Public Admission Price: 45p
Stand/Space Costs: £30/day, no extras.
Late Booking Opportunities: Some
Photographs: Yes
Selection Policy: B

JEAN WELCH SHOWS
3 Tentergate Avenue
Knaresborough
North Yorks HG5 9BQ
Tel: 01423 867144
Fax: 01423 867144
Contact: Malcolm
Number of Events: 13
Number of Stands: 50
Public Admission Price: £2
Stand/Space Costs: £48/day, no extras.
Late Booking Opportunities: Nearly always
Photographs: No
Selection Policy: D

JETS QUALITY CRAFT FAIRS
74 Hazel Way
Crawley Down
West Sussex
RH10 4EU
Tel: 01342 713375
Fax: 01342 713375
Contact: Mrs J Edmonds
Number of Events: 10
Stand/Space Costs: On application.
Late Booking Opportunities: Some
Photographs: Yes
Selection Policy: B

JOHN & JENNIFER FORD
October Hill
Upper Longdon
Rugeley
Staffs
WS15 1QB
Tel: 01543 491000
Contact: Jennifer Ford
Number of Events: 1
Number of Stands: 110
Public Admission Price: £4.50
Stand/Space Costs: On application.
Late Booking Opportunities: Rare
Photographs: Yes
Selection Policy: B
Exhibitors must retail products related to
lacemaking.

KATHARINE HOUSE HOSPICE
Weston Road
Stafford
Staffs
ST16 3SB
Tel: 01785 254645 or 255785
Fax: 01785 247803
Contact: Mrs Margaret Reeves
Number of Events: 1
Number of Stands: 70
Public Admission Price: 75p (accompanied children free).
Stand/Space Costs: £25-£30/day.
Electricity charged extra.
Late Booking Opportunities: Some
Photographs: Yes
Selection Policy: B

KELD CRAFT FAIRS
Finley House
Harmby
Leyburn
North Yorks DL8 5PE
Tel: 01969 624815
Contact: John Morgan

Number of Events: 73
Number of Stands: 20
Public Admission Price: Nil
Stand/Space Costs: £22/day, no extras.
Late Booking Opportunities: Some
Photographs: No
Selection Policy: C

KEVIN MURPHY CRAFT FAIRS
Chapel Farm
St Johns Chapel
Eastacombe
Barnstaple
Devon EX31 3PB
Tel. 01271 343160
Contact: Kevin Murphy
Number of Events: 45
Number of Stands: 50
Public Admission Price: 60p
Stand/Space Costs: £30/day, no extras.
Late Booking Opportunities: Some
Photographs: Yes
Selection Policy: B

KINGFISHER PROMOTIONS
6 School Lane
Wilburton
Cambs
CB6 3RW
Tel: 01353 740725
Fax: 01353 740725
Contact: Anita Foster
Number of Events: 18
Number of Stands: 55
Public Admission Price: £1
Stand/Space Costs: £35/day, no extras.
Late Booking Opportunities: Some
Photographs: Yes
Selection Policy: B

KINGS BROMLEY & DISTRICT HORTICULTURAL SOCIETY
c/o 82 Alrewas Road
Kings Bromley
Staffs
DE13 7HP
Tel: 01543 472378
Contact: M J Smith
Number of Events: 1
Number of Stands: 30-40
Public Admission Price: £4
Stand/Space Costs: £15/day.
Table Hire charged extra.
Late Booking Opportunities: Nearly always
Photographs: No
Selection Policy: C

KIRKLEES METROPOLITAN COUNCIL
Queensgate Market
Princess Alexandra Walk
Huddersfield
West Yorks HD5 9JZ
Tel: 01484 223730
Fax: 01484 223735
Contact: Mrs J Edgar or Mrs H Maddran
Number of Events: 2
Number of Stands: 120
Public Admission Price: Nil
Stand/Space Costs: £20/day, no extras.
Late Booking Opportunities: Nearly always
Photographs: No
Selection Policy: C, but still purely craft.
Also weekly crafts in Holmfirth; see
section on Alternative Craft
Marketing Options.

KNIGHTS GARDEN CENTRE
Rosedene Nursery
Woldingham
Surrey CR3 7LA
Tel: 01883 653188
Fax: 01883 652221
Contact: Carol Challand
Number of Events: 1
Number of Stands: 20+
Public Admission Price: Nil
Stand/Space Costs: £20/day.
Tables charged extra.
Late Booking Opportunities: Some
Photographs: Yes
Selection Policy: B
July fair; dates to be confirmed.

L.A.C.E.
Lee's Arts & Crafts Exhibitions
6 Bradley Gardens
Rosegrove, Burnley
Lancs BB12 6JT
Tel: 01282 452637
Fax: 01282 710289
Email: jwhittaker@compuserve.com
Contact: Jim Whittaker
Number of Events: 8-10
Number of Stands: 5-6
Public Admission Price: Nil
Stand/Space Costs: £25/day (tables not provided).
Late Booking Opportunities: Some
Photographs: No
Selection Policy: C
Organiser of week-long shopping centre
events in Lancashire and Yorkshire; see
section on Alternative Craft Marketing
Options.

LAMBETH COUNTRY SHOW
c/o The Pyramids Centre
The Esplanade
Southsea
Hants PO5 3ST
Tel: 01705 799977
Fax: 01705 359990
Contact: Pam Buck
Number of Events: 1
Number of Stands: Unknown
Public Admission Price: Nil
Stand/Space Costs: £135 maximum.
Extras: Chairs £3; Tables £6; Electricity by
arrangement.
Late Booking Opportunities: Nearly always
Photographs: Yes
Selection Policy: B

LAMPORT HALL TRUST
Lamport Hall
Lamport, nr Northampton
Northants NN6 9HD
Tel: 01604 686272
Fax: 01604 686224
Contact: G P S Drye
Number of Events: 2
Number of Stands: 100
Public Admission Price: £2.80
Stand/Space Costs: £75/day, no extras.
Late Booking Opportunities: Some
Photographs: Yes
Selection Policy: C

LANCASTRIAN FAIRS
19 Dovedale Drive
Burnley
Lancs BB12 8XD
Tel: 01282 430670
Contact: Kevin Townson
Number of Events: 210
Number of Stands: 15-50
Public Admission Price: 50p
Stand/Space Costs: £15/day, no extras.
Late Booking Opportunities: Some
Photographs: No
Selection Policy: D
See also section on Alternative Craft
Marketing Options.

LANE END CRAFT FAIR
8 Widdenton View
Lane End
Bucks
HP14 3DU
Tel: 01494 882739
Contact: Connie Smith
Number of Events: 1

Number of Stands: 25
Public Admission Price: Nil
Stand/Space Costs: £11/day, no extras.
Late Booking Opportunities: Some
Photographs: Yes
Selection Policy: A/B

LAUDERDALE ARTS & CRAFTS
22A Calabria Road
London
N5 1JA
Tel: 0411 419788
Contact: Elizabeth Nelson
Number of Events: 15
Number of Stands: 50
Public Admission Price: Voluntary
Contributions.
Stand/Space Costs: £25+/day, no extras.
Late Booking Opportunities: Nearly
always
Photographs: Yes
Selection Policy: B

LAUREL CRAFTS
6 Springhill Lane
Penn
Wolverhampton
West Midlands
WV4 4SH
Tel: 01902 330159
Fax: 01902 330159
Contact: Lin
Number of Events: 13
Number of Stands: 30+
Public Admission Price: 50p
Stand/Space Costs: £30/day, no extras.
Late Booking Opportunities: Rare
Photographs: Yes
Selection Policy: B

LINDA POWELL
98 Victoria Road
Formby
Merseyside L37 1LP
Tel: 01704 833207
Fax: 01704 870060
Contact: Linda Powell
Number of Events: 1
Number of Stands: 70
Public Admission Price: Nil
Stand/Space Costs: £40/day.
Electricity charged extra.
Late Booking Opportunities: Some
Photographs: No
Selection Policy: D
Organiser of The Ideal Home Marquee at
The Liverpool Show.

LIVE PROMOTIONS LTD
The Millstone
St Thomas Road, Spalding
Lincs PE11 2XY
Tel: 01775 768661
Fax: 01775 768665
Email: livepromotions@btinternet.com
Website: www.truckfest.co.uk
Number of Events: 4
Number of Stands: Varies
Public Admission Price: Varies
Stand/Space Costs: On application.
Late Booking Opportunities: Rare
Photographs: No Selection Policy: D

LIVING CRAFTS
1 The Chowns, Harpenden
Herts AL5 2BN
Tel: 01705 426523/01582 761235
Fax: 01705 426523
Contact: Jean or Robin Younger
Number of Events: 1
Public Admission Price: £3-£6.50.

LIVING HERITAGE CRAFT SHOWS LTD
PO Box 36
Uttoxeter
Staffs ST14 8PY
Tel: 01283 820548
Fax: 01283 821200
Number of Events: 60
Number of Stands: 40-150
Public Admission Price: £1-£3.50
Stand/Space Costs: £50-£100 for a 12ft
stand; no extras.
Late Booking Opportunities: Some
Photographs: Yes
Selection Policy: B

LONDON BOROUGH OF ENFIELD
Countryside and Tourism Team
Civic Centre, Silver Street
Enfield
Middx EN1 3XJ
Tel: 0181 982 7043
Fax: 0181 982 5450
Contact: David Smith

LONDON BOROUGH OF REDBRIDGE
Leisure Services
8th Floor Front, Lynton House
255-259 High Road, Ilford
Essex IG1 1NY
Tel: 0181 478 3020 Extn: 3532
Fax: 0181 478 9129
Contact: Arts & Entertainment Team
Number of Events: 1

Number of Stands: 100
Public Admission Price: £3 (adults)
Stand/Space Costs: £90-£110/day.
Electricity and Tables charged extra.
Late Booking Opportunities: Some
Photographs: Yes
Selection Policy: B

LONG MELFORD COUNTRY FAIR
26 Third Avenue
Glemsford, Sudbury
Suffolk CO10 7QJ
Tel: 01787 280941
Fax: 07070 603220
Email: robert.basham@lineone.net
Website: website.lineone.net~robert.basham
Contact: Sandy Basham
Number of Events: 1
Number of Stands: 80
Public Admission Price: £3-£4
Stand/Space Costs: £35 for the weekend.
Electricity and Tables charged extra.
Late Booking Opportunities: Some
Photographs: No Selection Policy: B

LUDLOW CASTLE FESTIVAL OF CRAFTS
Lane Cottage
Norbury, Bishops Castle
Salop SY9 5DX
Tel: 01588 650307
Fax: 01588 650307
Contact: Prue Dakin
Number of Events: 2
Number of Stands: 60
Public Admission Price: £3
Stand/Space Costs: £60/day.
Electricity charged extra – £20 for three days
Late Booking Opportunities: Some
Photographs: Yes
Selection Policy: B

LUTON MUSEUM SERVICE
Luton Museum & Art Gallery
Wardown Park, Luton
Beds LU2 7HA
Tel: 01582 546723
Fax: 01582 546763
Email: worrellk@luton.gov.uk
Contact: Karen Worrell
Number of Events: 2
Number of Stands: 50-70
Public Admission Price: £1 or £2
Stand/Space Costs: £20/day.
Electricity charged extra.
Late Booking Opportunities: Rare
Photographs: Yes
Selection Policy: B

M B COUNTY FAIRS
Bradsole
Abbey Road, Dover
Kent CT15 7DL
Tel: 01304 829822
Fax: 01304 829822
Number of Events: 22
Number of Stands: 100+
Public Admission Price: £1+
Stand/Space Costs: £18/day.
Electricity charged extra at £1 per day.
Late Booking Opportunities: Some
Photographs: No
Selection Policy: C

M&B CRAFTS
6 Corbett Road
Carterton
Oxon OX18 3LD
Tel: 01993 213422
Contact: Mrs Myrtle Slade
Number of Events: 19
Number of Stands: 14
Public Admission Price: Nil
Stand/Space Costs: £16/day, no extras.
Late Booking Opportunities: Rare
Photographs: Yes
Selection Policy: B

MADE IN SCOTLAND LTD
Station Road
Beauly, Inverness-shire
IV4 7EH
Tel: 01463 782578
Fax: 01463 782409
Email: mis@enterprise.net
Website: www.made-in-scotland.co.uk
Contact: Peter Guthrie
Number of Events: 2
Number of Stands: 500-800
Public Admission Price: N/A, Trade Only events.
Stand/Space Costs: £125-£130 per square metre.
Electrics and Stand Extras charged extra.
Late Booking Opportunities: Some
Photographs: Yes
Selection Policy: D
Trade Only shows in Aviemore and Glasgow.

**PLEASE MENTION THE
CRAFTWORKER'S YEAR BOOK
WHEN CONTACTING
EVENT ORGANISERS**

MARATHON EVENT MANAGEMENT LTD
The All England Jumping Course
London Road
Hickstead
West Sussex RH17 5NX
Tel: 01273 833884
Fax: 01273 835556
Email: marathon@btinternet.com
Contact: Philip Bunn
Number of Events: 5
Number of Stands: 200
Public Admission Price: £7
Stand/Space Costs: £70/day.
Electricity charged extra.
Late Booking Opportunities: Some
Photographs: Yes
Selection Policy: A

MARIE MARGARET PROMOTIONS
77 Cedar Lawn Avenue
Barnet
Herts EN5 2LP
Tel: 0181 440 2773
Fax: 0181 440 2773
Email: mariemargaret@msn.com
Contact: Marie Margaret
Number of Events: 20
Number of Stands: 30
Public Admission Price: Nil
Stand/Space Costs: £30/day, no extras.
Late Booking Opportunities: Some
Photographs: No
Selection Policy: C

MARY HOLLAND CRAFT FAIRS LTD
PO Box 43
Abingdon
Oxon OX14 2EX
Tel: 01235 521873
Fax: 01235 521873
Contact: Pauline
Number of Events: 5
Number of Stands: 30-100
Public Admission Price: £3.50-£3.90
Stand/Space Costs: £50-£60/day, no extras.
Late Booking Opportunities: Rare
Photographs: Yes
Selection Policy: A/B

MARY SHORTLE OF YORK
9 Lord Mayor's Walk
York
North Yorks YO3 7HB
Tel: 01904 425168
Fax: 01904 425168
Email: msho35911@aol.com

Contact: Mary Shortle
Number of Events: 14
Number of Stands: 50-100
Public Admission Price: £2.50
Stand/Space Costs: £40/day, no extras.
Late Booking Opportunities: Some
Photographs: No
Selection Policy: D

MASCOT CRAFT & GIFT FAIRS
PO Box 129
Tadworth
Surrey KT20 5YR
Tel: 01737 812989
Fax: 01737 814740
Email: acw@clara.co.uk
Contact: Michael Sharp
Number of Events: 12
Number of Stands: 80-150
Public Admission Price: £1
Stand/Space Costs: £30/day, no extras.
Late Booking Opportunities: Some
Photographs: No
Selection Policy: C

MAURTRAID CRAFT SHOWS
202 Buckingham Road
Bletchley
Milton Keynes
Bucks MK3 5JB
Tel: 01908 271833
Contact: Sue Preedy
Number of Events: 8
Number of Stands: 70-95
Public Admission Price: Usually Free
Stand/Space Costs: £70-£90/day, no
extras.
Late Booking Opportunities: Some
Photographs: Yes
Selection Policy: B
Mainly shopping centre events; see
section on Alternative Craft
Marketing Options.

MELTON MOWBRAY SHOW
PO Box 5421
Melton Mowbray
Leics LE13 0WT
Tel: 01664 500335
Fax: 01664 500335
Number of Events: 1
Number of Stands: Up to 100
Public Admission Price: Nil
Stand/Space Costs: On application.
Late Booking Opportunities: Some
Photographs: Yes
Selection Policy: C

MERIDIENNE EXHIBITIONS LTD
The Fosse
Fosse Way, Radford Semele
Warks CV31 1XN
Tel: 01926 614101
Fax: 01926 614293
Email: 100544.1675@compuserve.com
Contact: Carole Muddeman
Number of Events: 5
Organiser of the Midlands and National
Woodworking Exhibitions, Engineering in
Miniature and Model events

MGA FAIRS
PO Box 282
Overstone
Northampton NN6 0SD
Tel: 01604 642185
Fax: 01604 642185
Email: gmaldis@aol.com
Contact: Marion or George Aldis
Number of Events: 10
Number of Stands: 55-90
Public Admission Price: £2
Stand/Space Costs: £35/day.
Tables charged extra.
Late Booking Opportunities: Rare
Photographs: Yes
Selection Policy: A

MIDAS FAIRS
PO Box 175, Beaconsfield
Bucks HP9 1UL
Tel: 01494 674170 (24hr ansafone)
Contact: Joy Alder
Number of Events: 3
Number of Stands: 65
Public Admission Price: £1.50
Stand Costs: £45-£50 per fair, no extras
Late Booking Opportunities: Some
Photographs: Yes
Selection Policy: B

MIDDLESEX COUNTY SHOW
PO Box 148, Pinner
Middx HA5 5LT
Tel: 0181 866 1367
Fax: 0181 866 1367
Contact: Ann Sullivan
Number of Events: 1
Number of Stands: 200
Public Admission Price: £6-£7
Stand/Space Costs: £55/day.
Electricity charged extra.
Late Booking Opportunities: Rare
Photographs: No
Selection Policy: D

MINIATURA DOLLS HOUSE SHOWS

41 Eastbourne Avenue
Hodge Hill
Birmingham
West Midlands
B34 6AR
Tel: 0121 749 7330
Fax: 0121 749 7330
Contact: Muriel Hopwood
Number of Events: 4
Number of Stands: 200+
Public Admission Price: £5-£9
Stand/Space Costs: On application.
Late Booking Opportunities: Rare
Photographs: Yes
Selection Policy: B
These are highly specialised events.

MONMOUTHSHIRE COUNTY COUNCIL

Markets & Fairs Office
Town Hall, Cross Street
Abergavenny
Monmouthshire
NP7 5TN
Tel: 01873 735811
Fax: 01873 735829
Contact: G B Harris
Number of Events: 10+
Number of Stands: 96
Public Admission Price: Nil
Stand/Space Costs: £16/table for the day.
Late Booking Opportunities: Rare
Photographs: No
Selection Policy: C
See section on Alternative Craft Marketing
Options for details on weekly markets.

NATIONAL CRAFTS FAIR

National House
28 Grosvenor Road
Richmond
Surrey
TW10 6PB
Tel: 0181 940 4608
Fax: 0181 891 0115
Mobile: 0370 626424
Contact: Anthony James
Number of Events: 2
Number of Stands: 90-110
Public Admission Price: £2.50
Stand/Space Costs: £60/day.
Extras: Electricity £25; Tables £5.
Late Booking Opportunities: Some
Photographs: Yes
Selection Policy: A

NATIONAL EISTEDDFOD OF WALES

40 Parc Ty Glas
Llanishen
Cardiff CF4 5WU
Tel: 01222 763777
Fax: 01222 763737
Email: eira@eisteddfod.org.uk
Website: www.eisteddfod.org.uk
Contact: Eira Bowen
Number of Events: 1
Number of Stands: 300
Public Admission Price: £6.50
Stand/Space Costs: On application.
Late Booking Opportunities: Some
Photographs: No
Selection Policy: D

NATIONWIDE EXHIBITIONS (UK) LTD

PO Box 20, Fishponds
Bristol BS16 5QU
Tel: 0117 970 1000
Fax: 0117 970 1001
Email: user@nwe.co.uk
Website: www.nwe.co.uk
Contact: Robert Ewin
Number of Events: 7
Number of Stands: Varies
Stand/Space Costs: On application.

NEWCASTLE ARMSTRONG BRIDGE CRAFT MARKET

Public Health & Environmental Dept
Civic Centre, Newcastle upon Tyne
Tyne & Wear NE1 8PB
Tel: 0191 232 8520 Extn: 6112
Fax: 0191 211 4962
Email: phep@dial.pipex.com
Contact: P Sweet
Number of Events: 52
Number of Stands: 70
Public Admission Price: Nil
Stand/Space Costs: £114 per year; see
section on Alternative Craft Marketing
Options.
Late Booking Opportunities: None
Photographs: No
Selection Policy: C

NICKY MCGARRY

31 Seahill Road
Holywood
Co Down
BT18 0DJ
Tel: 01232 422274
Fax: 01232 422274
Contact: Nicky McGarry
Number of Events: 8

Number of Stands: 35
Public Admission Price: £1.50
Stand/Space Costs: £30/day.
Display Boards charged extra.
Late Booking Opportunities: Some
Photographs: Yes
Selection Policy: B
Organises events in Northern Ireland.
Dates to be confirmed.

NORTH LANARKSHIRE LEISURE
Buchanan Business Park
Cumbernauld Road, Stepps
Glasgow G33 6HR
Tel: 0141 304 1800
Fax: 0141 304 1902
Contact: Jillian Ferrie
Number of Events: 3
Number of Stands: 50+
Public Admission Price: £1
Stand/Space Costs: £18/day, no extras.
Late Booking Opportunities: Some
Photographs: No
Selection Policy: C

NORTH OF ENGLAND HORTICULTURAL SOCIETY
4a South Park Road
Harrogate
North Yorks HG1 5QU
Tel: 01423 561049
Fax: 01423 536880
Contact: Roger Brownbridge
Number of Events: 2
Number of Stands: 70
Public Admission Price: £8
Stand/Space Costs: £50/day.
Extra frontage available at additional cost
Late Booking Opportunities: Rare
Photographs: Yes
Selection Policy: B

NORTH TYNESIDE COUNCIL
Events Unit
40a Bell Street
North Shields
Tyne & Wear NE30 1HF
Tel: 0191 200 5415
Fax: 0191 200 8910
Contact: Carol Alevroyianni
Number of Events: 2
Number of Stands: 50
Public Admission Price: Nil
Stand/Space Costs: £25-£50/day, no extras
Late Booking Opportunities: Some
Photographs: Yes
Selection Policy: B

NORTHAMPTON BOROUGH COUNCIL
Cliftonville House
Bedford Road
Northampton
Northants
NN4 7NR
Tel: 01604 238791
Fax: 01604 238796
Email: events@northampton.gov.uk
Contact: Alison Coles
Number of Events: 1
Number of Stands: 80
Public Admission Price: Nil
Stand/Space Costs: £75/day.
Late Booking Opportunities: Rare
Photographs: Yes
Selection Policy: B

NORTHERN EXHIBITIONS
Clent House
Back Lane
Hunsingore
West Yorks LS22 5JB
Tel: 01423 359259
Fax: 01423 359259
Contact: Richard Clark
Number of Events: 5
Number of Stands: Varies
Public Admission Price: N/A; Trade Fairs.
Stand/Space Costs: On application.
Late Booking Opportunities: On application
Photographs: Yes
Selection Policy: Please apply
Gift Trade Fairs in the north of England, plus one in Scotland.

NOTTINGHAM CITY COUNCIL
Markets & Fairs Office
Glasshouse Street
Nottingham
Notts
NG1 3LP
Tel: 0115 915 6970
Fax: 0115 915 6973
Contact: Richard Noble or Dawn Hurt
Number of Events: 2
Number of Stands: 30 (summer), 60 (christmas).
Public Admission Price: Nil
Stand/Space Costs: £26/day, no extras.
Late Booking Opportunities: Some
Photographs: Yes
Selection Policy: C

OAK CRAFT FAIRS
7 Sandstone Avenue
Walton
Chesterfield
Derbys S42 7NS
Tel: 01246 569698
Email: roboak@globalnet.co.uk
Contact: Chris Warriner
Number of Events: 15
Number of Stands: 60
Public Admission Price: £1.50
Stand/Space Costs: £100.
Electricity is charged extra at the
marquee events.
Late Booking Opportunities: Some
Photographs: Yes
Selection Policy: B

OAKLEAF CRAFT FAIRS
Enfield
Sandleheath
Fordingbridge
Hants
SP6 1PA
Tel: 01425 654663
Fax: 01425 654663
Contact: Mike Hodder
Number of Events: 25
Number of Stands: 15-30
Public Admission Price: 40p-50p
Stand/Space Costs: £18-£20/day, no
extras.
Late Booking Opportunities: Some
Photographs: Yes
Selection Policy: B

OKEHAMPTON AGRICULTURAL SHOW
Landymoor
Cowsen Lane
Sourton, Okehampton
Devon
EX20 4HY
Tel: 01837 861478
Fax: 01837 861617
Email: jtennant@globalnet.co.uk
Contact: Melanie Tennant
Number of Events: 1
Number of Stands: 40
Public Admission Price: £4.50
Stand/Space Costs: £20/day.
Extras: Chairs £2; Tables £8.20.
Late Booking Opportunities: Some
Photographs: No
Selection Policy: C

OLD SPITALFIELDS MARKET
See Urban Space Management

ORCHARD EVENTS LTD
1 Newton Grove
Chiswick
London W4 1LB
Tel: 0181 742 2020
Fax: 0181 995 0977
Contact: Nicky Stephenson
Number of Events: 3
Number of Stands: 270
Public Admission Price: £4-£5
Stand/Space Costs: £75/day.
Electricity and Tables charged extra.
Late Booking Opportunities: Some
Photographs: Yes
Selection Policy: B

OYSTER EXHIBITIONS
93a Mumbles Road
Swansea
West Glam SA3 5TW
Tel: 01792 405019
Fax: 01792 402778
Contact: Zoe Bragg or Robert Thomas
Number of Events: 1
Number of Stands: 200

P&O EVENTS LTD
Earls Court Exhibition Centre
Warwick Road
London
SW5 9TA
Tel: 0171 370 8185
Fax: 0171 370 8235

PACH MONUMENTALS
22 Woodford Avenue
Gants Hill
Essex IG2 6XG
Tel: 0181 529 4881
Fax: 0181 551 9743
Email: sdias1932@yahoo.com
Contact: Sam Dias
Number of Events: 12
Number of Stands: 25
Public Admission Price: Nil
Stand/Space Costs: £18/day, no extras.
Late Booking Opportunities: Nearly always
Photographs: Yes
Selection Policy: D

PATCHINGS ART CENTRE
Oxton Road
Calverton
Notts
NG14 6NU
Tel: 0115 965 3479
Fax: 0115 965 5308

Contact: John Bell
Number of Events: 1
Number of Stands: 150
Public Admission Price: £4.50 (concessions).
Stand/Space Costs: £125 for the full four days, no extras.
Late Booking Opportunities: Rare
Photographs: Yes
Selection Policy: A

PESTALOZZI CHILDREN'S VILLAGE TRUST
Sedlescombe
nr Battle, East Sussex
TN33 0RR
Tel: 01424 870444
Fax: 01424 870655
Email: dir@mistral.co.uk
Website: www3.mistral.co.uk/dec/
Contact: Pam Thomas
Number of Events: 1
Number of Stands: 20+
Public Admission Price: £2 (£5 family ticket)
Stand/Space Costs: £30 indoors; £25 outdoors.
Tables charged extra at £3.
Late Booking Opportunities: Nearly always
Photographs: No
Selection Policy: C/D - should reflect cultural tradition or ethnic goods if possible. This is a registered charity.

PORTISHEAD SUPPORTERS
10 Woodhill Avenue
Portishead
North Somerset
BS20 7EX
Tel: 01275 847033
Contact: Mrs Rita Daniels
Number of Events: 2
Number of Stands: 35
Public Admission Price: Nil
Stand/Space Costs: £20/day, no extras.
Late Booking Opportunities: Some
Photographs: No
Selection Policy: C

POTWALLOPING FESTIVAL
c/o The Flat
21 Nelson Road
Westward Ho
Devon
EX39 1LF
Tel: 01237 470205 (evenings only)
Email: roz.evans@virgin.net
Contact: Roz Evans

Number of Events: 1
Number of Stands: 50
Public Admission Price: Nil
Stand/Space Costs: £7 per table/day.
Electricity charged extra at £5 per day.
Late Booking Opportunities: Rare
Photographs: Yes
Selection Policy: B

PRIORY COURT CRAFT FAIRS
Priory Court
Cuckoo Lane
Liverpool
Merseyside
L25 3PL
Tel: 0151 428 3083
Fax: 0151 428 3083
Contact: Mark Broadbent
Number of Events: 3
Number of Stands: 25
Public Admission Price: Varies
Stand/Space Costs: £35/day.
Electricity charged extra.
Late Booking Opportunities: Some
Photographs: No
Selection Policy: C

QUALITY CRAFT & GIFT FAIRS
55 Alwoodley Lane
Alwoodley
Leeds
West Yorks
LS17 7PU
Tel: 0113 267 1896
Fax: 0113 230 0225
Contact: Diane or Stuart Morris
Number of Events: 18-20
Number of Stands: 40-50+
Public Admission Price: Zero-£1, depending on status.
Stand/Space Costs: £35/day, no extras.
Late Booking Opportunities: Some
Photographs: Yes
Selection Policy: B, though quality bought-in crafted goods will also be considered.

QUALITY CRAFT FAIRS
The Inglenook
Threshers Bush
Harlow
Essex
CM17 0NP
Tel: 01279 411002
Fax: 0171 247 3710
Contact: Joyce Boyask
Number of Events: 16

QUILT EVENTS LTD

PO Box 300
Hethersett
Norwich
Norfolk NR9 3DB
Tel: 01603 812259
Fax: 01603 812097
Email: quiltex@webex.co.uk
Website: www.webex.co.uk/quiltex/
quiltex.html
Contact: Jane Lawrence
Number of Events: 12
Number of Stands: 30-100
Public Admission Price: £5
Stand/Space Costs: £300 for three days, no
extras.
Late Booking Opportunities: Some
Photographs: Yes
Selection Policy: A

QUINTET PROMOTIONS

4 Claremount Court
Dipe Lane
West Boldon
Tyne & Wear NE36 0NF
Tel: 0191 536 2684
Contact: Margery Walsh
Number of Events: 30
Number of Stands: 25-60
Public Admission Price: 50p-£1 (under 18
years free).
Stand/Space Costs: £20/day, no extras.
Late Booking Opportunities: Some
Photographs: Yes
Selection Policy: B

R J EXHIBITIONS

Waveney
Upper Tilehouse Street, Hitchin
Herts SG5 2EF
Tel: 01462 453261
Contact: Bob Sims
Number of Events: 8
Number of Stands: 50
Public Admission Price: £2
Stand/Space Costs: £45/day, no extras.
Late Booking Opportunities: Some
Photographs: No
Selection Policy: C

R J HEYDON

5 Church Street
Aylesbury
Bucks
HP20 2QP
Tel: 01296 415333
Fax: 01296 397092

Contact: John Heydon
Number of Events: 2
Number of Stands: 20-40
Public Admission Price: Zero-£1
Stand/Space Costs: £25-£30/day.
Late Booking Opportunities: Some
Photographs: No
Selection Policy: C/D

R&S FAIRS

PO Box 818
Westcliff-on-Sea
Essex SS0 8HQ
Tel: 01702 345222
Fax: 01702 345234
Contact: Belinda Sheridan
Number of Events: 2
Number of Stands: 100+
Public Admission Price: £1.50
Stand/Space Costs: £35/day, no extras.
Late Booking Opportunities: Some
Photographs: No
Selection Policy: B

RAINBOW FAIR

Navigation Wharf
Carre Street, Sleaford
Lincs NG34 7TW
Tel: 01529 414793
Fax: 01529 414985
Contact: Mrs L Gough
Number of Events: 27
Number of Stands: 200-300
Public Admission Price: £3 (approx)
Stand/Space Costs: On application.
Late Booking Opportunities: Rare
Photographs: Yes
Selection Policy: B

RED ROSE FOREST

Dock Office
Trafford Road
Salford Quays
Manchester M5 2XB
Tel: 0161 872 1660
Fax: 0161 872 1680
Email: team@redroseforest.co.uk
Website: www.nwnet.co.uk/redroseforest
Contact: Kerry Welsh
Number of Events: 5
Number of Stands: 150
Public Admission Price: £2.50
Stand/Space Costs: £25 or £50/day.
Tables and Chairs charged extra.
Late Booking Opportunities: Some
Photographs: No
Selection Policy: C

RICHMOND FELLOWSHIP CRAFT FAIR
8 Addison Road
Kensington
London W14 8DJ
Tel: 0171 603 6373
Fax: 0171 602 8652
Contact: Connie Harman
Number of Events: 1
Number of Stands: 38
Public Admission Price: £3
Stand/Space Costs: £100.
Late Booking Opportunities: Rare
Photographs: Yes
Selection Policy: A
December craft fair held in aid of the
Richmond Fellowship for Community
Mental Health.

RITA DANIELS/POSSET FUNDRAISERS
10 Woodhill Avenue
Portishead
North Somerset BS20 7EX
Tel: 01275 847033
Contact: Mrs Rita Daniels
Number of Events: 2
Number of Stands: 33
Public Admission Price: Nil
Stand/Space Costs: £25/day, no extras.
Late Booking Opportunities: Rare
Photographs: No
Selection Policy: C

ROMOR EXHIBITIONS LTD
PO Box 448
Bedford MK40 2ZP
Tel: 01234 345725
Fax: 01234 328604
Contact: Anthony Rose
Number of Events: 12
Number of Stands: 80-150+
Public Admission Price: £1-£4
Stand/Space Costs: £30-£40/day. Tables
and (sometimes) Electricity charged extra
– please ask
Late Booking Opportunities: Nearly
always
Photographs: Yes
Selection Policy: A/B

ROYAL INTERNATIONAL AIR TATTOO
Building 15
RAF Fairford
Glos
GL7 4DL
Tel: 01285 713300 Extn: 3391
Fax: 01285 713268
Email: RAFBFE@rafbfe.telme.com

Contact: Tom Watts
Number of Events: 1
Number of Stands: 500+
Stand/Space Costs: On application
Late Booking Opportunities: Some
Photographs: Yes
Selection Policy: B

ROYAL NORFOLK SHOW
The Showground
Dereham Road
New Costessey, Norwich
Norfolk NR5 0TT
Tel: 01603 748931
Fax: 01603 748729
Contact: Mrs D M Akers
Number of Events: 1
Number of Stands: 30
Public Admission Price: £9
Stand/Space Costs: £150.
Electricity and Tables charged extra.
Late Booking Opportunities: Some
Photographs: Yes
Selection Policy: B

RUDGWICK STEAM & COUNTRY SHOW
Show Office
Windacres Barn
Rudgwick
West Sussex RH12 3EG
Tel: 01403 822378/0973 262613
Contact: Terry Hand
Number of Events: 1
Number of Stands: 200
Public Admission Price: £2.50-£4,
depending on status.
Stand/Space Costs: £30/day.
Electricity and Tables charged extra.
Late Booking Opportunities: None
Photographs: No
Selection Policy: C

RURAL CRAFTS ASSOCIATION
Brook Road
Wormley
Godalming
Surrey GU8 5UA
Tel: 01428 682292
Fax: 01428 685969
Contact: Trevor Sears
Number of Events: 61
Number of Stands: 100+
Public Admission Price: £4
Stand/Space Costs: £80+/day.
Late Booking Opportunities: Some
Photographs: Yes
Selection Policy: B

SELBY GAME FAIR LTD

Chapel House
Newland
Selby
North Yorks YO8 8QT
Tel: 01757 618333
Fax: 01757 618333
Email: scarflace@demon.co.uk
Contact: Michelle
Number of Events: 4
Number of Stands: 100
Public Admission Price: £5
Stand/Space Costs: £40/day.
Electricity, Tables and Chairs charged extra.
Late Booking Opportunities: Nearly always
Photographs: No

SHERBORNE CRAFT MARKET

c/o The Old Forge
Holton, Wincanton
Somerset BA9 8AX
Tel: 01963 33384
Fax: 01963 33384
Contact: Susan Higginson
Number of Events: 1
Number of Stands: 45
Public Admission Price: 50p
Stand/Space Costs: £35/day, no extras.
Late Booking Opportunities: Rare
Photographs: Yes
Selection Policy: B

SHIRES EVENTS

1 Lower Farm Cottage
Halse, Brackley
Northants NN13 6DY
Tel: 01280 705842
Contact: Mr K McManus
Number of Events: 6
Number of Stands: 80+
Public Admission Price: £3-£4
Stand/Space Costs: £50/day.
Electricity charged extra. Caravan sites also available.
Photographs: Yes
Selection Policy: B

SKELTON SHOW

Tonlyn
Fairybread Lane
Stainton
Cumbria
CA11 0DX
Tel: 0468 630143
Fax: 01768 242321
Contact: John Slee

Number of Events: 1
Number of Stands: 60 (plus 120 trade stands).
Public Admission Price: £4
Stand/Space Costs: £20 per table/day.
Tables charged extra at £5.
Late Booking Opportunities: Rare
Photographs: No
Selection Policy: C

SMALLHOLDER SHOWS

1 Brookside
Henfold Lane
Beare Green
Surrey
RH5 4QH
Tel: 01306 741302
Fax: 01306 741302
Contact: P & C Rainger
Number of Events: 3
Number of Stands: 200
Public Admission Price: £4
Stand/Space Costs: £35/day.
Electricity, Tables and Chairs charged extra.
Late Booking Opportunities: Rare
Photographs: No
Selection Policy: D

SOCIETY OF DESIGNER CRAFTSMEN

24 Rivington Street
London
EC2A 3DU
Tel: 0171 739 3663
Fax: 0171 739 3663
Email: secretary@designcraft.org.uk
Website: www.cogent-comms.co.uk/crafts/dcraft
Contact: Richard O'Donoghue
Number of Events: 3-4
Number of Stands: 40
Public Admission Price: Nil
Stand/Space Costs: Varies.
Late Booking Opportunities: None
Selection Policy: A/B
Only Society members take part in the exhibition.

SOMETHING SPECIAL CRAFT & GIFT FAYRES

31 Richmond Road
Lee-on-Solent
Hants
PO13 9NT
Tel: 01705 550419
Contact: Roz Dennison
Number of Events: 8

Number of Stands: 70
Public Admission Price: Nil
Stand/Space Costs: £22-£40/day.
Electrical Supply charged extra at £3.
Late Booking Opportunities: Rare
Photographs: No
Selection Policy: C

SOUTH WEST TRUCKERS

23 Hamlyn Close
Newbarn Park
Taunton
Somerset
TA1 4NT
Tel: 01823 276143
Contact: Shirley Brinicombe
Number of Events: 1
Number of Stands: 50
Public Admission Price: £3
Stand/Space Costs: £5 per foot frontage/
day, no extras.
Late Booking Opportunities: Please
enquire
Photographs: No
Selection Policy: C

SOUTHWATER PROMOTIONS

29 Woodlands Way
Southwater, nr Horsham
West Sussex
RH13 7HY
Tel: 01403 730113
Contact: Mrs M Brooker
Number of Events: 3
Number of Stands: 35
Public Admission Price: Nil
Stand/Space Costs: £32/day, no extras.
Late Booking Opportunities: Rare
Photographs: Yes
Selection Policy: B

SPECIAL EVENTS - SOUTHEND-ON-SEA BOROUGH COUNCIL

PO Box 6
Southend-on-Sea
Essex
SS2 6ER
Tel: 01702 215166
Fax: 01702 215465
Contact: Lisa Tidder
Number of Events: 3

SPRINGFIELDS EXHIBITION CENTRE

Springfields Gardens
Camelgate
Spalding
Lincs

PE12 6ET
Tel: 01775 724843/01775 713253
Fax: 01775 711209
Contact: Brian Willoughby
Number of Events: 4

ST DONATS ARTS CENTRE

St Donats Castle
nr Llantwit Major
Vale of Glamorgan
CF61 1WF
Tel: 01446 792151
Fax: 01446 794711
Email: admin.sdac@which.net
Contact: Sharon Stone
Number of Events: 2
Number of Stands: 40
Public Admission Price: Nil-£5, depending
on status.
Stand/Space Costs: £60/day, no extras.
Late Booking Opportunities: Some
Photographs: Yes
Selection Policy: B

ST HELENS SHOW

St Helens MBC
Rivington Centre, Rivington Road
St Helens
Merseyside
WA10 4ND
Tel: 01744 455349
Fax: 01744 455350
Contact: Jenny Lloyd
Number of Events: 1
Number of Stands: 150
Public Admission Price: Nil
Stand/Space Costs: On application.
Late Booking Opportunities: Rare
Photographs: No
Selection Policy: C/D

STAMFORD ARTS CENTRE

(Craft Showcases)
27 St Marys Street
Stamford
Lincs
PE9 2DL
Tel: 01780 763203
Fax: 01780 766690
Contact: Carol Palmer
Number of Events: 12 Craft Exhibitions
Public Admission Price: Nil
Photographs: Yes
Selection Policy: B
See section on Alternative Craft Marketing
Options.

STAMPS UNLIMITED
The Stamp Cupboard
The Old Post Office
8 Swan Street, Kingsclere
Berks
RG20 5PJ
Tel: 01635 299110
Fax: 01635 299295
Contact: Mike Payne
Number of Events: 1
Number of Stands: 30+
Public Admission Price: £2.50
Stand/Space Costs: £140, no extras.
Late Booking Opportunities: Nearly always
Photographs: N/A
Selection Policy: By invitation only

STANCIE KUTLER CRAFTS
c/o Nantwich Civic Hall
Market Street
Nantwich
Cheshire
CW5 6LN
Tel: 01270 624288
Contact: Stancie Kutler
Number of Events: 2

STAPEHILL ABBEY, CRAFTS & GARDENS
276 Wimborne Road West
Stapehill
nr Wimborne
Dorset
BH21 2EB
Tel: 01202 861686
Fax: 01202 894589
Contact: Sheena Tinsdale
Number of Events: 2
Number of Stands: 30
Public Admission Price: £2.50
Stand/Space Costs: £25/day.
Electrical Power charged extra at £5.
Late Booking Opportunities: Some
Photographs: No
Selection Policy: C
Also permanent craft units on site and
special events; see section on Alternative
Craft Marketing Options.

STOKE ROW STEAM RALLY
6 Wayside Green
Woodcote
nr Reading
Berks
RG8 0QJ
Tel: 01491 681483
Fax: 01491 681483

Contact: Mark Casson
Number of Events: 1
Number of Stands: 30
Public Admission Price: £3
Stand/Space Costs: £10/day, no extras.
Late Booking Opportunities: Some
Photographs: No
Selection Policy: C

TAUNTON AGRICULTURAL SHOW LTD
The Showground
Netherday Farm
Thurlbear, Taunton
Somerset
TA3 5AX
Tel: 01823 353066
Fax: 01823 354340
Contact: Tony Richards
Number of Events: 1
Number of Stands: 48
Public Admission Price: £5.50 (adults).
Stand/Space Costs: £50 for a standard site.
No Tables/Chairs provided. Electricity
charged extra at £45.
Late Booking Opportunities: Some
Photographs: No
Selection Policy: C

THE ARTS CENTRE
Biddick Lane
Fatfield
Washington
Tyne & Wear
NE38 8AB
Tel: 0191 219 3455
Fax: 0191 219 3466
Contact: Marie Kirbyshaw
Number of Events: 12
Number of Stands: 60
Public Admission Price: Nil
Stand/Space Costs: £14/fair.
Table charged extra at £3.
Late Booking Opportunities: Rare
Photographs: Yes
Selection Policy: B

THE COUNTRY LIVING FAIRS
BDC Events
52 Upper Street
London
N1 0QH
Tel: 0171 359 3535
Fax: 0171 288 6446
Contact: Richard Pearson
Number of Events: 2
Number of Stands: 330
Public Admission Price: £8.50-£10

Stand/Space Costs: Varies, but around
£240 per square metre.
Some extra charges.
Late Booking Opportunities: Some
Photographs: Yes
Selection Policy: A

THE CRAFT & CIDER COUNTRY FAYRE
14 Parsonage Road
Berrow
Somerset TA8 2NL
Tel: 01278 784414 (day + evenings)
Fax: 01278 784414
Contact. Alan Bevan
Number of Events: 1
Number of Stands: 80-100
Public Admission Price: £3.50
Stand/Space Costs: £50/day, no extras.
Late Booking Opportunities: Some
Photographs: Yes
Selection Policy: B/C

THE CRAFT GUILD OF WEST LANCASHIRE
1 Westgate
Pennylands
Skelmersdale
Lancs WN8 8LP
Tel: 01695 51999
Fax: 01695 51222
Contact: Theresa Gaskell
Number of Events: 9-10
Number of Stands: 15
Public Admission Price: Nil
Stand/Space Costs: £25+/day, no extras.
Late Booking Opportunities: Only The
Craft Guild members may show.
Photographs: Yes
Selection Policy: A

THE CRAFT MOVEMENT
PO Box 1641
Frome
Somerset
BA11 1YY
Tel: 01373 813333
Fax: 01373 813636
Contact: Joan Clink
Number of Events: 8
Number of Stands: 90+
Public Admission Price: £4
Stand/Space Costs: £100+/day.
An additional charge is made for extra
lights or tables/chairs.
Late Booking Opportunities: Some
Photographs: Yes
Selection Policy: A

THE CRAFT TENT COMPANY
c/o Thimble House, 80 Lime Road
Wednesbury
West Midlands WS10 9NF
Tel: 0121 556 4281
Contact: David or Jacqui Duffill
Number of Events: 8
Number of Stands: 30
Public Admission Price: Varies
Stand/Space Costs: £17.50/day.
Electricity charged extra.
Late Booking Opportunities: Some
Photographs: Yes
Selection Policy: B

THE CRAFTER'S MARKETPLACE
Unit 4, The Coliseum Centre
off London Road
Derby
Derbys DE1 2NY
Tel: 01332 267750
Fax: 01332 267751
Contact: Cliff Bloomfield
A specialist craft retailing operation open
all year round. See section on Alternative
Craft Marketing Options for details.

THE EXHIBITION TEAM LTD
Events House, Wycombe Air Park
Marlow
Bucks SL7 3DP
Tel: 01494 450504
Fax: 01494 450245
Number of Events: 28
Number of Stands: 150
Public Admission Price: £3
Stand/Space Costs: £100/day.
Extras: Service Charge and any Extra
Tables required.
Late Booking Opportunities: Rare
Photographs: Yes
Selection Policy: B

THE FARNHAM MALTINGS
Bridge Square, Farnham
Surrey GU9 7QR
Tel: 01252 713637
Fax: 01252 718177
Email: farnmalt@aol.com
Contact: Ms Tozzy Bridger
Number of Events: 2
Number of Stands: 70
Public Admission Price: £2.50
Stand/Space Costs: On application.
Late Booking Opportunities: Some
Photographs: Yes
Selection Policy: B

THE GREAT YORKSHIRE TRACTION ENGINE CLUB
Low Wood, Low Dalby
Pickering
North Yorks YO18 7LT
Tel: 01751 460312
Contact: Rebecca Swiers
Number of Events: 1
Number of Stands: 30
Public Admission Price: £1.50-£4,
depending on status.
Stand/Space Costs: £30 for the two days,
no extras.
Late Booking Opportunities: Some
Photographs: No
Selection Policy: B/C

THE LONDON DOLLSHOUSE FESTIVAL
25 Priory Road
Kew
Richmond
Surrey TW9 3DQ
Tel: 0181 948 1893
Fax: 0181 332 2894
Email:
caroline@dollshousefestiv.demon.co.uk
Website:
www.dollshousefestiv.demon.co.uk
Contact: Caroline Hamilton or Gillie
Towers
Number of Events: 1
Number of Stands: 170
Public Admission Price: £5
Stand/Space Costs: Confirm with organ-
iser, but Electricity will be
charged extra at £10.
Late Booking Opportunities: Rare
Photographs: Yes
Selection Policy: A

THE MALCOLM GROUP EVENTS LTD
Ground Floor
3 Brunswick Place
Hove
East Sussex BN3 1EA
Fax: 01273 723249
Email: malcolm@fastnet.co.uk
Website: www.mgel.com
Contact: C Geisler
Number of Events: 3
Number of Stands: 200
Public Admission Price: £5
Stand/Space Costs: £125/day.
Extras: Electricity £20; Tables £15; Chairs £5
Late Booking Opportunities: Some
Photographs: No
Selection Policy: C

THE NATIONAL TRUST
Castle Ward
Strangford
Downpatrick
Co Down
BT30 7LS
Tel: 01396 881204
Fax: 01396 881729
Contact: Mike Gaston or Hazel McKibbin
Number of Events: 10-20
Number of Stands: 20-30
Public Admission Price: £3.50 per car.
Stand/Space Costs: £20/day, no extras.
Late Booking Opportunities: Nearly
always
Photographs: Yes, sometimes
Selection Policy: B

THE NATIONAL TRUST
East Riddlesden Hall
Bradford Road
Keighley
West Yorks
BD20 5EL
Tel: 01535 607075
Fax: 01535 691462
Contact: Liz Houseman
Number of Events: 2
Number of Stands: 25
Public Admission Price: £1
Stand/Space Costs: £15/day, no extras.
Late Booking Opportunities: Some
Photographs: Yes
Selection Policy: B

THE NATIONAL TRUST
Florence Court
Enniskillen
Co Fermanagh
BT92 1DB
Tel: 01365 348249
Fax: 01365 348873
Contact: Property Manager
Number of Events: 2
Number of Stands: 25
Public Admission Price: £1-£4
Stand/Space Costs: £10/day, no extras.
Late Booking Opportunities: Some
Photographs: No
Selection Policy: C

THE NATIONAL TRUST
Wimpole Hall
Arrington
nr Royston
Cambs
SG8 0BW

Tel: 01223 207257
Fax: 01223 207838
Email: aweusr@smtp.ntrust.org.uk
Contact: Craft Fair Manager
Number of Events: 2
Number of Stands: 40
Public Admission Price: £2
Stand/Space Costs: £50/day, no extras.
Late Booking Opportunities: Some
Photographs: Yes
Selection Policy: B

THE RURAL LIVING SHOW

Prioryfield House
20 Canon Street
Taunton
Somerset
TA1 1SW
Tel: 01823 323363
Fax: 01823 271072
Contact: Louise Walker
Number of Events: 1
Number of Stands: 130
Public Admission Price: £2
Stand/Space Costs: £50/day, no extras.
Late Booking Opportunities: Rare
Photographs: Yes
Selection Policy: B

THE SUSSEX GUILD

c/o Huntswood
St Helena Lane
Streat, nr Hassocks
West Sussex
BN6 8SD
Tel: 01273 890088
Contact: J Fisher
Number of Events: 7
Number of Stands: Varies
Public Admission Price: Varies
Stand/Space Costs: Varies
Late Booking Opportunities: None
Photographs: Yes
Selection Policy: A/B
Exhibitors/Members must be residents of
Sussex or adjoining counties.

THE YFC COUNTRY FAYRE

c/o Ansells Farm
Langford
Lechlade
Glos
GL7 3LD
Tel: 01367 860540
Fax: 01367 860540
Contact: Heather Kirby
Number of Events: 1

Number of Stands: 40
Public Admission Price: £4
Stand/Space Costs: £20/day.
Electricity charged extra.
Late Booking Opportunities: Rare
Photographs: No
Selection Policy: C

THURLOW STEAM RALLY & SHOW

c/o 4 London Road
Great Chesterford
Saffron Walden
Essex CB10 9NY
Tel: 01799 530548/01440 783457
Contact: Jacki Charles or Don Loveday
Number of Events: 1
Number of Stands: Up to 40
Public Admission Price: £2.50-£3.50,
depending on status.
Stand/Space Costs: £22 for the weekend.
Tables charged extra at £2.
Late Booking Opportunities: Nearly always
Photographs: No
Selection Policy: C/D

TIVERTON CRAFT FAIR

c/o 29 Old Road
Tiverton
Devon EX16 4HJ
Tel: 01884 253556
Fax: 01884 253556
Contact: Celia Rufey
Number of Events: 1
Number of Stands: 70+
Public Admission Price: Nil
Stand/Space Costs: £30/day, no extras.
Late Booking Opportunities: Rare
Photographs: Yes
Selection Policy: B

TOWERLANDS CENTRE

Panfield Road
Braintree
Essex CM7 5BJ
Tel: 01376 326802
Fax: 01376 552487
Contact: Ray Bunn or Angela Adams
Number of Events: 2
Number of Stands: 150
Public Admission Price: £1.50
Stand/Space Costs: £20/day.
Tables and Electricity charged extra.
Additional space also
available at extra cost.
Late Booking Opportunities: Some
Photographs: No
Selection Policy: C

TOWN & COUNTRY CRAFT FAIRS

Hill Cross
Ashford, Bakewell
Derbys DE45 1QL
Tel: 01629 812008/01234 355569
Fax: 01629 813413
Contact: Pat Paulett
Number of Events: 13
Number of Stands: 50
Public Admission Price: £1
Stand/Space Costs: £40/day.
Electricity charged extra at the marquee
event.
Late Booking Opportunities: Nearly always
Photographs: Yes
Selection Policy: C

TOWN & COUNTRY FESTIVAL

RASE
National Agricultural Centre
Stoneleigh Park
Warks CV8 2LZ
Tel: 01203 696969
Fax: 01203 696900
Email: vickys@rase.org.uk
Website: www.rase.org.uk
Contact: Victoria Stephens
Number of Events: 1
Number of Stands: 210
Public Admission Price: £6.50
Stand/Space Costs: £199 for the three
days. Tables and General Stand Equipment
charged extra.
Late Booking Opportunities: Some
Photographs: Yes
Selection Policy: Generally A/B, but an
imported craft section also allowed.

TRADE PROMOTION SERVICES LTD

Exhibition House
Warren Lane
London SE18 6BW
Tel: 0181 301 8600
Fax: 0181 855 3506
Email: tps@tps.emap.co.uk
Website: www.gift-gardenmart.com
Number of Events: 6
Number of Stands: 2000-5000
Public Admission Price: N/A, Trade Only
Events.
Stand/Space Costs: Shell Schemes from
£130 to £175 per square
metre, depending on the event.
Late Booking Opportunities: Some
Photographs: No
Spring Fair, Autumn Fair, Housewares
International etc.

TRADITIONAL CRAFTS LTD

Box 31, Medway Bridge Marina
Manor Lane, Rochester
Kent ME1 3HS
Tel: 01634 849778
Fax: 01634 849778
Contact: Alison
Number of Events: 9
Number of Stands: 120
Public Admission Price: £3
Stand/Space Costs: £80/day, no extras.
Late Booking Opportunities: Some
Photographs: Yes
Selection Policy: B

TY MAWR COUNTRY PARK

Cae Gwilym Lane
Cefn Mawr
Wrexham
Clwyd LL14 3PE
Tel: 01978 822780
Contact: Liz Carding
Number of Events: 1
Number of Stands: 50
Public Admission Price: Nil
Stand/Space Costs: £12 for the one-day
fair. Table and Chair Hire available.
Late Booking Opportunities: Some
Photographs: No
Selection Policy: D

URBAN SPACE MANAGEMENT

56 Camden Lock Place
Camden
London NW1 8AF
Tel: 0171 247 6590
Fax: 0171 247 6178
Contact: Keely Wootten
Number of Events: 800+
Number of Stands: Varies, according to
location
Stand/Space Costs: £5-£45/day, depending
on which day and where.
The company manages Camden Lock
Market, Greenwich Market and Old
Spitalfields Market. See section on
Alternative Craft Marketing Options for
details on each of these.

VBR CRAFTS

64 Red Rose
Binfield
Berks RG42 5LD
Tel: 01344 455909
Contact: Valerie Batt-Rawden
Number of Events: 2
Number of Stands: 55

Public Admission Price: Nil
Stand/Space Costs: £33 for one day or £60
for two days. Tables charged extra, where
required.
Late Booking Opportunities: Nearly always
Photographs: Yes
Selection Policy: B

WALES CRAFT COUNCIL
Henfaes Lane
Welshpool Industrial Estate
Welshpool
Powys SY21 7BE
Tel: 01938 555313
Fax: 01938 556237
Contact: Judith Thomas
Number of Events: 2
Number of Stands: 170
Stand/Space Costs: On application.
Late Booking Opportunities: Nearly always
Photographs: No
Selection Policy: C
These are Trade Only shows.

WALFORD MILL CRAFT CENTRE
Stone Lane, Wimborne
Dorset BH21 1NL
Tel: 01202 841400
Fax: 01202 840132
Contact: Philip Goulden
Craft shop and exhibition gallery and craft
school; see section on
Alternative Craft Marketing Options.

WEST COUNTRY CRAFT FAIRS
**Unit 6, Underwood Business Park
Wookey Hole Road, Wells
Somerset BA5 1AF
Tel: 01749 677049
Fax: 01749 677049
Contact: Fred Wilcox
Number of Events: 31
Number of Stands: 40
Public Admission Price: 50p
Stand/Space Costs: £30/day, no extras.
Late Booking Opportunities: Some
Photographs: Yes
Selection Policy: B
See also section on Alternative Craft
Marketing Options.**

WEST LAKES CRAFTSMEN
1 High Station
Dearham
Maryport
Cumbria
CA15 7LB

Tel: 01900 814035/01697 320741
Contact: Trevor Brown or Jean Sherwen
Number of Events: 40
Number of Stands: 15-40
Public Admission Price: Nil
Stand/Space Costs: £8-£20 per 6ft table/day
Selection Policy: B/C
Non-profit making organisation showing at
village halls, agricultural shows, vintage
rallies + marquees in Lake District/Solway
Coast

WEST OF ENGLAND FAIRS
24 Ganders Park
Edginswell Lane, Torquay
Devon TQ2 7JF
Tel: 01803 875635
Fax: 01803 875635
Contact: Mrs June Cogings
Number of Events: 3
Number of Stands: 40-60
Public Admission Price: £1.50-£2.50
Stand/Space Costs: £30/day, no extras.
Late Booking Opportunities: Some
Photographs: No
Selection Policy: B

WEST PENNINE PROMOTIONS
271 Tyldesley Road
Atherton
Manchester
Tel: 01942 870695
Contact: Geoffrey Grundy
Number of Events: 30
Number of Stands: 25-30
Public Admission Price: 50p
Stand/Space Costs: £20/day, no extras.
Late Booking Opportunities: Some
Photographs: No
Selection Policy: C

WILTSHIRE COUNTY SHOW
c/o Imperial Charity
34a George Street
Warminster
Wilts BA12 8QB
Tel: 01985 216644
Fax: 01985 217400
Contact: David Smith or David McCance
Number of Events: 1
Number of Stands: 65-85
Public Admission Price: £5
Stand/Space Costs: £40/day.
Extras: Electricity £10; Tables £5; Chairs £3.
Late Booking Opportunities: Some
Photographs: Yes
Selection Policy: a combination of A, B & C.

WIRRAL SHOW CRAFT MARQUEE
142 Sandbrook Lane
Moreton
Wirral
Merseyside
L46 0QL
Tel: 0151 677 7095
Contact: Mrs A Cordon
Number of Events: 1
Number of Stands: 65
Public Admission Price: Nil
Stand/Space Costs: £35/day, no extras.
Late Booking Opportunities: Rare
Photographs: No
Selection Policy: C

WMH LEISURE
71 West Street
Sittingbourne
Kent
ME10 1AN
Tel: 01795 474660
Fax: 01795 472926
Email: wilchesson@gardenshows.com
Website: www.gardenshows.com
Contact: Will Chesson
Number of Events: 2
Number of Stands: 50
Public Admission Price: £3
Stand/Space Costs: £25.
Extras: Electricity £15; Tables £10.
Late Booking Opportunities: Some
Photographs: No
Selection Policy: C

WOODLAND CRAFTS
"Butskiln", Street End
Sidlesham Common
Chichester
West Sussex
PO20 7QD
Tel: 01243 641306
Fax: 01243 641306
Contact: Paul Bishopp
Number of Events: 35
Number of Stands: 30-150
Public Admission Price: £1-£3
Stand/Space Costs: £25-£50/day.
Electricity and Tables (varies) charged
extra.
Late Booking Opportunities: Some
Photographs: Yes
Selection Policy: B or C, depending on
event
See also section on Alternative Craft
Marketing Options.

WORTHING LEISURE
Pavilion Theatre
Marine Parade, Worthing
West Sussex BN11 3PX
Tel: 01903 239999 Extn 2503
Fax: 01903 821124
Contact: Rosie Gray
Number of Events: 13
Number of Stands: 69
Public Admission Price: Nil
Stand/Space Costs: £26/day.
Larger space available at an additional
cost of £2.
Late Booking Opportunities: Some
Photographs: No
Selection Policy: D

WYESIDE ARTS CENTRE
Castle Street, Builth Wells
Powys LD2 3BN
Tel: 01982 552555
Fax: 01982 552515
Contact: Natalie Bass
Number of Events: Permanent showcase
Number of Stands: 10
Public Admission Price: Nil
Stand/Space Costs: Percentage levied on
sales.
Late Booking Opportunities: Some
Photographs: No
Selection Policy: B
See section on Alternative Craft Marketing
Options for details.

YORKRAFT FAIRS
Mossgiel
Spa Well Lane
West Cowick, Goole
East Yorks DN14 9EA
Tel: 01405 861509
Fax: 01405 861509
Contact: Pete or Therese
Number of Events: 30
Number of Stands: 10-15
Public Admission Price: Nil
Stand/Space Costs: £10/day, no extras.
Late Booking Opportunities: Some
Photographs: Yes
Selection Policy: B

PLEASE MENTION THE
CRAFTWORKER'S YEAR BOOK
WHEN CONTACTING
EVENT ORGANISERS

REPRESENTATIVE BODIES IN CRAFT

ASSOCIATIONS AND FEDERATIONS

AN TUIREANN
Struan Road, Portree
Isle of Skye IV51 9EG
Tel: 01478 613306
Fax: 01478 613156
Contact: Karen Ferguson
Email: antuireann.demon.co.uk
Membership: Non-juried, paid membership
(one year £12, life £100).
An Tuireann is a registered charity.

ASSOCIATION FOR CONTEMPORARY JEWELLERY
c/o The School of Jewellery
Vittoria Street, Birmingham
West Midlands B1 3PA
Tel: 0121 331 5940
Fax: 0121 331 5943
Contact: Maria Hanson
Membership: Non-juried, paid membership.

ASSOCIATION FOR APPLIED ARTS
6 Darnaway Street
Edinburgh EH3 6BG
Tel: 0131 220 5070
Fax: 0131 225 5660
Contact: Anne Lightwood
Membership: Non-juried, paid membership.
Restricted to Scotland.

ASSOCIATION OF BLAIRGOWRIE CRAFTWORKERS
Tel: 01250 873623
Contact: Don Amer
Website: www.scottish-towns.co.uk/
perthshire/blairgowrie/abc/index.html
Membership: Juried for Full membership;
new category of Associate Membership
recently introduced. Fees payable for both.

ASSOCIATION OF CREATIVE CRAFTS AND ART (ACCA)
PO Box 41
Driffield
East Yorks YO25 8YX
Tel: 01377 253900
Fax: 01377 255918
Contact: Margaret Griffiths
Membership: Juried.

ASSOCIATION OF GUILDS OF WEAVERS, SPINNERS & DYERS
2 Bower Mount Road
Maidstone
Kent
ME16 8AU
Tel: 01622 678429
Contact: Anne Dixon
Membership: Association of the 100+ guilds
of this type throughout the UK.

ASSOCIATION OF ILLUSTRATORS
32-38 Saffron Hill
London EC1N 8SG
Tel: 0171 831 7377
Fax: 0171 831 6277
Contact: Samantha Taylor
Email: st@a-o-illustrators.demon.co.uk
Website: www.aoi.co.uk
Membership: Restricted to illustrators.

ASSOCIATION OF WOODTURNERS OF GREAT BRITAIN
c/o Keeper's Cottage
Lee, Ellesmere
Salop SY12 9AE
Contact: Peter Einig
Email: petereinig@mcmail.com
Website: www.woodturners.co.uk
Membership: Non-juried, paid membership.

BASKET MAKERS ASSOCIATION
King William Cottage
Yalberton Road
Paignton
Devon
TQ4 7PE
Contact: Hilary Burns
Membership: Non-juried, paid membership.

BRIGANTIA
The Old Vicarage
Bondgate, Helmsley
North Yorks
YO62 5BP
Tel: 01439 770657
Fax: 01439 770691
Contact: Tracie Jarvis
Email: info@brigantia.co.uk
Website: www.brigantia.co.uk
Membership: Juried and restricted to the
North Yorkshire area.

BRITISH ARTIST BLACKSMITHS ASSOCIATION
111 Main Street, Ratho
Midlothian EH28 8NW
Tel: 0131 333 1300
Fax: 0131 333 3354
Contact: Phil Johnson
Email: phil@rathobyres.demon.co.uk
Membership: Non-juried, paid membership.

BRITISH ASSOCIATION OF DECORATIVE & FOLK ARTS
1 Bentley Close
Horndean
nr Waterlooville
Hants PO8 9HH
Tel: 01705 571516
Fax: 01705 356658
Contact: Sue Goodhand
Email: s.goodhand@virgin.net
Membership: Non-juried, paid membership.

BRITISH CERAMIC CONFEDERATION
Federation House
Station Road
Stoke-on-Trent
Staffs ST4 2SA
Tel: 01782 744631
Fax: 01782 744102
Contact: Francis Morrall
Email: bcc@ceramfed.co.uk
Membership: Confederation representing British ceramic producers from all sectors; also the employers' federation.

BRITISH CHINESE ARTISTS' ASSOCIATION
Interchange Studios
Dalby Street
London NW5 3NQ
Tel: 0171 267 6133
Fax: 0171 482 5292
Contact: Andy Cheung
Website: www.livjm.ac.uk/~leagchan/can/canhome.html
Membership: Open.

BRITISH DECOY AND WILDFOWL CARVERS ASSOCIATION
26 Shendish Edge
Hemel Hempstead
Herts HP3 9JZ
Tel: 01442 247610
Contact: Mrs Janet Morris
Membership: Non-juried, paid membership.

BRITISH DOLL ARTISTS ASSOCIATION
31 Braeside Crescent
Billinge, Wigan
Lancs WN5 7PQ
Tel: 01744 894784
Contact: Mrs Eileen Bramwell
Membership: Restricted to doll artists.

BRITISH WOODCARVERS ASSOCIATION
25 Summerfield Drive
Nottage, Porthcawl
Mid Glam CF36 3PB
Tel: 01656 786937
Fax: 01656 786937
Contact: J B Sullivan
Membership: Non-juried, paid membership.

CORNWALL CRAFTS ASSOCIATION
Trelowarren Gallery
Trelowarren
Mawgan in Meneage
Helston, Cornwall
TR12 6AF
Tel: 01326 221567
Fax: 01326 221567
Contact: Rod Shaw Sands
Membership: Non-juried, paid membership. Restricted to makers in Cornwall.

COUNTRY CRAFTS ASSOCIATION
29 Wallis Avenue
Lincoln
Lincs LN6 8AS
Tel: 01522 687911
Fax: 01522 687911
Contact: Colin Hornsey
Membership: Juried.

CRAFT POTTERS ASSOCIATION OF GREAT BRITAIN
21 Carnaby Street
London W1V 1LP
Tel: 0171 437 6781
Fax: 0171 287 9954
Contact: Tony Ainsworth
Email: tony.ainsworth@virgin.net
Membership: Juried.

DESIGNER JEWELLERS GROUP
24 Rivington Street
London EC2A 3DU
Tel: 0171 739 3663
Contact: The Secretary
Membership: Juried.

DORSET COUNTY ARTS & CRAFTS ASSOCIATION
21 St Anthony's Road
Bournemouth
Dorset BH2 6PB
Tel: 01202 553113
Fax: 01202 553113
Contact: Paul Newsome
Email: dcaca@pador.btconnect.co.uk
Membership: Restricted to Dorset.

DORSET POTTERY GROUP
Trumps In Cottage
Whitchurch Canonicorum
Bridport, Dorset DT6 6RH
Tel: 01297 489347
Contact: Alan Ashpool
Membership: Non-juried, paid membership.

DRY STONE WALLING ASSOCIATION OF GREAT BRITAIN
c/o YFC Centre
National Agricultural Centre
Stoneleigh Park, Warks
CV8 2LG
Tel: 0121 378 0493
Fax: 0121 378 0493
Contact: J Simkins
Email: j.simkins@dswagb.ndirect.co.uk
Website: www.dswagb.ndirect.co.uk
Membership: Open.

EXMOOR PRODUCERS ASSOCIATION
7-9 Fore Street
Dulverton
Somerset
TA22 9EX
Tel: 01398 324383
Fax: 01398 324383
Contact: Amanda Baker
Email: exmoor.producers@virgin.net
Website: www.exmoor-producers.co uk
Membership: Non-juried, paid membership.
Restricted to makers in the 'Greater Exmoor'
area.

FEDERATION OF BRITISH ARTISTS (MALL GALLERIES)
17 Carlton House Terrace
London
SW1Y 5BD
Tel: 0171 930 6844
Fax: 0171 839 7830
Contact: The Secretary
Membership: Juried; restricted to artists.

FIFE CRAFT ASSOCIATION
12 Valley Grove, Leslie
Glenrothes
Fife KY6 3BZ
Tel: 01592 743539 (any time)
Contact: Peter Leigh
Membership: Non-juried, paid membership.

FLOWERS & PLANTS ASSOCIATION
Covent House
New Covent Garden Market
London SW8 5NX
Tel: 0171 738 8044
Fax: 0171 622 5307
Email: press-office@flowers.org.uk
Website: www.flowers.org.uk
Membership: Open on payment of
membership fee.

INTERNATIONAL FELTMAKERS ASSOCIATION
South Graystone Farm
Lesmahagow
Lanarkshire ML11 0HL
Tel: 01555 894624
Contact: Jenny Mackay
Email: 101657.440@compuserve.com
Website: www.antel.demon.co.uk/ifa/
ifa.htm
Membership: Non-juried, paid membership.

KENT POTTERS ASSOCIATION
Fairview Barn
Upper Street
Broomfield
Kent ME17 1PS
Tel: 01622 863554
Contact: Janet Jackson
Membership: Open to potters on payment of
membership fee.

KNITTING CRAFT GROUP
Gurt of House
Boltby
Thirsk
North Yorks YO7 2DY
Tel: 01845 537280
Contact: Alec Dalglish
This group is linked to the Knitting &
Crochet Guild (see Guilds & Clubs) and
promotes hand knitting and crochet to
beginners.

LOCHABER CRAFT & FOOD PRODUCERS ASSOCIATION
Strathview
Strontian
Argyll PH36 4JA
Tel: 01967 402279
Contact: Catherine Campbell
Membership: By invitation only and restricted to producers in the Lochaber region.

MADE IN SCOTLAND LTD
Station Road
Beauly
Inverness-shire IV4 7EH
Tel: 01463 782578
Fax: 01463 782409
Contact: Peter Guthrie
Email: mis@enterprise.net Website: www.made-in-scotland.co.uk
Membership: Non-juried, paid membership.

NATIONAL ACRYLIC PAINTERS ASSOCIATION
134 Rake Lane, Wallasey
Wirral, Merseyside
L45 1JW
Tel: 0151 639 2980
Contact: Kenneth Hodgson
Membership: Juried.

NATIONAL ASSOCIATION OF DISABLED CRAFTWORKERS
Piethorn Cottage
Barrachan
By Mochrum
Wigtownshire DG8 9NF
Tel: 01988 860204
Fax: 01988 860204
Contact: Alex Conrade-Marshall
Freephone: 0800 0745285
Membership: Open to all disabled craftworkers; donations.

NEW FIBRE ART
Seaholme
East Bracklesham Drive
Bracklesham Bay
West Sussex PO20 8JW
Contact: Susan Cutts
Membership: Open for Associate Membership and juried for those wanting to exhibit; restricted to those in fibre art.

NORTH WALES POTTERS
Caecarrog
Aberhosan
Machynlleth
Powys SY20 8SE
Tel: 01654 703247
Fax: 01654 703247
Contact: Steve Mattison
Email: steve@carrog.co.uk
Website: www.ftech.net/~carrog/nwp.htm
Membership: Non-juried, paid membership. Restricted to potters in North Wales and Borders.

NORTHERN POTTERS ASSOCIATION
16 High Street
Whitwell
Worksop
Notts S80 4QU
Tel: 01909 724781
Contact: Brian Holland
Membership: Non-juried, paid membership.

OCHIL CRAFT ASSOCIATION
32 Mayfield Avenue
Tillicoultry
Clackmannanshire
Tel: 01259 750672
Contact: Moira Watson
Membership: Juried.

ORKNEY CRAFT INDUSTRIES ASSOCIATION
Outerdykes
Stenness
Orkney KW16 3HA
Tel: 01856 850207
Fax: 01856 850819
Contact: Andi Ross
Membership: Juried and restricted to makers in the Orkney Isles.

PATCHWORK ASSOCIATION
PO Box 300
Hethersett,
Norwich
Norfolk NR9 3DB
Tel: 01603 812259
Fax: 01603 812097
Contact: Jane Lawrence
Email: quiltex@webex.co.uk
Website: www.webex.co.uk/quiltex/quiltex.html
Membership: Non-juried, paid membership.

PEMBROKESHIRE CRAFT MAKERS
Venn Farm
Waterston Road, Milford Haven
Pembrokeshire SA73 1DN
Tel: 01646 690190
Fax: 01646 690190
Contact: Sheila Hickey
Membership: Juried and restricted to makers
in West Wales.

RUGBY CRAFT ASSOCIATION
10 Dewar Grove
Hillmorton, Rugby
Warks CV21 4AT
Tel: 01788 575761
Contact: Mrs Christine Hughes
Membership: Non-juried, paid membership.

SCOTTISH BASKETMAKERS CIRCLE
Drumnahoy Mill House
Sauchen, Inverurie
Aberdeenshire AB51 7JQ
Contact: Mrs S Paterson
Membership: Non-juried, paid membership
for basketmakers, chair seaters and willow
sculpturers.

SCOTTISH BORDERS CRAFT ASSOCIATION
c/o Kalemouth, Kelso
Roxburghshire TD5 8LE
Tel: 01835 850266
Fax: 01835 850266
Contact: Margaret Jeary
Membership: Non-juried, paid membership.
Open to craftworkers in the Scottish Borders
region.

SCOTTISH POTTERS ASSOCIATION
'Murrayfield'
Roslin Glen, Roslin
Midlothian EH25 0PX
Tel: 0131 440 2228
Contact: Maggie Longstaff
Membership: Non-juried, paid membership.

SOUTHEND SPINNERS & WEAVERS GUILD
48 Albert Road
Benfleet
Essex SS7 4DJ
Tel: 01268 752158
Contact: Pauline Everett
Email: pauline@teverett.freeserve.co.uk
Membership: Non-juried, paid membership.

THE GIFTWARE ASSOCIATION
10 Vyse Street
Birmingham
West Midlands B18 6LT
Tel: 0121 237 1105
Fax: 0121 237 1106
Contact: Wendy Webb/Patricia Hunt
Email: enquiries@giftware.org.uk
Website: www.giftware.org.uk
Membership: Non-juried, paid membership.

UIST CRAFT PRODUCERS
Sandbank
Grimsay
North Uist
Western Isles HS6 5HU   Tel: 01870
603180 Fax: 01870 603180
Contact: Theona Morrison
Membership: Restricted to makers within the
Uists, i.e. Berneray, North Uist, Benbecula,
South Uist and Eriskay.

WESTCOUNTRY POTTERS ASSOCIATION
Mill Lodge
Sea Lane
Kilve, Bridgwater
Somerset TA5 1EB
Tel: 01278 741314
Contact: Treston Holmes
Membership: Non-juried, paid membership.

GUILDS AND CLUBS

ABERGELE GUILD OF SPINNERS, WEAVERS & DYERS
Bryn Eglwys
Pont y Gwyddel
Llanfairtalhaiarn
Abergele LL22 9RB
Tel: 01745 540360
Fax: 01745 540412
Contact: Hilary Castle
Membership: Restricted to crafts mentioned.

AVON GUILD OF SPINNERS, WEAVERS & DYERS
Long Ashton Village Hall
Keedwell Hill, Long Ashton
Bristol
Tel: 01275 8778860
Contact: Maggie Robinthwaite
Membership: Non-juried, paid membership.

BORDER LACEMAKERS
c/o 6 Julian Heights
Fleur-de-Lys
Gwent
NP2 1TT
Tel: 01443 821445
Contact: Mrs Betty Bridge
Membership: Non-juried; restricted to the
Welsh Border areas.

BRADFORD & DISTRICT GUILD OF HANDWEAVERS, SPINNERS & DYERS
19 Copgrove Road
Leeds
West Yorks LS8 2SP
Tel: 0113 248 8108
Contact: Veronica Metcalfe
Membership: Non-juried, paid member-
ship.

BRECKNOCK GUILD OF SPINNERS, WEAVERS & DYERS
c/o Beilidu Farm
Pentre Bach
Brecon
Powys LD3 8UB
Tel: 01874 636664
Contact: Mrs L C Scott
Membership: Non-juried, paid member-
ship.

BRECON & RADNOR GUILD OF WEAVERS, SPINNERS & DYERS
Guidfa House
Crossgates
Llandrindod Wells
Powys LD1 6RF
Tel: 01597 851241
Fax: 01597 851875
Contact: Patsy Beswick
Membership: Restricted to these crafts.

BRITISH POLYMER CLAY GUILD
2 Stone House
Howey
Llandrindod Wells
Powys LD1 5PL
Tel: 01597 825517
Contact: Margaret Reid
Email: mfhreid@polyopol.kc2ltd.co.uk
Website: www.heaser.demon.co.uk/
polyclay/guild/britpol.htm
Membership: Non-juried, paid member-
ship. Open to those who use
polymer clay in any way.

BRITISH STICKMAKERS GUILD
31 Springfield Close
Andover
Hants SP10 2QR
Tel: 01264 396757
Contact: L W McIver
Website: ourworld.compuserve.com/
homepages/heathcote
Membership: Non-juried, paid membership.

BRITISH TOYMAKERS GUILD
124 Walcot Street
Bath
BA1 5BG
Tel: 01225 442440
Contact: Robert Nathan

CAMBRIDGESHIRE GUILD OF WEAVERS, SPINNERS & DYERS
4 Pound Hill
Cambridge
Cambs CB3 0AE
Contact: Mrs Noreen Roberts
Membership: Non-juried, paid membership.

CHESHIRE GUILD OF WEAVERS, SPINNERS & DYERS
14 Station Road
Parkgate
South Wirral
Cheshire L64 6QJ
Tel: 0151 336 1341
Contact: Muriel Tinker
Membership: Non-juried, paid membership.

CLWYD GUILD OF WEAVERS, SPINNERS & DYERS
8 Coleshill Street
Holywell
Flintshire CH8 7UP
Tel: 01352 715634
Contact: Carol Rutherford
Membership: Non-juried, paid member-
ship covering crafts mentioned.

COTSWOLD CRAFTSMEN
The Willows
44 Two Hedges Road
Bishop's Cleeve
Glos GL52 4AA
Tel: 01242 672334
Contact: Chris Eagles
Membership: By invitation and juried.
Restricted to makers from the Cotswolds
area.

CRAFT GUILD OF WEST LANCASHIRE
1 Westgate
Pennylands
Skelmersdale
Lancs WN8 8LP
Tel: 01695 51999
Fax: 01695 51222
Contact: Theresa Gaskell
Email:
tgaskell@westlancs.businesslink.co.uk
Membership: Restricted to craft and
artworkers.

CRAFT IN ACTION
Arcus Veni, 21 Upton Gardens
Upton upon Severn
Worcs WR8 0NU
Tel: 01684 592709
Contact: Christine Gledhill
Membership: Selected by invitation after
seeing details. Write or telephone for the
application form.

CREFFTAU'R CYMOEDD
(Crafts of the Valleys)
c/o 13 Acland Road
Bridgend
Mid Glam CF31 1TF
Tel: 01656 663372 (evenings only)
Contact: Sian Mayer
Membership: A promotional and social
group with juried membership.
Restricted to Glamorgan and cannot take
further members at present.

CROSS STITCH GUILD
Pinks Barn, London Road
Fairford
Glos GL7 4AR
Tel: 01285 713678
Fax: 01285 713678
Contact: Helen King
Membership: Non-juried, paid member-
ship.

CUMBRIA CRAFT GUILD
Hollin Howe
Lonsties, Keswick
Cumbria CA12 4TD
Tel: 01768 771458
Contact: Val Blenkiron
Membership: Non-juried, paid member-
ship. Restricted to makers in
Cumbria and surrounding areas; guild
exhibition is juried.

DESIGNER MAKERS IN BATH & BRISTOL
(formerly Avon Craft Guild)
c/o 2 Bathwick Terrace
Bath BA2 4EL
Tel: 01225 461825
Contact: Jill Bartlett
Membership: Juried. Restricted to designer
makers in the BA, BS and SN postcode
regions (former Avon County Council
boundaries).

DEVON GUILD OF CRAFTSMEN
Riverside Mill
Bovey Tracey
Devon TQ13 9AF
Tel: 01626 832223
Fax: 01626 834220
Email: devonguild@crafts.org.uk
Website: www.crafts.org.uk
Membership: Selected, paid membership.
Restricted to the South West region, up as
far as Bristol and across to Southampton.

DISS AND DISTRICT GUILD OF
WEAVERS, SPINNERS & DYERS
c/o Southview
Common Road
Shelfanger, Diss
Norfolk IP22 2DP
Tel: 01379 643563
Contact: Mrs P J Ross
Membership: Non-juried, paid membership.

EAST SUSSEX GUILD OF
WEAVERS, SPINNERS & DYERS
Great Streele Cottage
Framfield
Uckfield
East Sussex TN22 5SA
Tel: 01825 890425
Fax: 01825 890464
Contact: Mrs S Hoblyn
Membership: Non-juried, paid membership.

EAST SUSSEX GUILD OF
CRAFTWORKERS
Little Clays
Willingford Lane
Burwash Weald, Etchingham
East Sussex TN19 7HR
Tel: 01435 882707
Contact: Alf Case
Membership: Juried, paid membership.
Restricted to makers in East Sussex and
boundaries only.

EGG CRAFTERS GUILD OF GREAT BRITAIN
The Studio
7 Hylton Terrace
North Shields
Tyne & Wear NE29 0EE
Tel: 0191 258 3648
Contact: Joan Cutts
Membership: Non-juried, paid membership.

EMBROIDERERS' GUILD
Apartment 41
Hampton Court Palace
Surrey KT8 9AU
Tel: 0181 943 1229
Fax: 0181 977 9882
Contact: Gale Williams
Email: gwilliams@embroiderersguild.org.uk
Membership: Non-juried, paid membership.

EMBROIDERERS' GUILD, CARMARTHEN BRANCH
Ty Carian, Adpar
Newcastle Emlyn SA38 9EL
Tel: 01239 711224
Contact: Mrs Irene Popkins
Membership: Non-juried, paid membership for embroiderers.

EMBROIDERERS' GUILD, GWENT BRANCH
c/o 2 Winchester Close
Newport
Gwent NP9 3BL
Tel: 01633 815018
Contact: M Walker
Membership: Non-juried, paid membership

EMBROIDERERS' GUILD, KINGSTON BRANCH
c/o 123 Horton Hill, Epsom
Surrey KT19 8SY
Tel: 01372 815118
Fax: 01372 815118
Contact: Sue Marshall
Membership: Non-juried, paid membership.

EMBROIDERERS' GUILD, SWANSEA BRANCH
8 Bron-y-Bryn
Killay
Swansea SA2 7NP
Tel: 01792 205935
Contact: Jane Riseborough
Membership: Non-juried, paid membership.

EMBROIDERERS' GUILD, WEST BRIDGFORD BRANCH
61 Shelford Road, Radcliffe-on-Trent
Notts NG12 1AJ
Tel: 0115 933 6268
Fax: 0115 933 6591
Contact: Liz Welch
Email: lizzie@dial.pipex.com
Membership: Open.

GALLOWAY CRAFT GUILD
76 King Street
Castle Douglas
Kirkcudbrightshire DG7 1AP
Tel: 01644 440604
Contact: Clive Donovan
Membership: Non-juried, paid membership.
Restricted to makers in the Dumfries & Galloway region plus Ayrshire.

GLAMORGAN GUILD OF WEAVERS, SPINNERS & DYERS
4 Heol Don, Whitchurch
Cardiff CF4 2AU
Tel: 01222 627326
Contact: Jean Roberts
Membership: Open to crafters of types mentioned. Restricted to Glamorgan.

GLOUCESTERSHIRE GUILD OF CRAFTSMEN
Lynch Cottage, Oakridge Lynch
Stroud
Glos GL6 7NZ
Tel: 01285 760365
Contact: Mary Noble
Membership: Juried.

GRAMPIAN GUILD OF WEAVERS, SPINNERS & DYERS
32 Woodburn Crescent
Aberdeen AB15 8JX
Tel: 01224 321231
Contact: Mrs Evelyn Duncan
Membership: Non-juried, paid membership.
Despite name, not necessarily restricted to these crafts.

GREAT YARMOUTH GUILD OF ARTISTS AND CRAFTSMEN
2 Bure Close, Great Yarmouth
Norfolk NR30 1QU
Tel: 01493 844187
Contact: Mrs A C Balls
Membership: Non-juried, paid membership.

GUILD OF BRITISH DECOUPEURS
"Chimneys", 18 Pembridge Close
Charlton Kings
Cheltenham
Glos GL52 6XY
Tel: 01242 235302
Contact: Madeleine Smith
Membership: Non-juried, paid membership.

GUILD OF DISABLED HOMEWORKERS
Market Street
Nailsworth
Glos GL6 0BX
Tel: 01453 835623
Fax: 01453 835623
Contact: Membership Secretary
Membership: Free and open membership for
the disabled.

GUILD OF ENAMELLERS
Uplands
Brighton Road
Lower Kingswood
Surrey KT20 6SX
Contact: G Winter
Membership: Non-juried, paid membership
for enamellers.

GUILD OF ESSEX CRAFTSMEN
34 Pembroke Road
Seven Kings, Ilford
Essex IG3 8PH
Tel: 0181 590 1417
Contact: David Nathan
Membership: By invitation only to those
living or working in Essex.

GUILD OF GLASS ENGRAVERS
35 Ossulton Way
London N2 0JY
Tel: 0181 731 9352
Fax: 0181 731 9352
Contact: Mrs Christine Weatherhead
Membership: Non-juried, international, paid
membership.

GUILD OF HEREFORDSHIRE CRAFTSMEN
Castle Weir
Lyonshall, Kington
Herefordshire HR5 3HR
Tel: 01544 340332/340312
Fax: 01544 340417
Contact: Miss E S Baker
Membership: Juried and restricted to makers
in Herefordshire.

GUILD OF LINCOLNSHIRE CRAFTSMEN
"Netherfield", 8 Lodge Lane
Nettleham, Lincoln
Lincs LN2 2RS
Tel: 01522 751843/0374 797099
Contact: Mrs Helen Cotten
Membership: Juried and restricted to
makers in Lincolnshire.

GUILD OF MASTER CRAFTSMEN
166 High Street
Lewes
East Sussex BN7 1XU
Tel: 01273 477374
Fax: 01273 486300
Contact: Lesley Pizzey
Membership: Restricted by craft type;
referees used.

GUILD OF NEEDLE LACE
Redwoods, Green Lane
Little Melton, Norwich
Norfolk NR9 3LE
Tel: 01603 810482
Fax: 01603 810482
Contact: Mrs D M Nash
Membership: Non-juried, paid membership.

GUILD OF STRAW CRAFTSMEN
c/o Westhope College
Craven Arms
Salop SY7 9JN
Tel: 01884 861293
Fax: 01884 861293
Contact: Anne Dyer
Membership: Restricted to straw craftsmen.

GWENT GUILD OF WEAVERS, DYERS & SPINNERS
Green Meadow Community Farm
Green Meadow, Cwmbran
Gwent NP44 5AJ
Tel: 01495 764559
Contact: S Morgan
Membership: Open to makers described.

GWYNEDD GUILD OF WEAVERS, SPINNERS & DYERS
c/o Tan-y-Mynydd
Ffordd Penmynydd, Llanfairpwll
Ynys Mon LL61 5JT
Tel: 01248 714218
Contact: Pat Denne
Email: m.p.denne@bangor.ac.uk
Membership: Open.

HALLAMSHIRE GUILD OF WEAVERS, SPINNERS & DYERS
62 Pingle Road
Sheffield
South Yorks S7 2LL
Tel: 0114 236 0969
Contact: Mrs H Stansfield
Membership: Open and centred on the Sheffield area.

HAMPSHIRE & BERKSHIRE GUILD OF CRAFTSMEN
7 Bournefield
Sherborne St John
nr Basingstoke
Hants RG24 9JB
Tel: 01256 851433
Contact: Olga Norris
Email: olganorris@compuserve.com
Membership: Juried and restricted to makers in Hampshire and Berkshire

HEREFORDSHIRE GUILD OF WEAVERS, SPINNERS & DYERS
56 Broomy Hill
Hereford
Herefordshire HR4 0LQ
Tel: 01432 269073
Contact: Judith Baresel
Membership: Non-juried, paid membership.

ISLE OF AXHOLME CRAFTS GUILD
c/o 9 Tower Hill
Westwoodside
nr Doncaster
South Yorks DN9 2DH
Tel: 01427 752941
Contact: A Tasker
Membership: Juried and restricted to makers in North Lincolnshire and South Yorkshire.

KENNET VALLEY GUILD OF SPINNERS, WEAVERS & DYERS
71 Maple Crescent
Newbury
Berks RG14 1LP
Tel: 01635 43846
Mobile: 0973 119980
Contact: Albert Moss
Membership: Non-juried, paid membership.

KENT GUILD OF SPINNERS, DYERS & WEAVERS
110 Grand Drive
Herne Bay
Kent CT6 8HS
Tel: 01227 741266
Fax: 01227 749502
Contact: Mrs S Brown
Email: SBrown6524@aol.com
Membership: Non-juried and free; restricted to Kent.

KNITTING & CROCHET GUILD
228 Chester Road North
Kidderminster
Worcs DY10 1TH
Tel: 01562 754367
Contact: Anne Budworth
Email: RGB-UK@compuserve.com
Website: www.rgb.ndirect.co.uk/guild
Membership: Non-juried, paid membership.

LACE GUILD
The Hollies
53 Audnam
Stourbridge
West Midlands DY8 4AE
Tel: 01384 390739
Fax: 01384 444415
Contact: Margaret Watts
Email: hollies@laceguild.demon.co.uk
Website: www.laceguild.demon.co.uk
Membership: Non-juried, paid membership.

LINCOLNSHIRE GUILD OF WEAVERS, SPINNERS & DYERS
190 Grantham Road
Sleaford
Lincs NG34 7NU
Contact: Mrs J Mounter
Membership: Non-juried, paid membership for those working in the fields mentioned.

LLYN GUILD OF WEAVERS, SPINNERS & DYERS
Maes Mawr
Llanllyfni
Caernarfon
Gwynedd
Tel: 01286 881809
Contact: Jean Rickford
Membership: Non-juried, paid membership.

LONDON & HOME COUNTIES GUILD OF WEAVERS SPINNERS & DYERS
c/o Flat 2
12 Lee Road
London SE3 9RT
Tel: 0181 355 0278
Contact: Charlotte Grierson
Membership: Non-juried, paid membership.

MAKERS GUILD IN WALES
Craft in the Bay
Cory's Building
57 Bute Street
Cardiff CF1 6AJ
Tel: 01222 484611
Fax: 01222 491136
Contact: Molly Curley
Membership: Juried and restricted to makers only in Wales.

MID-HERTS GUILD OF SPINNERS, WEAVERS & DYERS
29 Chantry Lane
Hatfield
Herts AL10 9HS
Tel: 01707 269225
Contact: Ruth Waters
Membership: Non-juried, paid membership.

MIDDLE ESSEX GUILD OF WEAVERS, SPINNERS & DYERS
7 The Paddocks
Great Totham
Maldon
Essex CM9 8PF
Tel: 01621 891817
Contact: Mrs Susan Munton
Membership: Non-juried, paid membership.

MILTON KEYNES CRAFT GUILD
c/o The National Hockey Stadium
Silbury Boulevard
Central Milton Keynes
Bucks MK9 1HA
Tel: 01908 694764
Fax: 01908 694764
Contact: Clare Layton
Email: clare@layton2.demon.co.uk
Membership: Juried for Full Membership; non-juried for Associate Membership. Restricted to central and south Buckinghamshire.

MONTGOMERYSHIRE GUILD OF WEAVERS, SPINNERS & DYERS
Corndon Lodge
White Gritt, Minsterley
Salop SY5 0JL
Tel: 01588 650282
Contact: Marjo Hofland
Membership: Non-juried, paid membership.

NORFOLK & SUFFOLK GUILD OF WEAVERS, SPINNERS & DYERS
69 Pinewood Avenue
Lowestoft
Suffolk NR33 9AJ
Tel: 01502 565931
Contact: Mrs S Holford

NORFOLK CRAFTSMEN'S GUILD
Rosecroft, Rode Lane
Carleton Rode, Norwich
Norfolk NR16 1NW
Tel: 01953 860706
Contact: Mrs Rosemary Kingsland
Membership: Juried.

NORTHAMPTONSHIRE GUILD OF DESIGNER CRAFTSMEN
28 High Street
Milton Mansor
Northants NN7 3AS
Contact: Bob Walder
Membership: Juried.

NORTHANTS SPINNERS, WEAVERS & DYERS GUILD
c/o Stone House
14 Bedford Road, Denton
Northants NN7 1DR
Tel: 01604 890534
Contact: Doug Littler
Membership: Non-juried, paid membership. Restricted to spinners/weavers/dyers in Northants and immediate environs.

OSWESTRY & WELSH BORDER CRAFT CIRCLE
c/o Croesoswallt Crafts
Powis Hall, Oswestry
Salop SY11 1PZ
Tel: 01691 652423 (evenings only)
Contact: Sue Franklin
Membership: Group marketing/running occasional fairs. Juried, but no vacancies. Nevertheless welcome visit at stall in Powis Hall.

OXFORDSHIRE CRAFT GUILD
7 Goddards Lane
Chipping Norton
Oxon OX7 5NP
Tel: 01865 763679
Fax: 01865 763724
Contact: Mr I C King
Email: sarinn@aol.com
Membership: By invitation for Full and
Associate Membership; also
Friends of Guild option. Restricted to
Oxfordshire.

PEMBROKESHIRE GUILD OF WEAVERS, SPINNERS & DYERS
Rose Cottage
Sandyhill Road
Saundersfoot
Pembrokeshire SA69 9HN
Tel: 01834 812544
Contact: Sue Hoyland
Membership: Non-juried, paid membership.

PETERBOROUGH GUILD OF SPINNERS, WEAVERS & DYERS
15 Audley Gate
Peterborough
Cambs PE3 9PG
Tel: 01733 263947
Contact: Mrs J Phillips
Website: ourworld.compuserve.com/
homepages/markswingler/SWD.htm
Membership: Non-juried, paid membership.

QUILLING GUILD
4 Marquis Close
Bishop's Stortford
Herts CM23 3PH
Tel: 01279 466936 (evenings only)
Fax: 01279 466936
Contact: P Herring
Email: peter.herring29@virgin.net
Membership: Non-juried, paid membership;
restricted to quillers.

QUILTERS' GUILD OF THE BRITISH ISLES
Room 190
Dean Clough
Halifax
West Yorks HX3 5AX
Tel: 01422 347669
Fax: 01422 345017
Contact: The Administrator
Membership: Open. Celebrating 20th
anniversary in 1999.

SECOND TURNING TEXTILE GROUP
83 Bramcote Drive West
Beeston
Notts NG9 1DU
Tel: 0115 925 5265
Contact: Adela Davies
Membership: This is an Exhibiting Group, by
invitation only.

SHETLAND GUILD OF SPINNERS, WEAVERS & DYERS
Shetland Textile Museum
Weisdale Mill, Weisdale
Shetland ZE2 9LW
Tel: 01595 830419 or 860281
Fax: 01595 830419
Contact: Susan Johnson
Membership: Non-juried, paid membership.

SIRHOWY VALLEY LACEMAKERS
c/o 6 Julian Heights
Fleur-de-Lys
Gwent NP2 1TT
Tel: 01443 821445
Contact: Mrs B R Bridge
Membership: Open.

SOMERSET GUILD OF WEAVERS, SPINNERS AND DYERS
c/o 3 Southmead
West Camel, Yeovil
Somerset BA22 7QQ
Tel: 01935 850144
Contact: Mrs C Mellish
Membership: Non-juried, paid membership.

SURREY GUILD OF CRAFTSMEN
1 Moushill Lane
Milford, Godalming
Surrey GU8 5BH
Tel: 01483 424769 (10.30am-5pm)
Contact: Helena Greig
Membership: Associate Membership is
open; Full Membership is juried. Restricted
to Surrey and surrounding areas.

THE SUSSEX GUILD
6 Marlpit Road
Sharpthorne
nr East Grinstead
West Sussex RH19 4PD
Tel: 01342 810591
Contact: Basil Hall
Membership: Juried and restricted to makers
in Sussex and the adjoining counties.

WESSEX CRAFTSMEN
3 West Park Road
Corsham
Wilts SN13 9LN
Tel: 01249 712395
Contact: Colin Ringwald
Membership: Non-juried, paid membership.

WESSEX GUILD OF CRAFTSMEN
91 Green Lane
Clanfield
Hants PO8 0LG
Tel: 01705 571744
Contact: Allan Parsons
Membership: Juried, restricted by craft type
and specific to Hampshire and West Sussex.

WEST ESSEX & EAST HERTS GUILD OF SPINNERS, WEAVERS & DYERS
c/o The Harrons
Broadley Common
Waltham Abbey
Essex EN9 2DH
Tel: 01992 892436
Contact: Mrs Pat Holder
Membership: Non-juried, paid membership.

WORCESTERSHIRE GUILD OF WEAVERS, SPINNERS & DYERS
73 Pershore Road
Evesham
Worcs WR11 6LU
Tel: 01386 49948
Contact: Ros Parkinson
Membership: Open.

YORK & DISTRICT GUILD OF WEAVERS, SPINNERS & DYERS
Weavery, New Road
Brandesburton
nr Driffield
East Yorks YO25 8RX
Tel: 01964 543123
Contact: Mrs Enid Parker
Membership: Non-juried, paid membership.

**PLEASE MENTION THE
CRAFTWORKER'S YEAR BOOK
WHEN CONTACTING
GUILDS OR SOCIETIES**

SOCIETIES

ABINGDON SILVER GROUP
4 St James Road
Radley
nr Abingdon
Oxon OX14 3AQ
Tel: 01235 524866
Fax: 01235 200122
Contact: John Huddleston
Email: ag@huddleston.co.uk
Website:ourworld.compuserve.com/
homepages/jjjj_huddleston/index.htm
Membership: Restricted to silversmiths.

AMBLESIDE HORTICULTURAL & CRAFT SOCIETY
8 Loughrigg Park
Ambleside
Cumbria LA22 0DY
Tel: 01539 432904
Contact: Mrs Dorothy Johnson
Membership: Open.

BEAD SOCIETY OF GREAT BRITAIN
1 Casburn Lane
Burwell
Cambs CB5 0ED
Contact: Carole Morris
Membership: Non-juried, paid membership.

BIRMINGHAM CALLIGRAPHY SOCIETY
19 Garman Close
Great Barr
Birmingham
West Midlands B43 6NB
Tel: 0121 358 2113
Contact: Jim Cairns
Membership: Non-juried, paid membership.

BRITISH SOCIETY OF ENAMELLERS
(Glass on Metal Artists)
30 Kensington Square
London W8 5HH
Tel: 0171 937 3601
Fax: 0171 376 1729
Contact: Alexandra Raphael
Membership: Juried and restricted to UK
based glass on metal artists.

BRITISH SOCIETY OF MASTER GLASS PAINTERS
6 Queen Square
London WC1N 2AR
Tel: 01943 602521
Contact: Ruth Cooke
Email: secretary@bsmgp.org.uk
Website: www.bsmgp.org.uk
Membership: Juried, free membership; send an SAE for details.

CALLIGRAPHY & LETTERING ARTS SOCIETY
54 Boileau Road
London SW13 9BL
Tel: 0181 741 7886
Fax: 0181 741 7886
Contact: Sue Cavendish
Email: suecavendish@compuserve.com
Website: www.clas.co.uk
Membership: Open.

DESIGNER BOOKBINDERS
6 Queen Square
London WC1N 3AR
Tel: 01248 602591
Fax: 01248 602591
Contact: Miss Lester Bath
Membership: Both Open and Juried grades of paid membership.

ESSEX CRAFT SOCIETY
Nightingale Cottage
Nightingale Hall Road
Earls Cole, Colchester
Essex CO6 2NR
Tel: 01787 222937
Contact: Sara Impey
Membership: Juried and restricted to makers in Essex.

LACE SOCIETY
Lynwood, Stratford Road
Oversley Green
Alcester
Warks B49 6PG
Tel: 01789 762594
Contact: Mrs Marjory Carter
Membership: Society devoted to lacemakers pursuing their chosen hobby. Apart from teaching, members are not professionals and do not make for sale. Numbers limited to 1250 members; some vacancies, strictly on application.

LONDON POTTERS
105 Albert Bridge Road
London SW11 4PF
Tel: 0171 228 7831
Contact: Mary Lambert
Membership: Open.

MARQUETRY SOCIETY
1 St Catherines Way
Down End
Fareham
Hants PO16 8RL
Tel: 01329 237005
Contact: Peter Metcalfe
Website: www.freespace.virgin.net/tedhiggs
Membership: Non-juried, paid membership.

NATIONAL SOCIETY OF MASTER THATCHERS
c/o 20 The Laurels
Tetsworth
Thame
Oxon OX9 7BH
Tel: 01844 281568
Fax: 01844 281568
Contact: Mrs C J Ashton-Moore
Email: NSMT@bigfoot.com
Website: NSMT.hypermart.net
Membership: Restricted to thatchers.

NORFOLK CONTEMPORARY CRAFT SOCIETY
Gilderswood Farm
Forcett St Peter
Norwich
Norfolk NR16 1LN
Tel: 01953 789362
Contact: Mrs B A Prior
Membership: Open for Associate Membership and Friends of the Society; Juried for Exhibiting Members.

PAPERWEIGHT
(Group for Paper Makers & Paper Artists)
Mardle Cottage
Higher Combe
West Buckfastleigh
Devon TQ11 0JD
Tel: 01364 643867
Contact: Brenda Turner
Membership: Non-juried, paid membership.

ROYAL SOCIETY OF PAINTER-PRINTMAKERS

Bankside Gallery, 48 Hopton Street
London SE1 9JH
Tel: 0171 928 7521
Fax: 0171 928 7521
Contact: Alison Rowe
Email: re&rws@bankside-gallery.demon.co.uk
Membership: Juried and restricted by art type.

ROYAL SOCIETY OF BRITISH SCULPTORS

108 Old Brompton Road
South Kensington
London SW7 3RA
Tel: 0171 373 5554
Fax: 0171 370 3721
Contact: Colette Bailey
Email: RBS@sculpturecompany.demon.co.uk
Membership: Juried and restricted to sculptors.

ROYAL WATERCOLOUR SOCIETY

Bankside Gallery, 48 Hopton Street
London SE1 9JH
Tel: 0171 928 7521
Fax: 0171 928 2820
Contact: Alison Rowe
Email: re&rws@banksidegallery.demon.co.uk
Membership: Juried and restricted by art type.

SCOTTISH ARTISTS & ARTIST CRAFTSMEN

No 6, 169 Great Junction Street
Edinburgh
EH6 5LG
Tel: 0131 554 3365
Fax: 0131 554 3365
Contact: Angela Carolan
Email: info@saacweb.org
Website: www.saacweb.org/
Membership: Non-juried, paid membership.

SOCIETY FOR ITALIC HANDWRITING

205 Dyas Avenue
Great Barr
Birmingham
West Midlands B42 1HN
Tel: 0121 358 0032
Fax: 0121 358 0032
Contact: Nicholas Caulkin
Membership: Open.

SOCIETY OF CRAFTSMEN

Kemble Gallery
29 Church Street
Hereford
Herefordshire
HR1 2LR
Tel: 01432 266049
Contact: Cilla Thomas
Membership: Juried, with members' work then being eligible for sale in craft shop.

SOCIETY OF DESIGNER CRAFTSMEN

24 Rivington Street
London EC2A 3DU
Tel: 0171 739 3663
Fax: 0171 739 3663
Contact: Richard O'Donoghue
Email: secretary@societydesigncraft.org.uk
Membership: Juried.

SOCIETY OF PORTRAIT SCULPTORS

27 Winchester Street
London
W3 8PA
Tel: 01825 750485
Fax: 01825 750485
Contact: David Houchin
Website: www.portrait-sculpture.org
Membership: Juried.

SOCIETY OF SCRIBES AND ILLUMINATORS

6 Queen Square
London WC1N 3AR
Tel: 01483 894155
Fax: 01483 894155
Contact: Clare Turvey
Email: scribe@calligraphy.org
Website: www.calligraphy.org
Membership: Non-juried, paid membership.

SOUTH WALES POTTERS

Black Mountain Pottery
Llanelieu Court
Talgarth
Powys
LD3 0EB
Tel: 01874 711518
Fax: 01874 711518
Contact: Pauline Paterson
Membership: Non-juried, paid membership. Restricted to potters in Wales and South West England.

SOUTH WEST TEXTILE GROUP

c/o Highfield Farm House
Woodhill
Stoke St Gregory
Somerset TA3 6EW
Contact: Jenny Blackburn
Membership: Artist led group concentrating on textiles and restricting its membership to South West England.

SUFFOLK CRAFT SOCIETY

Bridge Green Farm
Gissing Road
Burston
Norfolk IP22 3UD
Tel: 01379 740711
Contact: Monique Gregson
Membership: Juried and restricted to makers in East Anglia (mostly Suffolk). Higher standards required from those out of county.

TEXTILE SOCIETY

c/o Charlesbye Farm
Greetby Hill
Ormskirk
Lancs L39 2DT
Tel: 0181 523 2399
Contact: Mrs Lyn Broster
Membership: Non-juried, international, paid membership.

WEST WALES MARQUETRY GROUP

Wynnstay
Gilfachrheda
New Quay
Dyfed SA45 9SP
Tel: 01545 580018
Contact: Pat Austin
Membership: Non-juried, paid membership.

QUANGOS, REGIONAL AND OTHER BODIES

ARTS COUNCIL OF ENGLAND

14 Great Peter Street
London
SW1P 3NQ
Tel: 0171 973 6517
Fax: 0171 973 6590
Contact: Stephen Chappell
Email: enquiries@artscouncil.org.uk
Website: www.artscouncil.org.uk
The national funding body for the arts in England and responsible for developing, sustaining and promoting the arts.

ARTS COUNCIL OF NORTHERN IRELAND

MacNeice House
77 Malone Road
Belfast
BT9 6AQ
Tel: 01232 385200
Fax: 01232 661715
The national funding and development body for the arts in Northern Ireland.

ARTS COUNCIL OF WALES
VISUAL ARTS & CRAFT DEVELOPMENT

9 Museum Place
Cardiff
South Glam CF1 3NX
Tel: 01222 376500
Fax: 01222 221447
Email: information@ccc.acw.org.uk
Website: www.ccc.acw.org.uk
The national funding and development body for the arts in Wales.

CRAFTS COUNCIL

44a Pentonville Road
Islington
London
N1 9BY
Tel: 0171 806 2501
Fax: 0171 837 6891
Contact: Reference Desk
Email: reference@craftscouncil.org.uk
Website: www.craftscouncil.org.uk
Non-departmental governmental body, with both Open and Juried forms of membership.

EAST DEVON SMALL INDUSTRIES GROUP
East Devon Business Centre
Heathpark
Honiton
Devon EX14 8SF
Tel: 01404 41806
Fax: 01404 46865
Contact: Sue Bond or Geoff Hulley
This is a Local Enterprise Agency with free business advisory service.

EAST MIDLANDS ARTS BOARD
Mountfields House
Epinal Way
Loughborough
Leics LE11 0QE
Tel: 01509 218292
Fax: 01509 262214
Contact: Crafts Officer
The regional arts development agency for Leics, Northants, Derbys (except High Peak) and Notts.

EASTERN ARTS BOARD
Cherry Hinton Hall
Cherry Hinton Road
Cambridge
Cambs CB1 4DW
Tel: 01223 215355
Fax: 01223 248075
The regional arts development agency for Herts, Essex, Cambs, Lincs, Suffolk and Norfolk.

FFORWM CREFFT CYMRU
(Craft Forum Wales)
Snowdon Mill Art & Craft Centre
Snowdon Street
Porthmadog
Gwynedd LL49 9DF
Tel: 01766 510910
Fax: 01766 510 913
Contact: Bill Hildyard
Email: snowdon.mill@btinternet.com
Website: www.menternet.org.uk/crafts
Membership: A Community Cooperative with juried membership which is restricted to makers in Wales.

LONDON ARTS BOARD
Elme House
133 Long Acre
Covent Garden
London WC2E 9AF
Tel: 0171 240 1313
Fax: 0171 670 2400
The regional arts development agency for Greater London.

MADE IN CUMBRIA
County Offices
Busher Walk, Kendal
Cumbria LA9 4RQ
Tel: 01539 732736
Fax: 01539 729480
Contact: Richard Knowles
Email: RJK@madeincumbria.co.uk
Website: www.madeincumbria.co.uk
Membership: An Economic Development Initiative run by Cumbria County Council; non-juried, paid and restricted to those in Cumbria.

NORTH WEST ARTS BOARD
Manchester House
22 Bridge Street
Manchester M3 3AB
Tel: 0161 834 6644
Fax: 0161 834 6969
Contact: Crafts Officer
Email: nwarts-info@mcrl.poptel.org.uk
Wesbite: www.arts.org.uk
The regional arts development agency for Cheshire, High Peak of Derbyshire, Manchester, Lancashire and Merseyside.

NORTHERN ARTS
9-10 Osborne Terrace
Jesmond
Newcastle upon Tyne
Tyne & Wear NE2 1NZ
Tel: 0191 281 6334
Fax: 0191 281 3276
Contact: Visual Arts Department
Email: nab@norab.demon.co.uk
Website: www.arts.org.uk
The regional arts development agency for Cleveland, Co Durham, Tyne & Wear, Northumberland and Cumbria.

ORIGIN DYFED LTD
1 St Mary's Street
Carmarthen SA31 1TN
Tel: 01267 220377
Fax: 01267 220377
Contact: Louise Wiste
This is a Community Cooperative accepting members from within Dyfed on a non-juried, paid basis.

RURAL DEVELOPMENT COMMISSION
141 Castle Street
Salisbury
Wilts
SP1 3TP
Tel: 01722 336255
Fax: 01722 332769
Email: rdc.info@argonet.co.uk
Website: www.argonet.co.uk/rdc
Assisted training for saddlery, forgework, upholstery, wheelwrighting, wood machining, thatching and furniture making firms in rural England. To be merged with Countryside Commission in April 1999.

SCOTTISH ARTS COUNCIL
Crafts Department
12 Manor Place
Edinburgh
EH3 7DD
Tel: 0131 226 6051
Fax: 0131 225 9833
The national funding and development body for the arts in Scotland.

SOUTH EAST ARTS
(Crafts and Public Art)
Union House
Eridge Road
Tunbridge Wells
Kent TN4 8HF
Tel: 01892 507215
Fax: 01892 549383
Contact: Frances Lord
Email: info@seab.co.uk
Website: www.arts.org
The regional arts development agency for Kent, Surrey, East Sussex and West Sussex.

SOUTH WEST ARTS
Bradninch Place
Gandy Street
Exeter
Devon
EX4 3LS
Tel: 01392 218188
Fax: 01392 413554
Contact: Information Service
Email: swarts@mail.zynet.co.uk
Website: www.swa.co.uk
The regional arts development agency for Bristol/Bath/NE Somerset, Devon, Dorset (excl SE Dorset), Gloucestershire and Somerset.

SOUTHERN ARTS
13 St Clement Street, Winchester
Hants SO23 9DQ
Tel: 01962 855099
Fax: 01962 861186
Contact: Sandy White
Email: sandy.white@southernarts.co.uk
The regional arts development agency for Berks, Bucks, SE Dorset, Hants, Isle of Wight, Oxon and Wilts.

WALES CRAFT COUNCIL
Henfaes Lane
Welshpool
Powys SY21 7BE
Tel: 01938 555313
Fax: 01938 556237
Contact: Dawn Davies
The Membership Organisation for crafts in Wales.

WEST MIDLANDS ARTS
82 Granville Street, Birmingham
West Midlands B1 2LH
Tel: 0121 631 3121
Fax: 0121 643 7239
Contact: Information Services/Craft
Email: west.midarts@midnet.com
Website: www.west-midlands.arts.org.uk
The regional arts development agency for the West Midlands, Worcs, Herefordshire, Shropshire, Warks and Staffs.

WORSHIPFUL COMPANY OF FURNITURE MAKERS
Painters' Hall
9 Little Trinity Lane
London EC4V 2AD
Tel: 0171 248 1677
Fax: 0171 248 1688
Contact: Mrs J Wright, The Clerk
Email: clerk@furnituremkrs.co.uk
Website: www.furnituremkrs.co.uk
This is a City of London Livery Company, restricted to those working within the Furniture Industry.

WORSHIPFUL COMPANY OF GLAZIERS & PAINTERS OF GLASS
Glaziers Hall
9 Montague Close
London Bridge
London SE1 9DD
Tel: 0171 403 3300

Fax: 0171 407 6036
Contact: David Eking, Clerk
Membership: This is a City of London
Livery Company, with membership by
invitation only.

YORKSHIRE & HUMBERSIDE ARTS BOARD
21 Bond Street
Dewsbury
West Yorks WF13 1AX
Tel: 01924 455555
Fax: 01924 466522
The arts development agency covering
East, West, South and North Yorkshire.

NON UK BASED BODIES

CARLOW CRAFT GUILD
c/o Maureen Murphy
Knock Beg, Carlow
EIRE
Tel: 00 353 (0)503 42477
Fax: 00 353 (0)503 42477
Email: patrickjmurphy@tinet.ie
Membership: Juried and restricted to makers
in the Carlow area.

CLARE ASSOCIATION OF ARTISTS AND CRAFTWORKERS
Ballycroum, Caher
Co Clare
EIRE
Tel: 00 353 (0)61 925172
Fax: 00 353 (0)65 36501
Contact: Theresa Crichton
Membership: Non-juried, paid membership.
Restricted to County Clare.

CRAFT POTTERS SOCIETY OF IRELAND
45 Hazelwood, Shankill
Co Dublin
EIRE
Tel: 00 353 (0)1 282 3487
Contact: Sue Parker
Email: ceramicsireland@yahoo.com
Membership: Non-juried, paid membership.

CRAFTS COUNCIL OF IRELAND
Castle Yard, Kilkenny
Co Kilkenny
EIRE
Tel: 00 353 (0)56 61804

Fax: 00 353 (0)56 63754
Contact: Joanna Quinn
Email: craftsir@indigo.ie
Membership: Listed crafts only; Eire only

HANDWEAVERS GUILD OF CORK
31 Kiltegan Lawn
Rochestown Road, Cork
EIRE
Tel: 00 353 (0)21 89 55 68
Contact: Frances Leach
Membership: Non-juried, paid membership.

NEDERLANDSE VAKGROEP KERAMISTEN
(Dutch Ceramists Association)
Kleine Breedstraat 4
9101 LB Dokkum
HOLLAND
Tel: 00 31 (0)519 221187
Fax: 00 31 (0)519 221168
Contact: Jan Dekker
Email: goudhand@wxs.nl
Website: www.nvk-keramiek.nl
Membership: Juried.

PROFESSIONAL ORGANISATION OF DUTCH INTERIOR ARCHITECTS BNI
Falckstraat 53
1017 VV Amsterdam
HOLLAND
Tel: 00 31 (0)20 42 33 233
Fax: 00 31 (0)20 42 33 122
Contact: Mrs Marianne Ketel
Email: bni@open.net.com
Membership: BNI is a professional
organisation with a juried membership

SCULPTORS' SOCIETY OF IRELAND
119 Capel Street
Dublin 1
EIRE
Tel: 00 353 (0)1 872 2296
Fax: 00 353 (0)1 872 2364
Contact: Anne-Marie Ridge
Email: ssi@iol.ie
Website: www.iol.ie/~ssi
Membership: Non-juried, paid membership.

WORLD CRAFTS COUNCIL - EUROPE
Rheinstrasse 23
60325 Frankfurt am Main
GERMANY
Tel: 00 49 (0)69 743 2113
Fax: 00 49 (0)69 743 2113
Contact: Katrin Strauss
Membership: Non-juried, paid membership

DIRECTORY OF PUBLICATIONS

AN MAGAZINE
(formerly Artists Newsletter)
AN
PO Box 23
Sunderland
Tyne & Wear SR4 6DG
Tel: 0191 514 3600
Fax: 0191 564 1600
Email: subs@anpubs.demon.uk
Available by mail order. Price: Single
copy £3. Annual order (mailed) £25. Free
sample copy available on request.

ART & CRAFT MAGAZINE
Scholastic Ltd
Subscriptions Department
Westfield Road, Southam
Warks CV33 0JH
Tel: 01926 816250
Fax: 01926 815563
Email: scholastic@compuserve.com
Website: www.scholastic.co.uk
Available by mail order only. Price: Single
copy £2.35. Annual order (mailed)
£28.20.

ARTISTS & ILLUSTRATORS
Quarto Magazines
Subscriptions Department
Freepost (KE 8338)
Leicester LE87 4AF
Tel: 01858 435307
Fax: 01858 434958
Available via newsagent and direct by
mail order. Price: Single copy £2.40.
Annual order (newsagent) £28.80. Annual
order (mailed) £23.10.

BEAUTIFUL STITCHES
Aceville Publications Ltd
Subscription Department
Bradley Pavilions
Bradley Stoke North
Bristol BS32 0PP
Tel: 01454 620070
Fax: 01454 620080
Email: mail@maze.u-net.com
Available via newsagent and direct by
mail order. Price: Single copy £1.95.
Annual order via newsagent or direct by
mail order £11.70. Free sample copy
available on request.

CERAMIC REVIEW
Ceramic Review Publishing Ltd
21 Carnaby Street
London W1V 1PH
Tel: 0171 439 3377
Fax: 0171 287 9954
Email: ceramicr@globalnet.co.uk
Website: www.ceramic-review.co.uk
Available by mail order only. Price: Single
copy (mailed) £6.20. Annual order (mailed
UK) £32; (mailed overseas) £38 or US$70.

CRAFTS
Crafts Council
44a Pentonville Road
Islington
London N1 9BY
Tel: 0171 806 2542
Fax: 0171 837 0858
Available via newsagent and direct by mail
order. Price: Single copy £4.95. Annual
order (newsagent) £29.70. Annual order
(mailed) £27. Free sample copy on request.

CRAFTS BEAUTIFUL
Aceville Publications Ltd Subscription Dept
Bradley Pavilions
Bradley Stoke North
Bristol BS32 0PP
Tel: 01454 620070
Fax: 01454 620080
Email: mail@maze.u-net.com
Available via newsagent and direct by mail
order. Price: Single copy £2.60. Annual
order via newsagent or direct by mail order
£31.20 (various discounts available
throughout year). Free sample copy
available on request.

CRAFTSMAN MAGAZINE
PSB Design & Print Consultants Ltd
PO Box 5, Driffield
East Yorks YO25 8JD
Tel: 01377 255213
Fax: 01377 255730
Email: sales@craftsman-magazine.co.uk
Website: www.craftsman-magazine.co.uk
Available via newsagent and direct by mail
order. Price: Single copy £2.50. Annual
order (newsagent) £30. Annual
order (mailed) £25. Free sample copy
available on request.

SUBSCRIPTION OFFER

Subscribe to AN Magazine and get the essentials

Subscribe to AN (from only £25.00 per year) and get a free 'AN Essentials', the essential comprehensive artists' contact guide plus access to AN Advice, the free telephone helpline.

AN MAGAZINE
PO BOX 23, SUNDERLAND SR4 6DG
T: 0191 567 3589
F: 0191 564 1600
E: subs@anpubs.demon.co.uk

CREATIVE CRAFTS FOR THE HOME

Guild of Master Craftsmen Publications Ltd
166 High Street
Lewes
East Sussex
BN7 1XU
Tel: 01273 488005
Fax: 01273 478606
Available via newsagent and direct by mail order. Price: Single copy £2.95. Annual order (mailed) £32.95. Free sample copy available on request.

CREFFT/CRAFT NEWSLETTER

Arts Council of Wales
Visual Arts & Craft
Artform Development Division
9 Museum Place
Cardiff CF1 3NX
Tel: 01222 376500
Fax: 01222 221447
Available by mail order only. Price: Free to craftspeople working in Wales. Free sample copy available on request.

CROSS STITCH COLLECTION

Future Publishing Subscriptions Department
Freepost (BS 4900)
Somerton
Somerset
TA11 6BR
Tel: 01458 271142
Fax: 01225 822523
Email: subs@futurenet.co.uk
Website: www.futurenet.co.uk
Available via newsagent and direct by mail order. Price: Single copy £3.99. Annual order (newsagent) £23.94. Annual order (mailed) £17.99 Direct Debit or £20.50 Cheque/Credit Card.

CROSS STITCH GALLERY

Creative Crafts Publishing Ltd
Well Oast
Brenley Lane
Brenley
Faversham
Kent ME13 9LY
Tel: 01227 750215
Fax: 01227 750813
Email: CSG@hickmott.demon.co.uk
Available via newsagent and direct by mail order. Price: Single copy £3.99. Annual order (newsagent) £23.94. Annual order (mailed) £19.95.

CROSS STITCHER

Future Publishing
Subscriptions Department
Freepost (BS 4900)
Somerton
Somerset TA11 6BR
Tel: 01458 271109
Fax: 01225 822523
Email: subs@futurenet.co.uk
Website: www.futurenet.co.uk
Available via newsagent and direct by mail order. Price: Single copy £2.99. Annual order (newsagent) £35.88. Annual order (mailed) £26.99 Direct Debit or £30.50 Cheque/Credit Card.

DOLL MAGAZINE

Ashdown Publishing
Avalon Court
Star Road
Partridge Green
West Sussex RH13 8RY
Tel: 01403 711511
Fax: 01403 711521
Email: ashdown@ashdown.co.uk
Website: www.dollmagazine.com
Available via newsagent and direct by mail order. Price: Single copy £3.50. Annual order (mailed) £21.

DOLLS HOUSE WORLD

Ashdown Publishing
Avalon Court
Star Road
Partridge Green
West Sussex RH13 8RY
Tel: 01403 711511
Fax: 01403 711521
Email: ashdown@ashdown.co.uk
Website: www.dollshouseworld.com
Available via newsagent and direct by mail order. Price: Single copy £3.25. Annual order (mailed) £36.50.

E6000 JOURNAL

Alice Wilmshurst
Hawthornes
Whitecroft
nr Lydney
Glos GL15 4PF
Tel: 01594 562161
Email: aliceknit@aol.com
Available by mail order only.
Price: Single copy £2. Six issues (mailed) £10.

The BEST guide there is for all parchment craft enthusiasts...

The *Parchment*

A **craft** PUBLICATION

In every issue
GET PATTERNS
and step by step guides to a variety of parchment craft projects - with colour examples of at least **SIX finished items.** *plus hints, tips and cheats, news and views, puzzle plus subscribers' patterns for you to share*

NOW IN FULL COLOUR

Unique, user friendly bi-monthly parchment craft magazine,

SUBSCRIBE TODAY!
Just £15 per year or £7.75 for 3 issues

Express

FREE RING BINDER with every new subscription

Inside this issue ...
Christmas Decorations ● Gift Ideas
Ballerina in Blue ● Snowdrop Greetings
● Quick Cards ● Pot of Daffodils
Sunday Sail-Away ● Cones & Wax Catchers
News and views ● Prize puzzle
Hints, tips and cheats ● Problems
Area News ● Step by step guide

... don't just take our word for it - see what existing subscribers say!

● *First of all let me say how fantastic the new PE is. It is much appreciated & is pored over in priority to everything else when it arrives.* Bérengère Ross - France

● *Thank you very much for your magazine - it is beyond comment!* Linda Hiley - Australia

● *The new PE is lovely and when it arrives everything stops while I read every word.* Joy Verity - Essex

● *I was so thrilled to receive October's PE - it is a delight to behold!* Muriel Graves - Hampshire

● *I was so excited to read about this magazine, I would like to subscribe.* Lesley Zadow - Australia

● *Thank you so much for my first issue of PE. What a mine of information they are - I can't wait for the next one!* Yvonne Steel - Essex

● *I love the new format - congratulations to everyone.* Chris Parkington - Cleveland

● *PE is really what I have been looking for, information, instrucction, ideas, well - that's just for starters.* Mrs S Hall - Norfolk

If you like parchment craft ... you'll love

Parchment **Express**

Please reply to: Magmaker Ltd
Cromwell Court, New Road, St Ives, Cambs PE17 4BG

Parchment **SUBSCRIPTION**
Express ORDER FORM

Please register my subscription to Magmaker Ltd

☐ 1 year at £15 (6 issues)
☐ Half year at £7.75 (3 issues)

Please find enclosed my cheque
(made payable to Magmaker Ltd) for £........................ **OR**
Please charge to my credit/debit card

Card No. [ ][ ][ ][ ][ ][ ][ ][ ][ ][ ][ ][ ][ ][ ][ ][ ]

Exp. [ ][ ] / [ ][ ] Signed ....

Name ....

Address ....

....

.... Postcode ....

Please return to: Magmaker Ltd,   CWY
Cromwell Court, New Road, St Ives, Cambs PE17 4BG

ENGINEERING IN MINIATURE

TEE Publishing
The Fosse, Fosse Way
Radford Semele
nr Leamington Spa
Warks CV31 1XN
Tel: 01926 614101
Fax: 01926 614293
Email: 100544.1675@compuserve.com
Website: www.fotec.co.uk/mehs/tee
Available via newsagent and direct by mail
order. Price: Single copy £2.10. Annual
order (mailed UK) £25.20; (mailed Europe
airmail) £33; (mailed rest of world airmail)
£45.80.

FURNITURE & CABINETMAKING

Guild of Master Craftsmen Publications Ltd
166 High Street
Lewes
East Sussex BN7 1XU
Tel: 01273 488005
Fax: 01273 478606
Available via newsagent and direct by mail
order. Price: Single copy £2.95. Annual
order (newsagent) £39. Free sample copy
available on request.

GIFTS INTERNATIONAL

Nexus Subscriptions Department
Tower House, Sovereign Park
Lathkill Street
Market Harborough
Leics LE16 9EF
Tel: 01858 435344
Fax: 01322 667633

GIFTS TODAY

Lema Publishing, Unit 1
Queens Mary's Avenue
Watford
Herts WD1 7JR
Tel: 01923 250909
Fax: 01923 250995
Available by mail order only.
Price: Single copy £5. Annual order
(mailed) £50. Free sample copy available on
request.

GLOBAL CERAMIC REVIEW

44 Kingsway
Stoke-on-Trent
Staffs ST4 1JH
Tel: 01782 411433
Fax: 01782 747061
Email: sales@global-ceramic.com
Website: www.global-ceramic.com
Available by mail order only.
Price: Single copy £10. Annual order
(mailed); special offer to CWYB readers
£40 (normally £60). Free sample copy
available on request.

GOOD WOODWORKING

Future Publishing Subscriptions Department
Freepost (BS 4900)
Somerton
Somerset TA11 6BR
Tel: 01458 271115
Fax: 01225 822523
Email: subs@futurenet.co.uk
Website: www.futurenet.co.uk
Available via newsagent and direct by mail
order. Price: Single copy £2.60. Annual
order (newsagent) £31.20. Annual
order (mailed) £24.99.

INSPIRATIONS FOR YOUR HOME

GE Magazines Ltd
Tower Publishing Ltd
Tower House, Sovereign Park
Lathkill Street, Market Harborough
Leics LE16 9EF
Tel: 01858 435348
Fax: 01858 432164
Email: becca@inspirations-mags.co.uk
Available via newsagent and direct by mail
order. Price: Single copy £2.40. Annual
order (newsagent) £28.80. Annual order
(mailed) £23. Free sample copy available on
request.

JOURNAL FOR WEAVERS, SPINNERS & DYERS

Association of Guilds of WS&D
4 St Jude's Close
Queen's Gore, Southsea
Hants PO5 3HQ
Available by mail order only.
Price: Single copy £3.40.

KNITTING MACHINE JOURNAL

Alice Wilmshurst
Hawthornes
Whitecroft, nr Lydney
Glos GL15 4PF
Tel: 01594 562161
Email: aliceknit@aol.com
Available by mail order only. Price: Single
copy £1.75. Four issues (mailed) £6.

Get crafty...

Ideas for your home, for gifts or for your business

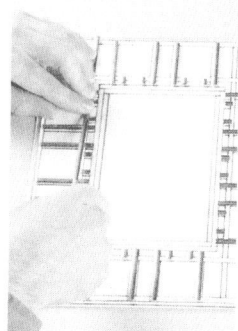

More projects than any other craft magazine

On sale every month £2.40
Available from WH Smith, John Menzies
and all good newsagents

SUBSCRIPTION HOTLINE 01858 435 322

...AFTS

...s Centre

...cn Road
Harold Wood
Romford
Essex RM3 0JF
Tel: 01708 379897
Fax: 01708 379804
Email: crafts@atlas.co.uk
Available via newsagent and mail order
only. Price: Annual order (newsagent)
£13.50. Annual order (mailed) £18.
Free sample copy available on request.

NEEDLECRAFT
Future Publishing
Subscriptions Department
Freepost (BS 4900)
Somerton
Somerset TA11 6BR
Tel: 01458 271125
Fax: 01225 822523
Email: subs@futurenet.co.uk
Website: www.futurenet.co.uk
Available via newsagent and direct by mail
order. Price: Single copy £2.99. Annual
order (newsagent) £35.88. Annual
order (mailed) £26.59 Direct Debit or
£30.50 Cheque/Credit Card.

NEW STITCHES
Creative Crafts Publishing Ltd
Well Oast, Brenley Lane
Brenley
Faversham
Kent
ME13 9LY
Tel: 01227 750215
Fax: 01227 750813
Email: CSG@hickmott.demon.co.uk
Available via newsagent and direct by mail
order. Price: Single copy £3.25. Annual
order (newsagent) £39. Annual order
(mailed) £32.50.

NEWSLETTER/STOPRESS
Crafts Council of Ireland
Castle Yard
Kilkenny
Co Kilkenny
EIRE
Tel: 00 353 56 61804
Fax: 00 353 56 63754
Email· craftsir@indigo.ie
Free sample copy available on request.

PARCHMENT EXPRESS
Magmaker Ltd
Cromwell Court
New Road
St Ives
Cambs
PE17 4BG
Tel: 01480 496130
Fax: 01480 495514
Available by mail order only.
Price: Single copy £2.50. Annual order
(mailed) £15.

PASSAP KNITTING MACHINE JOURNAL
Alice Wilmshurst
Hawthornes
Whitecroft
nr Lydney
Glos
GL15 4PF
Tel: 01594 562161
Email: aliceknit@aol.com
Available by mail order only.
Price: Single copy £2.50. Four issues
(mailed) £8.

POPULAR CRAFTS
Nexus Subscriptions Department
Tower House, Sovereign Park
Lathkill Street
Market Harborough
Leics LE16 9EF
Tel: 01858 435344
Fax: 01322 667633
Available via newsagent and direct by mail
order.
Price: Single copy £2.40. One-year order
(mailed) £31.20.
Two-year order (mailed) £61.40.
Free sample copy available on request.

PRACTICAL CRAFT
Magmaker Ltd
Cromwell Court
New Road
St Ives
Cambs PE17 4BG
Tel: 01480 496130
Fax: 01480 495514
Available via newsagent and direct by mail
order.
Price: Single copy £2.25. Annual order
(both via newsagent and
mailed direct) £27.
Sample copy available for £1.

'Practically the best

practical

craft

The monthly hobbycraft magazine with fresh,
appealing and achievable projects to
suit most areas of interest.

Dedicated to creative enjoyment
on a tabletop scale

Parchment
Craft is
featured in
every month's
Practical
Craft

practical *a.* given to action
rather than theory; relating to
action or real existence; useful

Follow Pauline Loweth and other designers
through every edition of Practical Craft in
unique parchment craft projects

*Available from your newsagent at £2.25 or for
subscription details contact:* **Practical Craft,
Cromwell Court, New Road, St Ives, Cambs PE17 4BG**

..., rublishing
United House
North Road
London N7 9DP
Tel: 0171 700 6740
Fax: 0171 607 6411
Available by mail order only.
Price: Annual order (mailed) £35.
Free sample copy available on request.

PROGRESSIVE GREETINGS WORLDWIDE

Max Publishing
United House
North Road
London N7 9DP
Tel: 0171 700 6740
Fax: 0171 607 6411
Available by mail order only.
Price: Annual order (mailed) £35.
Free sample copy available on request.

QUICK & EASY CROSS STITCH

Future Publishing
Subscriptions Department
Freepost (BS 4900)
Somerton
Somerset TA11 6BR
Tel: 01458 271138
Fax: 01225 822523
Email: subs@futurenet.co.uk
Website: www.futurenet.co.uk
Available via newsagent and direct by mail
order. Price: Single copy £2.85. Annual
order (newsagent) £34.20. Annual order
(mailed) £25.99 Direct Debit or £28.99
Cheque/Credit Card.

ROUTING

Nexus Subscriptions Department
Tower House
Sovereign Park
Lathkill Street
Market Harborough
Leics
LE16 9EF
Tel: 01858 435344
Fax: 01322 667633
Available via newsagent and direct by mail
order. Price: Single copy £2.95. One-year
order (mailed) £17.70. Two-year order
(mailed) £35.40. Free sample copy available
on request.

SHOWMAN'S DIRECTORY

Lance Publications
45 Bridge Street
Godalming
 Surrey GU7 1HL
Tel: 01483 422184
Fax: 01483 425697
Email: lanpub@showmans-directory.co.uk
Website: www.showmans-directory.co.uk
Available by mail order only.
Price: £17. The annual guide to town,
county, country, agricultural, air, steam and
dog shows; also directory of breeds and
other societies.

SLIP KNOT

Knitting & Crochet Guild
c/o 228 Chester Road North
Kidderminster
Worcs DY10 1TH
Tel: 01562 754367
Email: rgb_uk@compuserve.com
Website: rgb.ndirect.co.uk/guild/
Available only to members of the Knitting &
Crochet Guild.
Price: Annual subscription to the guild is
£16. Free sample copy available if you send
four 20p stamps.

STITCH IT, SELL IT!

Future Publishing
Subscriptions Department
Freepost (BS 4900)
Somerton
Somerset TA11 6BR
Tel: 01458 271150
Fax: 01225 822523
Email: subs@futurenet.co.uk
Website: www.futurenet.co.uk
Available via newsagent and direct by mail
order. Price: Single copy £3.99. Annual
order (newsagent) £23.94. Annual
order (mailed) £17.99 Direct Debit or
£20.50 Cheque/Credit Card.

TEDDY BEAR CLUB INTERNATIONAL

Aceville Publications Ltd
Subscription Dept
Bradley Pavilions
Bradley Stoke North
Bristol BS32 0PP
Tel: 01454 620070
Fax: 01454 620080
Email: teddy@maze.u-net.com
Website: www.teddybearmagazine.com

Don't Let your business pale into insignificance due to lack of information.

To discover over 1,200 contacts for organisers of outdoor and special events in the UK, you will need to purchase the

Showman's Directory.

Telephone 01483 422184

or send a cheque for £17.00 made
payable to Lance Publications
45 Bridge Street
Godalming, Surrey GU7 1HL

Available via newsagent and direct by mail order. Price: Single copy £3.25. Annual order via newsagent or direct by mail order £39 (various discounts available throughout the year). Free sample copy available on request.

TEDDY BEAR TIMES

Ashdown Publishing
Avalon Court
Star Road, Partridge Green
West Sussex RH13 8RY
Tel: 01403 711511
Fax: 01403 711521
Email: ashdown@ashdown.co.uk
Website: www.teddybeartimes.com
Available via newsagent and direct by mail order. Price: Single copy £3.25. Annual order (mailed) £36.50.

THE ART & DESIGN DIRECTORY

Avec Designs Ltd
PO Box 1384
Long Ashton
Bristol BS41 9DF
Tel: 01275 394639
Fax: 01275 394647
Available by mail order only
Price: £24.50 (mailed). Provides comprehensive reference source for art and design courses: A4, 420 pages, 8th edition.

THE DOLLS' HOUSE MAGAZINE

Guild of Master Craftsmen
Publications Ltd
166 High Street
Lewes
East Sussex BN7 1XU
Tel: 01273 488005
Fax: 01273 478606
Available via newsagent and direct by mail order. Price: Single copy £3.25. Annual order (mailed) £35.95. Free sample copy available on request.

THE QUILTER

The Quilters' Guild of
The British Isles
Room 190, Dean Clough
Halifax
West Yorks HX3 5AX
Tel: 01422 347669
Fax: 01422 345017
Available by mail order only.
Price: Annual order (mailed) £22.50.

THE ROUTER

Guild of Master Craftsmen
Publications Ltd
166 High Street
Lewes
East Sussex BN7 1XU
Tel: 01273 488005
Fax: 01273 478606
Available via newsagent and direct by mail order. Price: Single copy £2.95. Annual order (mailed) £33.25. Free sample copy available on request.

THE SCROLLSAW

Guild of Master Craftsmen
Publications Ltd
166 High Street
Lewes
East Sussex
BN7 1XU
Tel: 01273 488005
Fax: 01273 478606
Available via newsagent and direct by mail order. Price: Single copy £2.95. Annual order (mailed) £11.95. Free sample copy available on request.

THE WORLD OF EMBROIDERY

Michael Spender
PO Box 42
East Molesey
Surrey KT8 9BB
Tel: 0181 943 1229
Fax: 0181 977 9882
Email: jlongley@embroiderers.guild.co.uk
Website: www.hiraeth.com/world-emb/
Available by mail order only.
Price: Single copy £3.95. Annual order (mailed) £23.70.

TOY SOLDIER & MODEL FIGURE

Ashdown Publishing
Avalon Court
Star Road
Partridge Green
West Sussex
RH13 8RY
Tel: 01403 711511
Fax: 01403 711521
Email: ashdown@ashdown.co.uk
Website: www.toy-soldier.com
Available by mail order only.
Price: Single copy £3.50. Annual order (mailed) £21.

TRADITIONAL WOODWORKING

Waterways World The Well House,
High Street Burton-on-Trent
Staffs DE14 1JQ
Tel: 01283 742950 Fax: 01283 742966
Available via newsagent and by mail order.
Price: Single copy £2.45. Annual order by
post £41.50. Free sample copy on request

WOODCARVING

Guild of Master Craftsmen Publications Ltd
166 High Street, Lewes
East Sussex BN7 1XU
Tel: 01273 488005 Fax: 01273 478606
Available via newsagent and direct by mail
order. Price: Single copy £3.25. Annual
order (mailed) £28.50. Free sample copy
available on request.

WOODTURNING

Guild of Master Craftsmen Publications Ltd,
166 High Street, Lewes
East Sussex BN7 1XU
Tel: 01273 488005 Fax: 01273 478606
Available via newsagent and by mail order.
Price: Single copy £3.25. Annual order
(mailed) £43. Free sample copy on request.

WOODWORKER

Nexus Subscriptions Department
Tower House, Sovereign Park
Lathkill Street
Market Harborough
Leics LE16 9EF
Tel: 01858 435344
Fax: 01322 667633
Available via newsagent and direct by mail
order. Price: Single copy £2.45. One-year
order (mailed) £31.85. Two-year order
(mailed) £63.70. Free sample copy available
on request.

WORKBOX

Ebony Media Ltd
Heathland Business Park
Heathland Road
Liskeard, Cornwall PL14 4DH
Tel: 01579 340100
Fax: 01579 340200
Email: workbox@ebony.co.uk
Website: www.ebony.co.uk/workbox/
Available via newsagent and direct by mail
order. Price: Single copy £1.95. Annual
order (mailed) £10. Free sample copy
available on request.

steps
e
c
o
n
d

ISBN
09527501-2-0
£6.50

a guide to
careers in the
craft world

A one stop resource book
for recent graduates.
Covering every step from
CV's to Business Plans
Illustrated with case studies
by gallery owners
and makers.

Special Offer £5 incl P&P

Cheques to 'Craft Galleries'
@ Burton Cottage Farm
East Coker, Yeovil
Somerset BA22 9LS
Tel & Fax : 01935 862731

INDEX OF ADVERTISERS

While every effort is made to ensure the veracity of all the information we carry,
much of it is provided by event organisers and craft bodies themselves and accepted in good faith.
Please note then that, as publishers, we cannot accept any liability, financial or otherwise,
for any error or omission.

The 2000 Edition of The Craftworker's Year Book will be published in December 1999

For inquiries relating to: listings phone **01782 749919**, trade sales or advertising
0181 298 0929 and retail sales **0181 770 7087**

© **The Write Angle Press 1999**